GREAT LIVES OBSERVED

Gerald Emanuel Stearn, *General Editor*

EACH VOLUME IN THE SERIES VIEWS THE CHARACTER AND ACHIEVEMENT OF A GREAT WORLD FIGURE IN THREE PERSPECTIVES—THROUGH HIS OWN WORDS, THROUGH THE OPINIONS OF HIS CONTEMPORARIES, AND THROUGH RETROSPECTIVE JUDGMENTS—THUS COMBINING THE INTIMACY OF AUTOBIOGRAPHY, THE IMMEDIACY OF EYEWITNESS OBSERVATION, AND THE OBJECTIVITY OF MODERN SCHOLARSHIP.

ROBERT S. MAXWELL, *editor of this volume in the Great Lives Observed series, is Professor of History at Stephen F. Austin State College. Among his other books are* La Follette and the Rise of Progressives in Wisconsin *and* Emanuel L. Philipp: Wisconsin Stalwart. *His many articles on the Progressive Movement have appeared in numerous publications.*

GREAT LIVES OBSERVED

La Follette

Edited by ROBERT S. MAXWELL

No man in public life expresses the ideals of American Democracy so fully as does La Follette in his thought, his acts, his living. No man in public life today has done so much toward the attainment of those ideals.

—LOUIS D. BRANDEIS, JANUARY 3, 1912

A SPECTRUM BOOK

PRENTICE-HALL, INC., ENGLEWOOD CLIFFS, N.J.

To Merle Curti, "scholar, teacher, friend"

A SPECTRUM BOOK

Current printing (last number): 10 9 8 7 6 5 4 3 2 1

P 13-522433-0

C 13-522441-1

Library of Congress Catalog Card Number: 69–15341

Printed in the United States of America

Prentice-Hall International, Inc. (*London*)

Contents

PART THREE

LA FOLLETTE IN HISTORY

Introduction

In the history of the United States the reform heritage and the recurrent eras of reform have loomed large. Among these seemingly cyclical reform drives, the Progressive Movement has excited much interest and promoted much scholarly research and popular writing. Conventionally assigned to the dates between 1901 and 1917, the Progressive Movement actually extended beyond both these dates, gaining strength from forces which became apparent in the 1890's and continuing on into the 1920's to provide "a bridge" for liberal ideas and ideals to make their way to the New Deal.

The Progressive Era had several unusual aspects which distinguished it from other periods of reform. The movement thrived in an era of prosperity and operated on all levels of government. It included large segments of both major parties as well as the most important third party movement in this century. It introduced significant reforms in the social and economic realms as well as in the political world. The movement developed under intellectual leadership and drew support from farmers, trade unionists, small businessmen, college and university faculty, and even an occasional millionaire. Although the Progressive Movement included many prominent political or intellectual leaders during the pre-World War I era, for students of Progressivism three names stand out—Theodore Roosevelt, Woodrow Wilson, and Robert M. La Follette, Sr. Perhaps because he did not achieve the presidency and because his reform career extended over a quarter of a century (far longer than either of his chief rivals), La Follette, even more than Roosevelt or Wilson, has come to epitomize the Progressive. He was optimistic, moralistic, rational, and a convert to the necessity of planning. He was not afraid of the expansion of government for general social welfare, and he was confident that the future belonged to democracy and that the "cure for the ills of democracy was more democracy." Thus "Fighting Bob" La Follette cast a long shadow on the history of twentieth century America and, indirectly, of the world. In many respects he was the personification of the Progressive Era.

Robert Marion La Follette was born on a farm in Primrose Township, Dane County, Wisconsin, on June 14, 1855. His parents, Josiah and Mary Ferguson La Follette, were of French Huguenot and Scotch-Irish ancestry and had reached Wisconsin by way of North Carolina, Kentucky, and Indiana. His father died within a year of young La Follette's birth, leaving his widow and five children to cope with farm life on the Wisconsin frontier. A few years later his mother remarried, and La Follette grew up in the home of his stepfather, John Saxton, an elderly, pious disciplinarian. During these years La Follette attended a variety of country schools, worked at a number of village jobs, and helped on the family farm.

In the fall of 1875 La Follette entered the freshman class at the University of Wisconsin. He moved his mother, now again a widow, and his sister to a house in Madison near the university and worked afternoons and evenings to help pay expenses. Later he bought the college paper, the *University Press,* which he ran with skill and profit during the rest of his university career. As he had been poorly prepared for college, La Follette did not excel as a scholar, but he carried his course load adequately, took an active part in the university literary societies, and engaged in campus politics with considerable success. The outstanding event of La Follette's senior year was winning the interstate Oratorical Contest. At this time the event included competition among the colleges and universities of six states and ranked in the students' esteem with a major athletic championship.

La Follette chose for his oratorical effort a character study of Iago, the villain in Shakespeare's *Othello.* After winning the university and state contests he journeyed to Iowa City, Iowa, where he again triumphed over the best collegiate orators in the Midwest. Upon his return to Madison, townspeople and students accorded him a hero's welcome, drawing his carriage with willing hands from the railroad station to the campus, accompanied by bands, marchers, and a line of carriages. Many years later, classmates recalled this incident as their most vivid remembrance of the young Bob La Follette.

Although La Follette made only mediocre grades, he was deeply impressed by certain of his professors, especially President John Bascom from whom he acquired, in his own words, "a proper attitude toward public affairs." Most problems became to him a question of right or wrong, and he regularly stressed a moral and ethical view of political questions. Shortly afterward he read and reread Henry George's *Progress and Poverty,* which also left a permanent impression. Thus John Bascom and Henry George were perhaps the most influential forces in molding the thought and character of the young La Follette.

During the next four years La Follette studied law, was admitted to the bar, married his university classmate Belle Case, and served two terms as district attorney for Dane County. According to his own account his election to the county post was strongly opposed by Madison Republican Boss Elisha Keyes. But as Keyes' power was waning and as he was seeking political office himself, it is probable that his opposition was not as strenuous as La Follette recalled it in his autobiography some thirty years later. In 1884 La Follette successfully sought a seat in Congress. Using the same campaign methods that had won him the district attorney's post, he visited every town in his district and talked personally to as many voters as possible. This pattern of establishing a personal bond with voters and enlisting the aid of young party members, especially young university men, became a hallmark of La Follette campaigns which he followed throughout his career.

In Washington in 1885 La Follette met such party leaders as Joseph Cannon, Thomas B. Reed, and William McKinley. Appointed to the Indian Affairs Committee, La Follette gained the reputation of being studious, industrious, and high-minded. Although honest and idealistic, La Follette, during his congressional years, was a regular party man, a loyal Republican, and essentially conservative, giving little hint of the reformer that he was to become. He was a member of the Congresses that passed the Interstate Commerce Act, the Sherman Anti-Trust Act, and the McKinley Tariff Act.

When the Democratic landslide of 1890 terminated La Follette's tenure as representative, he returned to Madison expecting to become a leader in the state Republican organization. The next year (1891) he quarreled violently with Senator Philetus Sawyer, the most powerful Republican leader in the state, over the senator's efforts to involve him in the settlement of the "Treasury Cases." La Follette charged that Sawyer attempted to bribe him "to fix things" with the presiding judge, his brother-in-law Robert Siebecker. From then on La Follette fought against Sawyer and his friends and pledged that he would break the hold of the "machine" on Wisconsin politics. Sawyer in turn vowed that La Follette would never again hold public office in the state. This marked the beginning of La Follette's career as a reform leader and an independent progressive Republican.

After repeated failures, La Follette finally won the Republican nomination for governor in 1900. By this time Sawyer had died and the old Republican organization had so far disintegrated that La Follette gained the support of a number of regular Republicans such as industrialist Emanuel Philipp, millionaire Isaac Stephenson, and Congressman Joseph Babcock, who had previously backed Sawyer. As La Follette extended an olive branch to his erstwhile opponents, the ensuing election was something of a "harmony campaign" which La Follette and the entire Republican ticket won by a landslide.

La Follette at once pushed his program of primary elections, increased taxation of railroads and other corporations, and more stringent antimonopoly laws. This split the party into stalwart and progressive factions and brought charges that La Follette was a Populist, Socialist, or Anarchist. His program was initially blocked in the legislature, but "Fighting Bob" won re-election in 1902 and 1904, routing the conservatives completely and establishing himself as the political leader of Wisconsin. During these campaigns La Follette developed the "Roll Call" technique of reading the record on his opponents' activities in the legislature to their home town audiences, a standard practice in La Follette campaigns from then on. When he at last resigned the governorship to accept a seat in the United States Senate, he left a comprehensive package of reform legislation which placed Wisconsin in the forefront of the Progressive Movement. In addition to the primary election laws and corporation taxation measures, he had established an effective railroad commission, a civil service commission, and a tax commission. In all of these ventures La Follette drew heavily on the University of Wisconsin faculty for expert advice and assistance, creating a close working alliance between university and statehouse which became famous as "The Wisconsin Idea." Still more progressive legislation was sponsored by La Follette lieutenants who followed him as governor from 1906 to 1914. La Follette himself continued to exert leadership for progressive reform in his home state and was largely responsible for the reform programs achieved by his successors.

Upon taking his seat in the Senate, early in 1906, La Follette apparently expected to carry his Wisconsin reforms to the nation as a whole and to develop an enlarged "Wisconsin Idea" for the entire country. Although President Theodore Roosevelt welcomed him warmly, the Rough Rider did not include the new senator in the inner councils of the party nor did he frequently ask La Follette's advice on reform measures. During this first session La Follette threw himself into the fight for the Hepburn bill for railroad regulation, seeking to strengthen the commission's powers and to include a physical valuation feature on which to base rates. Although most of La Follette's proposals were not included in the Hepburn Act, they were enacted into law later as separate measures.

When the end of Roosevelt's second term approached in 1908, La Follette would have been happy to succeed him. However, the President bestowed his blessing on Secretary of War William Howard Taft, who, with Roosevelt's support, easily won the nomination and the election. La Follette stifled his disappointment and turned his attention to the election of 1912, which he was convinced would be "a progressive year." Many of Taft's policies alienated him, and early in 1911 La Follette joined with other liberal members of Congress to organize the National Progressive Republican League, dedicated to replacing Taft with a more progressive candidate in the election of 1912. Ex-President Roosevelt had also become disenchanted with Taft as President, but the Rough Rider steadily declined to seek the presidency again himself or to join the League. As a consequence La Follette became an active candidate with the support of the NPRL and began an extensive speaking tour of the country seeking to win delegates for the Republican convention.

Although La Follette attracted large audiences and gained considerable popular response, many progressives feared that Taft's position as incumbent President and his control of patronage and the party machinery would make him too difficult for La Follette to unseat at the convention. Many League members and avowed supporters of La Follette turned again privately to Roosevelt urging him to take over leadership of the progressives and become an avowed candidate against Taft. Roosevelt protested and vacillated for a time but then agreed to enter the race if it appeared that he had responded to a draft. At this time La Follette unwittingly all but took himself out of the race and gave his supporters an excuse to switch to Roosevelt. Overworked and ill, La Follette gave a very incoherent and rambling speech to the annual meeting of the Periodical Publishers Association in Philadelphia on February 2, 1912. The press reported that he had broken down and would be forced to withdraw from the campaign. Needless to say, most of his followers flocked to the banner of the Rough Rider.

La Follette refused, however, to give up. After a brief rest, he returned to the campaign and continued his vigorous tour. He bitterly attacked Roosevelt, charging that the ex-President had planned to run long before his announcement and had used him as a "stalking horse" to test progressive sentiment before committing himself to the race. He charged that Roosevelt was no true progressive and had been too ready to accept "a half-loaf" of reform legislation.

At the Republican Convention the delegates were almost evenly divided between supporters and opponents of Taft. The control of the convention rested with disputed delegates claimed by both Roosevelt and Taft. La Follette refused to make common cause with the Roosevelt forces against Taft and even refused to support Governor Francis McGovern of the Wisconsin delegation for chairman of the convention when it became apparent that the Roosevelt delegates would also back him. When the Taft-picked national committee decided all contests in favor of the President and the convention then proceeded to renominate Taft, the Roosevelt followers bolted the convention, formed the Progressive Party and nominated Roosevelt for President on an advanced progressive platform. La Follette refused to support either candidate and in his weekly periodical, *La Follette's Magazine,* he denounced them both. From his editorials it appears that he was pleased with the election of Democrat Woodrow Wilson over his two erstwhile friends.

La Follette played an independent political role during the first Wilson administration. He supported such "New Freedom" measures as the Underwood Tariff, the Clayton Anti-Trust Act, and the Federal Trade Commission though most members of his party were in opposition. He also won administration support for his measure to better working conditions at sea and improve safety standards which was passed as La Follette's Seamen's Law.

With the outbreak of World War I in 1914 La Follette became one of the leaders of the small group of isolationists in Congress dedicated to keeping America at peace. He urged a ban on loans or credits to the belligerents and supported a resolution declaring that travel in war areas should be at the citizen's own risk. He favored an embargo on all arms and munitions and proposed a popular referendum before Congress should declare war. After the break in diplomatic relations in 1917, La Follette was one of the "little group of willful men" who opposed President Wilson's proposal to arm American merchantmen. On April 4, La Follette was one of six senators who voted against a Declaration of War against Germany.

Although La Follette took pains to point out that he supported the administration's war program wherever possible and would not attempt to block the war effort merely because he had opposed the war declaration, the press soon accused him of being pro-German. He opposed the conscription bill and the administration's measure to finance the war largely by bond issues. La Follette favored a pay-as-you-go plan which would raise approximately 80 per cent of the war costs by increased taxation. He also opposed the espionage law as unconstitutional and unsuccessfully sought a congressional resolution for a Declaration of American War Aims. As might be expected, old friends turned against him and some newspapers called for his ouster from the Senate.

Because of a misquotation of a remark which La Follette made in a speech in St. Paul, there arose an even greater hue and cry, and a resolution to expel him from the Senate was introduced and referred to a senatorial committee. This committee held hearings and investigated the charges for more than a year. Senators vied for the opportunity to denounce La Follette and compared him to Judas and Benedict Arnold. Cartoonists pictured the Wisconsin senator being presented the Iron Cross by the Kaiser. A majority of faculty members of the University of Wisconsin (his alma mater) signed a round robin letter denouncing his war stand, and the Madison Club expelled him from membership. For the moment La Follette was an outcast—alone, friendless, and reviled.

In November 1918 the war ended, and as a result of the recent congressional elections, the Senate discovered that La Follette held the balance of power. With La Follette in his seat the Republicans could organize the Senate by the narrow margin of 49–47. The Senate speedily quashed the charges and dismissed the resolution to expel by a vote of 50 to 21. La Follette was now free to turn to more important matters.

During most of the next year and a half the principal business before the Senate was the Versailles Treaty which also incorporated the Covenant of the League of Nations. La Follette was indignant at the lack of candor by the administration concerning the secret promises and compromises of the peace conference. He was sick at the spectacle of the great nations dividing up the spoils of war, disregarding the interests and rights of smaller nations and minority groups. He distrusted the obligations proposed under the League of Nations. Consequently La Follette became a leader of the group which opposed the treaty and the League in any form. He later voted to attach the fifteen Lodge reservations and amendments to the treaty as he considered these an improvement on the Wilson version. But on the record votes he opposed the treaty in either form. After the final defeat of the treaty, La Follette was content. He considered it "an instrument to enforce an unjust peace which could only lead to future wars."

In spite of the threats of the superpatriots during the war, La Follette triumphantly won re-election for a fourth term in the Senate in 1922. During these years of Republican ascendancy, he steadily followed an independent course. He opposed the Esch-Cummins Act and the Fordney-McCumber Tariff, and voted for the bonus bill to compensate veterans of the World War. It was La Follette who introduced the Senate resolution calling for an investigation of the Teapot Dome and Elk Hills oil leases by the Department of the Interior. Together with Thomas Walsh who served as the prosecutor of the investigating committee, La Follette was responsible for uncovering the bribes and manipulations which were part of the Teapot Dome scandal and which eventually sent Secretary of the Interior Albert Fall to prison.

In the summer of 1923 La Follette made an extended trip to Europe to study conditions there—as he said "to learn." In addition to the countries of western Europe, he visited Soviet Russia, Italy under Mussolini, and Germany where French troops were still occupying the Ruhr. He returned with the opinion that Italian fascism and Russian communism were equally intolerable and that were he a citizen of either country he would fight the regime unceasingly. Germany, he felt, was being ground down by the victors even beyond the terms of the Versailles Treaty. He was certain that these conditions would lead to a new world war.

The war had split and divided the progressives, leaving them temporarily fighting among themselves. By 1924, however, the progressives had regrouped in Congress and had formed a cohesive minority which advocated a positive program of reform. This included federal aid to agriculture, a public power program coupled with further regulation of the great utilities companies, reform of the national banking structure, legislation to encourage collective bargaining by labor unions and to end the excessive use of the federal court injunction in labor disputes. They also urged a more realistic foreign policy including the diplomatic recognition of Soviet Russia. The acknowledged leader of the progressives and their chief spokesman in the Senate was Robert La Follette. Now sixty-nine, with a lofty pompadour of white hair and as straight and vigorous as ever, La Follette had outlived most of his enemies and had emerged as the unquestioned champion of liberalism and the common man in the entire country.

When both major parties nominated conservative and undynamic candidates for the presidency in their 1924 conventions, his progressive friends (some of whom had sought to organize a viable liberal third party movement since 1920) persuaded La Follette to undertake a campaign for President on an Independent and Progressive ticket. At an enthusiastic convention in Cleveland, liberals of many shades (Communists were excluded) unanimously endorsed La Follette for President and Burton K. Wheeler of Montana, a nominal Democrat, as his running mate. La Follette ran a vigorous and exciting race, advocating a comprehensive pattern of reforms. Republican and Democratic opponents feared that he would sweep the Midwest and Plains states, thus throwing the election into the House of Representatives. Although he lacked adequate campaign funds (his final report showed that he spent only one-sixteenth as much as the Republicans), La Follette carried his appeal to every section of the country, personally speaking in most of the states of the union. In the election, La Follette polled almost five million votes, carried his home state of Wisconsin, and ran second in eleven other states (all in the West and Midwest). Although defeated, La Follette had sounded the call for a new reform drive and had helped provide a "bridge" from the Progressive Era to the New Deal.

As punishment for his third party campaign, the Republican leadership in the Senate stripped La Follette, together with fellow progressives Smith Brookhart, Edwin F. Ladd, and Lynn Frazier, of their committee assignments and in effect read them out of the party. This largely deprived the Republican Party of its liberal wing and did much to impair the immediate future of the G.O.P.

La Follette had had a long, productive, and exciting career. He had left his mark on the legislation, standards of public service, and politics of his time. Four days after his seventieth birthday, he died in Washington on June 18, 1925. Old enemies as well as old friends vied to pay tribute to his memory and his long years of independent and courageous service. Wisconsin promptly elected his oldest son, Robert M. La Follette, Jr., to fill the vacant Senate seat, and for another twenty years "Young Bob" La Follette was to play an important part as a progressive leader of a new generation. The state also authorized a statue of "Fighting Bob" to be placed in Statuary Hall in the nation's capitol as one of her two most famous sons. In 1959 a Senate Committee under the direction of (then) Senator John F. Kennedy chose five outstanding senators whose contributions and service should be honored by having their portraits hang in the new Senate lounge. In addition to early immortals Henry Clay, John C. Calhoun, and Daniel Webster, and contemporary Robert A. Taft, the committee chose Robert M. La Follette, Sr. It was a distinguished company.

Chronology of the Life of La Follette

1855	(June 14). Born in Primrose Township, Dane County, Wisconsin, son of Josiah and Mary Ferguson La Follette.
1856	His father died.
1856–1873	La Follette grew up in rural Wisconsin, mother remarried (John Saxton), young La Follette attended school, worked on farm and at village jobs.
1873	La Follette with mother and sister, moved to Madison, attended local academy to prepare for university, worked at various jobs to support family.
1875–1879	Attended University of Wisconsin, participated in literary clubs, edited the *University Press.* In senior year won interstate oratorical contest with oration on *Iago.* Graduated in 1879.
1880–1884	Studied law, admitted to the Bar, married classmate Belle Case, won election to two terms as District Attorney of Dane County.
1884	Elected to Congress.
1885–1890	Member of Congress, met Joseph G. Cannon, Thomas B. Reed, and William McKinley.
1890–1891	Defeated for re-election. Returned to Madison and resumed practice of law.
1891	Broke with Philetus Sawyer over Treasury Cases; La Follette charged that Sawyer attempted to bribe him to influence the court.
1894	La Follette's candidate and friend, Nils P. Haugen, defeated for Republican nomination as governor.
1896	La Follette failed to win Republican nomination for governor.
1898	La Follette again failed to win Republican nomination for governor.
1900	La Follette won nomination in "Harmony Campaign." Was elected to governorship in a vigorous campaign which (temporarily) united all factions.
1901	As governor pushed for program of reform including direct primary, increased corporation taxation, and antimonopoly legislation. Blocked by stalwarts.
1902	Won re-election in bitter campaign. La Follette developed "Roll Call" technique. Organized political machine.

1904	Won third term as governor in historic battle and carried referendum on Primary Elections. Emerged as leading political power in Wisconsin.
1905	Elected to the United States Senate but did not relinquish governorship and take seat until January 1906.
1909	Established *La Follette's Weekly Magazine*.
1911	Re-elected to Senate. Helped to organize the National Progressive Republican League.
1912	Unsuccessfully campaigned for Republican nomination for President. Did not participate in post-convention campaign for any candidate.
1914	Progressives in Wisconsin split. Conservative elected governor.
1915–1916	Supported a strong policy of neutrality. Opposed preparedness program.
1916	Re-elected to Senate for third term (first election by popular vote).
1917	Voted against Armed Ship bill, Declaration of War, and Selective Service Act. Denounced as pro-German by superpatriots, Senate considered resolution to expel La Follette from seat.
1918	Attacks on and off the floor of the Senate continued. Senate Committee considered disloyalty charges.
1919	Disloyalty charges dismissed. La Follette takes leading part in the defeat of the Versailles Treaty.
1920	Campaigned in Wisconsin for John J. Blaine as governor. Returned state to Progressive ranks.
1922	Re-elected to the Senate by the people of Wisconsin for fourth term. La Follette's resolution set off Teapot Dome investigation.
1924	Ran for President on Independent and Progressive ticket with Burton K. Wheeler as vice-presidential candidate. Polled almost five million votes, but ran third.
1925	Stripped of committee assignments by Republican caucus. Died June 18, 1925.

PART ONE

LA FOLLETTE LOOKS AT THE WORLD

1

The Bosses and Reform[1]

In his crusade against the "Bosses" which led to his election as Governor of Wisconsin in 1900 La Follette was recognized as the spokesman for the progressive and reform-minded people of the state. He was identified in the public mind with certain specific proposals: reform of the tax structure, including more equitable taxation of the great corporations, direct primary elections, and vigorous prosecution of monopolies and trusts. In his campaign speeches he spoke often of the "Menace of the Political Machine" and offered his reforms to break its hold on the political life of the state. In his first message as governor to the Wisconsin Legislature in 1901, La Follette specifically outlined his program of reform. In this speech La Follette abandoned the traditional habit of sending the annual message to be read by a clerk and delivered the address in person, thus giving his proposals a much more forceful and dramatic effect.

MESSAGE OF GOVERNOR ROBERT M. LA FOLLETTE TO THE SENATE AND ASSEMBLY OF WISCONSIN, JANUARY 10, 1901

GENTLEMEN OF THE SENATE AND ASSEMBLY:

It is alike a privilege and a pleasure to congratulate you as the chosen representatives of the people of the State assembled under the law to express their will in your legislative acts. The session before you promises to be one of arduous labor and unusual responsibility. In compliance with the Constitution and established precedent, I submit the information and recommendations which follow. . . .

[1] From the *Journal of the Assembly,* January 10, 1901. State of Wisconsin (Madison, 1901), pp. 18–49.

Tax Reform

One of the great reforms of the Wisconsin Progressives was the development of a professional, expert, Tax Commission. Under the leadership of La Follette's friend Nils Haugen, who was a member of the Commission for twenty years, the Wisconsin Tax Commission reorganized the tax structure of the state, equalized property taxes, brought railroad and other corporate taxes to a more equitable basis, and sponsored the first modern graduated state income tax. In this excerpt from his 1901 message to the Legislature, La Follette described the pressing need for the Commission and a general reform of the state's tax structure.

The general scope of legislation and the large number of subjects acted upon in each session is unfavorable to the exhaustive examination and consideration of a problem as intricate and complex as the complete revision and codification of the tax laws.

The creation of a commission to make such investigation as the character and importance of the subject demand, to report to the Legislature the results of its examination, and to make recommendations in aid of just and efficient tax laws, could not fail of public approval.

Chapter 206, Laws of 1899, authorizes the appointment of a Tax Commissioner and two assistants to the Commissioner, for the purpose of investigating the tax system of this State, reporting thereon to the Legislature, and formulating and recommending legislation.

Owing to the scope of the work, and the great loss sustained to the Commission in the death of the first Tax Commissioner, General Michael Griffin, I am advised that no complete plan of revision of the tax laws will be proposed in the report made at the opening of the session.

The disappointment experienced on this account will, I believe, be lessened by the aid which you will doubtless receive from the Commission during the session in remedying the evils existing in some directions, and mitigating, if not wholly correcting, them in others. I would, under no circumstances, urge undue haste in the work of the Commission. It is of the utmost importance to each citizen and every interest, that all the time necessary should be taken and every possible facility furnished to enable it to complete, in a satisfactory manner, recommendations for a revision of the tax laws.

But, though it may require another biennial period to perfect and complete this work of the Commission, the fact should, under no circumstances, be made the excuse or justification for delaying such corrections of manifest inequalities as it is possible for the present Legislature to effect. Indeed, the great task of the Commission in constructing a complete system may be aided by remedying every defect possible in the existing law, either by amendment or independent act at this session, thus advancing along the line of revision and testing results wherever possible. In the meantime, the excess of burden which has so long rested upon certain classes of our citizens would be transferred to those who have carried less than a proportionate share in the past. Every act of government should be fair and just, and no portion of the system which allows certain classes of property to escape taxation, wholly or in part, should be permitted to stand upon the statutes.

The forthcoming report of the Tax Commission may not offer any recommendations to you respecting amendments to existing laws with a view of equalizing, in so far as may be, the assessment and collection of taxes. Nevertheless, in this work which it plainly behooves you to undertake, you will, without doubt, be greatly aided by the Commission either by further report during the session, or by co-operation with your committees in charge of this subject, in framing, perfecting and amending legislation to that end. Such legislation may be incorporated in, and made a part of, the final system of taxation and adopted as the law of this State. But, in the meantime, you will have rendered a great service to your constituents by affording the largest measure of relief you can give them at this time.

One of the first questions you should consider in dealing with the subject of taxation is the law creating the Commission itself. A careful examination of it will, I believe, convince you that it requires either very radical amendment, or that it should be entirely recast and reenacted.

One provision of this law seems to me very objectionable as a matter of public policy. There is absolutely no limit or check whatever upon the expenditure of money which may be made under it. In terms it authorizes the employment of any number of persons, to be paid salaries as the Commissioner, who is empowered to place them on the pay roll, may determine. In addition to this, the law warrants the payment of expenses and disbursements on account of the Commissioner, his assistants and clerks, without limitation, itemized accounts, vouchers, or the approval of any other officer of the State. In this respect I think the law is without example or parallel in the statutes of the State. Certain it is, if there be precedent for such legislation it should not be enlarged. Such a discretion is very liable to be abused sooner or later. Under a provision nearly, if not quite, as bad, it is reported that a sister State has incurred an expense of over one hundred thousand dollars for one year's work by her Tax Commission.

Another feature of this law which I believe can be changed with great advantage to the important duties of the Commission and economy to the State is the transfer of all statistical work to the Bureau of Statistics. Work of this character requires the services of men trained to the business. It should be under the supervision and control of the Commissioner of Statistics, whose reputation would at once give authority to this branch of the work, and guarantee rapidity and accuracy in its execution. This would relieve the Commission of the burden of attempting to build up a statistical bureau, and of supervising that special class of work, with which they can be acquainted only to a limited extent. To obtain the best results it seems to me the Commission should be free to give their time wholly to the vigorous enforcement of existing law, a critical study of its practical operation, and the development of better methods suggested by intelligent and discriminating observation and experience. Their valuable time should not be spent in supervising an office force in the performance of clerical and statistical work. There has for some time been employed in this office, besides the Commissioner and his two assistants, a force costing $5,700 per annum. I urge upon your attention the advisability of relieving the Commission of the performance of all labor of this character, believing that in so doing you will save money for the State, and, at the same time, advance the important work of the Commission.

This act further provides that the Tax Commission shall report to the Legislature on the first day of the session the results of its investigation and such legislation as they have formulated for the equalization of taxes. The Constitution, and well-observed custom, make it the duty of the Executive to submit to the Legislature upon its assembling his views respecting legislation and such recommendations as he may have to make. The act charges the Executive with the appointment of members of the Tax Commission, thereby fixing upon him direct responsibility to the State for the performance of their duties. But no provision is made enabling him to become informed as to their work from time to time, or as to the character or contents of their report, or any legislation they may propose. It would seem to me advisable that the Commission should be required to furnish such information to the Executive respecting its work as he may call for from time to time; to confer and consult with him in the prosecution of the work; and at least sixty days before the meeting of the Legislature to make its report to the Executive, who should transmit the same to the Legislature upon its assembling, together with any recommendations based thereon.

In conclusion upon this point, I desire to say that the Tax Commissioner has extended to the Executive every courtesy with respect to work in his office; but as only the introduction to the report is completed at this time, I am deprived of the valuable aid to be expected from the recommendations of the Commission, which will finally be incorporated therein.

While the act provides that the Commission shall have general supervision of the system of taxation throughout the State, that it may require local officers whose duties pertain to the assessment and collection of taxes or the disbursement of public funds to report to it, no authority is given to prescribe and enforce any rules or exercise any control whatever for the correction of faults found, or to exact a more faithful performance of duty on the part of local assessors. Supervision thus limited serves no end, except as an aid in securing information; and the single purpose of the law would seem to be the securing of information, the report of the same to the Legislature, with recommendations respecting legislation thereon.

In extending the term of service over a period of ten years and fixing the salary of the Commission at $5,000 and the two Assistant Commissioners at $4,000 each, the Legislature was undoubtedly prompted by the desire to attract to this service men of ability and fitness, such as the work demands. It does not, however, appear reasonable that it should require ten years to revise the tax system, or that when a revision has been completed by the Legislature that it should require the services of the Commission as a standing committee on revision for six or eight years thereafter. The period covered by two biennial sessions of the Legislature would appear to be a generous allowance of time for a thorough and complete performance of all the work contemplated by the law.

It is in no sense a disparagement of the value of the Commission's services, or the importance of the work, which prompts me to recommend that either the powers and duties of the Commission be greatly extended or that the term of service be shortened to a time consistent with the accomplishment of the duties defined by the law as it now stands.

Even if the term of service is shortened, an enlargement of the powers and duties of the Commission along certain lines would aid greatly in the work and facilitate, I believe, perfecting a complete tax system. In the solution of any practical problem experience is of great value. If, while engaged in formulating and revising the law, the Commission's power is extended to a supervision of its operation and enforcement, time will be saved to the Commission and the State in the end. Observation of the working of the machinery of the law in its details on the ground will be of immensely greater practical value than a much longer period of time spent in the office in purely constructive work. The information so obtained will be reliable, the recommendations based thereon simple and practical, their application already demonstrated.

Hence, I recommend that you so legislate as to require the Commission not only to have a general supervision of the system of taxation, but to take such measures as will enforce the provisions of the law, that all property be placed on the assessment roll at the actual cash value; that it be required to institute proper proceedings enforcing penalties provided for public officers whose duties pertain to the assessment and collection of taxes, and against individuals and the officers of corporations failing to comply with the provisions of the law with respect to the disclosure of property for assessment; to prefer charges for the removal from office of any assessor who has violated the law respecting assessment, and, in the prosecution of the same, authorize the Commissioner to call upon the Attorney-General or any district attorney of the State to prosecute any violation of the law respecting the assessment and collection of taxes; to visit, through some member of the Commission, each county in the State, personally, and investigate the work of assessors, with authority to summon the assessors of the county to appear before such Commission, or any member thereof, and to submit to examination respecting the performance of their duties as such assessors; to have full power and authority to take testimony and examine individuals and officers of corporations, and require the production of books and papers; and where the offices and books and papers and any witnesses are located outside the State, whenever necessary, to be empowered to take depositions in order to procure such information as may be useful either in enforcing the law or in enabling the Commission to recommend legislation; to examine upon their own motion, or upon the information of any individual, into any complaint as to property liable to taxation that has not been assessed, or has been improperly assessed, or to take such proceedings as will insure its assessment under the law whether such property be owned by an individual, a copartnership, or corporation.

While the added powers and duties herein suggested will, in their performance, make some demands upon the time of the Commission, I believe that knowledge on the part of the assessors and tax officers that the Commission is clothed with such power and authority will go a long way toward securing strict obedience to the law on the part of such officers. With the certainty that they are liable to be called upon to report fully to the Commission with respect to the performance of their duties at any time, their work will be performed with a view of being subjected to scrutiny and investigation, which, in and of itself, will produce radical reform at the outset.

That the law with respect to the assessment of all property can be so amended, supervised and enforced as to secure uniformity of assessment and enormously increase the tax upon classes of property which now escape wholly or in part, there is not the slightest reason to doubt. With neighboring States adding two or three hundred millions to the assessed valuation of personal property in a short twelve months, we shall be derelict in our duty indeed, if we fail to strengthen the law wherever it is weak and provide for its vigorous enforcement. To this end the assessor should be clothed with authority, and it should be made his duty, to interrogate under oath individuals and the officers of corporations with respect to property. Failure to perform this duty in any case should be made the subject of such reasonable penalties as will make it possible to secure the conviction of any assessor who fails to perform his duty.

It should furthermore be made the duty of the assessor to report to the Tax Commission, for their information, and to the district attorney of the county any individual who refuses to answer fully, or is believed to have evaded or misstated with respect to his property, or the property of any corporation of which he is an officer. It should be made the duty of the district attorney upon receiving such information from any assessor, or upon the sworn complaint of any individual that property liable to taxation has not been assessed, or has been improperly assessed, in either case, to cite such individual or person complained of to appear before the circuit court, or a judge thereof, there to be examined and answer fully questions relative to such inquiry, and to be subject to proceedings in contempt for failure to so appear and so answer, and liable to prosecution for perjury for knowingly and wilfully answering untruthfully as to any material fact upon which he is interrogated.

It is not my purpose, nor would it be possible within the space properly assignable to this subject, to instance all the changes by amendment and otherwise urgently demanded in the tax laws.

I understand that the Tax Commission has devoted much time to investigation, with a view of determining whether the corporations, including railroads, street railways, telegraph and telephone systems, insurance, trust and guarantee companies, taxed by license fee, and express companies, sleeping-car, freight line and equipment companies, taxed by a special ad valorem method, are justly and proportionately taxed under existing laws. The facts thus secured, together with the Commission's conclusions deduced therefrom, will, I believe, be communicated to you at this session. Not being advised of the results of such investigation, or of the nature and contents of the report, I can, of course, submit nothing with reference thereto. . . .

One of the questions you will have to determine in dealing with this subject is whether railway companies shall be taxed directly by assessment upon the value of their property, or whether they shall continue to pay under the license system a certain percentage upon their gross earnings. The strong objection to a license fee upon gross earnings is that it allows the corporation to make its own report of the amount of its gross earnings, or, in other words, to assess itself. It is but just to note in this connection, that, as appears by the above tables, the railway companies have been fairer than the average of individuals, who, as to the great mass of personal property, assess themselves: the percentage of assessed of market value of the railways being 20 5–100 as against 12 9–100 for all other personal property in 1899. In no case, however, should the assessment be left to the tax payer, whether corporation or individual, without some check or safeguard for the State. If the railway companies are to be taxed directly by assessment upon the value of their property, then I have no hesitation in saying that the assessment should be made by a State Board of the highest possible character and ability. If the present system of a license fee fixed at a certain rate per cent, upon gross earnings, is to be continued, then I recommend that there be reposed in some representative of the State, either the Tax Commission or Board of Assessment, authority to increase the amount of gross earnings reported by any railway company, to such sum as will, in the judgment of the Commission or Board of Assessment, render the amount just and equitable as representing the actual gross earnings of the company reporting the same; that such be taken as *prima facie* evidence of the actual gross earnings of such railway company; but that any railway company considering itself aggrieved by the sum so fixed as gross earnings may appear before such Commission or Board of Assessment and be fully heard, and produce witnesses and evidence in their behalf in respect thereto. The final determination of the Commission or Board should in some form be subject to the supervision of the courts. Authority to increase the amount or value of personal property of the individual, as returned by him, is now conferred upon the assessor by statute. Like authority should be given the Tax Commission or Board of Assessment with respect to the corporation, if taxed upon its own report of gross earnings.

With no other class of property is there presented so flagrant an example of open disregard of the law as in the case of bonds, mortgages, securities, and the average amount of money in possession and on deposit. A conservative estimate, based upon the latest accessible data together with census figures for 1890, shows real-estate mortgages in Wisconsin amounting to $110,000,000. This takes no account of unrecorded securities computed at $165,000,000. It is therefore safe to say that not over five per cent of the taxable notes, bonds and mortgages in the State pays any tax whatever.

The average amount of money in possession and on deposit which the assessor succeeded in finding and returning as taxes in 1898 was only $7,163,444. On the first Monday in July, 1898, the state and private banks alone reported to the State Treasurer "money on deposit" amounting to $40,976,312.70. The report of the United States Comptroller of the Currency shows that on the 5th day of May, 1898, the very month in which assessments were made, there was in the national banks of Wisconsin $46,224,201.43. Or in both national, state and private banks on these two dates in 1898 an aggregate of $87,200,513.50. More than $80,000,000 of this money wholly escaped taxation that year.

I am aware that in the literature which has rapidly accumulated on the subject there is much speculative discussion of "perfect theories" and "new systems" which wholly eliminate the personal property tax. But there are certain elementary principles respecting taxation, the justice of which we believe in, the practical operation of which we well understand, and from which, I am sure, no mere academic discussion will tempt you to depart.

I know well it is urged that any attempt to place these shirking millions on the assessment rolls will be wholly futile, and end in paying a premium on perjury, increasing the interest rate, and driving money out of the State. But we should remember that no persistent, resolute, determined effort has been made to enforce the existing tax laws, much less correct even their more manifest defects and give to their provisions vitality and force. In some States there have been spasmodic attempts to reach some classes of property, quickly discouraged and discredited, however, by those interested in having others pay their taxes. It is only very recently that real, thorough-going tax reform has been generally inaugurated. And when some adequate penalty has been attached to an assessor's failure to perform his duty; when it is made some one's business to see to it that the assessor obeys the laws or pays the penalty; when individuals and corporations are subjected to the same searching examination as to concealment respecting taxable property that the fraudulent debtor now encounters in trying to avoid his other liabilities; when the attempt to make one's neighbor pay one's taxes meets the same public condemnation and the same legal punishment that the individual encounters in trying to defraud the individual or the corporation—then the first of these objections will be effectually disposed of. The so-called intangible property—notes, bonds and mortgages—will then become tangible and assessable property.

But it is asserted that the money will be driven out of the State before its owners will consent to pay the tax upon it. If it is driven out of the State where will it go? In every State in the Union today public sentiment is strongly aroused and organization everywhere moving to make all taxable property, individual and corporate, meet its assessments and pay its taxes.

On all sides laws are being revised, and, in some States, constitutional amendments are being adopted to secure this result. It is reasonably certain that the day is at hand when no State in the Union will offer an asylum of refuge for capital seeking to evade the payment of taxes. Temporary transfers of limited amounts may be made. A few individuals may seek a change of residence. But we can spare the citizen who will expatriate himself rather than pay his taxes. It will be but a little time before the tax-dodger will find himself without a home and a country. Furthermore, it is not believed that much incentive will remain for so removing property from the State, because adding to the assessor's rolls the immense volume of property which now escapes will largely reduce the rate of taxation upon all classes of property.

It is asserted that it will raise the interest rate to make money and mortgages pay taxes. Possibly it may increase the interest rate somewhat to enforce the law as to money and mortgages. In California, where they have a constitutional provision that real-estate mortgages shall be assessed to the owner of the mortgage, and the assessed valuation of the real estate reduced by the amount of the mortgage, two different claims are made by those opposed to the assessment of mortgages: one, that the interest rate is increased to an amount sufficient to make the borrower pay the taxes; another, that an agreement between the borrower and lender is insisted upon by the latter, requiring payment by commission or otherwise, sufficient to reimburse the lender for the amount of taxes which he is required to pay upon the mortgage. It is a fact, however, as shown by the last census, that the interest rate in California is lower than in adjoining States, though this may be in part due to independent causes. After much discussion of the subject, Missouri adopted at the recent election a constitutional amendment similar in effect to that of California. Whatever may be the exact fact as to the effect on interest rate as between the borrower and lender, the principle is to be commended, because it taxes each man justly on the record. The mortgagor has to the extent of the mortgage parted with an interest in the real estate. The mortgagee has acquired that interest, and each is taxed only upon his proportionate share. There is another aspect of the case worthy of attention. Any law which secures a correct return of property by the assessor is to be commended. It is a distinct gain for honesty, and lodges in the public mind a more wholesome respect for the law. The individual possessor of wealth and the corporation of large capital engaged in evading and violating the tax laws are doing much to beget a disregard and want of respect for all law, and to excuse violation of its letter and spirit with all classes. But there is further answer to be made to the objection to taxing money, because it is claimed it will increase the interest rate. It is a manifest injustice to each taxpayer to compel him to pay an additional tax, occasioned by allowing several hundred millions of money and securities to go untaxed in this State, in order to maintain a lower interest rate for the advantage of the comparatively few who borrow. It is a matter for congratulation in Wisconsin that the great proportion of those who borrow, both upon real estate and collateral security, borrow for the purpose of improving property, extending business operations, and carrying and maintaining lines of credit in conducting every-day commercial transactions. If some addition to the interest rate in this State should follow the taxing of notes, mortgages and money as an adjustment between borrowers and lenders, it is a proposition which will admit of no dispute that the individuals, co-partnerships, and corporations borrowing the money have no right to ask the other taxpayers to contribute directly or indirectly toward keeping the interest rate down, or, in other words, to the payment of a portion of that interest.

In conclusion upon this important subject, I have only this to add: It is not unlikely that a complete revision of tax legislation may result in reconstructing the system upon radically different lines. There are many reasons that may be urged therefor, entitled to more or less weight. But these questions will be settled when they are reached in order. Your responsibility is a present one. And I commend this subject to your most careful consideration, confident that you will meet it with courage and fidelity, and discharge every duty devolving upon you just, fairly and promptly.

A Primary Election Law

La Follette frequently referred to the direct primary as the "first plank" in his program of reform. He argued that all barriers that separated the elected official from the direct control of the voters must be removed if the Republic was to become in truth a democracy. When finally adopted in 1904, Wisconsin's direct primary law was the first to establish a comprehensive system of direct nominating elections in the United States. La Follette reinforced this measure with preferential primaries for United States Senator and President, and a second-choice primary (to prevent minority elections) in 1911. In this address, La Follette vigorously set forth the arguments for the principle of primary elections.

Commissioned by the suffrages of the citizens of this State to represent them, you will have neither in the session before you nor in any official responsibility which you may assume, a more important duty than that of perfecting and writing upon the statute books of Wisconsin a primary election law.

It is a fundamental principle of this republic that each citizen shall have equal voice in government. This is recognized and guaranteed to him through the ballot. In a representative democracy, where a citizen cannot act for himself for any reason, he must delegate his authority to the public official who acts for him. Since government, with us, is conducted by the representatives of some political party, the citizen's voice in making and administering the laws is expressed through his party ballot. Hence, to preserve his sovereign right to an equal share in government, he must be assured an equal voice in making his party ballot. This privilege is vital. This is the initial point of all administration. It is here government begins, and if there be failure here, there will be failure throughout. Control lost at this point is never regained; rights surrendered here are never restored. As the foundation is laid, so will the structure be reared. The naming of the men upon this party ticket is the naming of men who will make and enforce the laws. It not only settles the policy of the party, it determines the character of the government.

For many years the evils of the caucus and convention system have multiplied and baffled all attempts at legislative control or correction. The reason for this is elementary. The evils come not from without but from within. The system in all its details is inherently bad. It not only favors, but, logically and inevitably, produces manipulation, scheming, trickery, fraud and corruption. The delegate elected in caucus is nominally the agent of the voter to act for him in convention. Too frequently he has his own interest alone at heart, and, for this reason, has secured his selection as a delegate. As a consequence, he acts not for the voter, but serves his own purpose instead. This fact in itself taints the trust from the outset, and poisons the system at its very source.

No legitimate business could survive under a system where authority to transact its vital matters was delegated and re-delegated to agents and sub-agents, who controlled their own selection, construed their own obligations, and were responsible to nobody.

From the very nature of the case such a system must build up a strong central power. The opportunity offered to acquire a mastery of party nominations, thus controlling great political organizations, and with them patronage and legislation as well, was certain to be seized upon by men possessed of the talent of combination, manipulation and political management. Hence, to-day, it is well understood that the whole complicated business is managed by a central power, from which emanates all orders, and to which even "instructed" delegates in convention are, in some mysterious way, quickly made subservient. This controlling power is the established political machine. Its overthrow is always possible; but since it is the inevitable result and logical outgrowth of the system, such overthrow can only be temporary, and the machine will either be restored or give way to a new machine constructed upon the same lines and operated upon the same principle of supreme authority.

The officials nominated by the machine become its faithful servants and surrender judgment to its will. This they must do in self-preservation or they are retired to private life. Wielding a power substantially independent of the voter, it is quite unnecessary to regard him as an important factor in government. He can usually be depended upon in the elections, because campaigns are so managed as to make strong appeal to party feeling, and he has to vote his party ticket or support that of the opposition nominated by the same method. Under our system of party government the selection of the candidate is the vital question.

It is unfair to assail the men who constitute or control the machine. As long as the delegate system is preserved, so long will some political machine control in the politics of the State. But even if it were possible to conduct a political convention without interference or domination from the political machine, it ought not to be intrusted with the selection of men who are to make and execute the laws. If it were possible to eliminate all bargains and deals and dickers and corruption, if the delegates were controlled by the purest motives, and desired only faithfully to represent the voters, whose agents they are,—even then the nominating convention is under no circumstances a fit place to transact the most important business in a representative government. A political convention is never a deliberative body. It is impossible from the brevity of its life, the confusion of its proceedings, the intangible character of its records, to fix or attach any abiding sense of responsibility in its membership. Its business is rushed through under pressure for time. Excitement and impatience control, rather than reason and judgment. Noisy enthusiasm outweighs the strongest argument. Misstatements and misunderstandings will defeat the best candidate. The plain truth can hardly keep pace with hurrying events. It is rare, indeed, that the results of a convention are satisfactory to anybody excepting the few who secure some personal advantage or benefit from it.

It is strange that the citizen has so long remained patient under practices which compel him to hand over the most important of his prerogatives to others to be exercised for him, and with so little regard either to his wishes or his interests.

It is the essence of republican government that the citizen should act for himself directly wherever possible. In the exercise of no other right is this so important as in the nomination of candidates for office. It is of primary importance that the public official should hold himself directly accountable to the citizen. This he will do only when he owes his nomination directly to the citizen. If between the citizen and the official there is a complicated system of caucuses and conventions, by the easy manipulation of which the selection of candidates is controlled by some other agency or power, then the official will so render his services as to have the approval of such agency or power. The overwhelming demand of the people of this State, whom you represent, is that such intervening power and authority, and the complicated system which sustains it, shall be torn down and cast aside. This it is your duty, and high privilege as well, to accomplish in the session before you. This, it is well understood, cannot be accomplished by any temporizing measure or so-called caucus reforms. The defects of the caucus, convention and delegate system are fatal because organic. It cannot be amended, reconstructed or reorganized, and its perpetuation secured. Its end is decreed by the enlightened moral sentiment of the entire country. It can no more resist the development which is sweeping it aside than could the adoption of the Australian ballot be successfully opposed a short ten years ago. It may secure trifling delays by temporary expedients. Its advocates may insist on making it a fetish and being sacrificed with it. But its knell has been sounded in Wisconsin, where it is already defeated, and a decade will leave scarcely a trace of its complicated machinery in existence in any State in the Union.

The demand of the voter to-day is clear and explicit. He asks that there be restored to him the citizen's right to vote directly for the party nominee of his choice. He asserts that denial of this right, or doubt of his ability to exercise it, is an impeachment of the principle upon which State and National government is based. There is no valid objection which can be interposed to this reasonable demand upon the part of the citizen, and I submit that the Legislature should primarily address itself to the business of framing a law that shall accord to him, in full measure, the sovereign power of the ballot. The plan of such legislation will not be found difficult of practical application. The details should be plain and simple. The specific provisions of such legislation are to be determined by the Legislature, not by the Executive department of the State government. The legislation should be so framed as to insure to each voter an equal voice in the selection of the candidates of his party, without let or hindrance on the part of any man; accompanying this should be such provisions as will insure an accurate registration and determination of the will of the people as expressed in such primary election.

Care should be taken that sufficient time be given the voter carefully to consider the character and merits of each candidate seeking nomination at the hands of the people.

When this has been done, and not till then, the mandate of the people expressed at the polls last November, will have been obeyed.

A primary election conducted under such a law will enable every voter to express his personal choice by direct vote for the candidates of his party. It will take of his time but one visit to the election booth, and but long enough while there to mark his ballot.

In the pursuit of his regular occupation day by day, in the quiet of his home under conditions the most favorable for reaching a sound conclusion, the voter will have time and opportunity to form his opinions as to the merits of the various candidates, and a few moments, at the most, on primary election day will be required to record that carefully matured judgment. How much more likely is the citizen to attend upon a primary election under these circumstances than to give up a considerable share of the entire season in order to attempt to express his preference through the uncertain medium of an authority delegated to one set of men selected in one set of caucuses for County officers, another for Assemblymen, another for State officers, each followed by nominating conventions as well, a scene of confusion, wrangling, dispute and disorder, where weak men are badgered and corrupt men are bought.

It is to be expected that objection will be interposed to any plan offered. It is right that all objections should be fairly considered. I apprehend, however, that very little time will be consumed on your part upon the objection that under a primary election nominations would not be distributed with reference to geography or nationality. When primary elections are held upon the same day, there is no opportunity for advantage by either party over the other in this respect, and the selection of candidates will be made upon considerations of greater importance to the people than either the nationality or place of residence of the candidates.

The objection has been offered that cities would be able to control as against the country in a primary election, because of the better opportunity to poll a large vote where the population is dense. It is scarcely fair to make this objection as pertaining to primary elections. It would be quite as easy to poll a full vote in the country in a primary election as it is to get out a representative vote to a caucus under the present system, and it is no more of an objection against primary elections that the density of population in cities offers greater facility for polling the city vote than it is against the election of delegates in caucuses. Neither would there be stronger tendency, for any reason, for cities to unite as against the country with primary elections than with caucuses. In practice it has never been found possible to unite cities against the country in any political way. Any attempt to accomplish this would defeat itself by arousing and solidifying the agricultural sections of the State.

It has been further objected that a primary election would afford opportunity for the presentation of an unlimited number of candidates, resulting in such division of the vote that nomination by plurality will be made by a small majority. This is one of the defects of nominations by political conventions. Under the caucus and convention system we often have a large number of candidates located in such parts of the State as to divide the vote of the candidate most obnoxious to the machine, each candidate claiming local support because of residence, for the purpose of gathering up delegations that may be transferred in convention to the candidate selected by the machine. Nor is this pretense confined to encouraging candidates for one particular office, with a view of controlling the nomination of that office. It is not unusual, for instance, in a gubernatorial contest for the machine to encourage many candidates in different sections of the State to seek nomination for the other places on the State ticket, not for the purpose of nominating them for such offices, but to secure control of the delegations from counties or congressional districts, which are to be used in the convention for the purpose of nominating the candidate chosen by the machine for the head of the ticket. This sometimes goes to the extent of bringing out many candidates for the same office, rewarding such candidates for having gathered up their delegations for this purpose by appointment to some office within the control of the machine. Indeed, so many phases of this practice are possible under the caucus and convention system, one would scarcely expect its advocates to venture it as an argument against primary elections.

When it is taken into account that, under a primary election law, men of the highest talent and especial fitness for public life will readily consent to become candidates for public office—men who can scarcely be tempted to stand as candidates under the present system; when we consider that under such a law the nominations will be made by a majority of all voters in an orderly and decent contest, determined by direct vote of the citizen under all the sanctions of the law; and when it is likewise manifest that mere stalking horses and straw candidates could make but a very limited appeal for popular vote, it must be apparent to any fair-minded man that a primary election is certain to limit rather than enlarge the field of candidates.

If, however, upon trial it should be found desirable, or if, in your judgment, it should be deemed wise at the outset, this objection can be effectually met by providing that the voter at the primary election shall indicate upon his ballot his first and second choice of the candidates presented for each office. And that if no candidate has a majority over all candidates of first choice, then the candidate having the largest number of first and second choice votes shall be accorded the nomination. Rare indeed, if ever, would an occasion present itself where this plan would not decide that nomination by a majority of the votes. In considering this objection it should be borne in mind that in no case under the caucus and convention system where there are a large number of candidates for any office does a majority of the voters determine the nomination. After much shifting, compromising, and trading with respect to other offices on the ticket, the majority vote in the convention does not represent or express, in any way, a majority vote by the voters. Indeed, it not infrequently happens that the candidate nominated has scarcely been considered as a candidate during the selection of delegates, in which case, as well as when "dark horse" candidates are sprung upon conventions, absolutely no opportunity is given the voter to express any choice.

Furthermore, under the caucus and convention system, delegates are almost invariably elected solely with reference to the head of the ticket, whether for State or county offices. As to other candidates upon the ticket, the voter scarcely hears mention of them by name. Under a primary election, since the voter must himself, personally in the election booth, pass upon the fitness and qualification for the nomination of every candidate on the ticket, those who are standing for the other important places below the head of the ticket, whose nominations ought in all cases to be made with care, will find it necessary to make a canvass upon their own account and upon their own merits instead of being successful through some combination with one or the other of the candidates for the head of the ticket.

It is obvious that any fair, candid consideration of this question removes every objection that can be interposed. The great reform accomplished through the Australian ballot, and its education to the voters everywhere, ought to demonstrate that an honest, intelligent effort to give the people of Wisconsin a primary election law, providing for all nominations and to be made by direct vote, is not only wise and just, but practicable and feasible from every possible point of view.

The principle has been applied in several States with such a degree of success that the matter is no longer an experiment. These laws have placed the selection of the candidates of all parties, and consequently, the selection of all officials, in the hands of the people. The character of the officials selected, the increased interests of the people in the selection of the candidates for public office, alike plainly point the way of progress along which the people of this Commonwealth have bidden us proceed.

I have extended this discussion more at length and dealt more in detail in suggesting legislative enactment than would be warranted ordinarily. But in view of the history of the movement for this legislation in our State, I have been prompted by a sense of duty in so doing.

I commend the matter to your careful consideration, knowing that you will faithfully execute the command of the people.

The University of Wisconsin

La Follette's support for the state university and his personal friendship for President Charles R. Van Hise greatly assisted the institution in its drive to become a "university of the first rank." In turn, university scholars advised and served La Follette and his successors in a variety of capacities, cementing the bond between the campus and the state house that has been described as the "Wisconsin Idea." In this short excerpt, La Follette pleaded the cause of the university and incidently spoke of his own philosophy of education.

The Reports of the Board of University Regents and of the President of the University convey to you detailed information respecting the growth and needs of this institution. The value to the State from its continued development, and its reputation throughout the country, are so well established and so generally appreciated that its friends and supporters can have no cause of apprehension for the future. Its growth in influence and usefulness within the last decade has exceeded the anticipations and hopes of its most sanguine promoters. State provision for the increasing expenses inseparable from growth has been generous and prompt. The new burdens have been carried by the people without complaint. If the advocates of university expansion will keep in mind their obligation to the State, which can be done without lessening the zeal for the cause in which they have enlisted, I am sure that they will meet with few obstacles in legislative action or in public sentiment.

The plea sometimes made that State universities cannot afford to compete with institutions of learning lavishly endowed by multimillionaires is not valid. It is not necessary to engage in competition in extravagant expenditure. In point of fact, our own and certain other State universities in the West are competing successfully in work and growth with the oldest and most richly endowed colleges in the country, without expenditures which would bear comparison. You will not forget—indeed, the friends of the University will not permit you to forget—that the University of Wisconsin has its rivals in universities of neighboring commonwealths. Few citizens of Wisconsin will be found ready to argue that this State cannot afford to keep pace with adjoining States in educational work and advancement.

During the last biennial period the material improvements of the University have included the enlargement of Main Hall, the construction of a suitable building for the College of Engineering, and the completion of the Library Building for the State Historical Society and University. The first provision for the last-named structure was made under Governor W. H. Upham's administration, and largely through the instrumentality of his influence. As a permanent home for the invaluable historical records and volumes of the State, as well as an important auxiliary to all University work, this splendid structure will stand an enduring monument to the enterprise of its distinguished projectors.

Additions to "the means of acquiring a thorough knowledge of the various branches of learning," during the last two years, include the reorganization of the College of Engineering and the establishment of the School of History and the School of Commerce. The purpose of this last school is to furnish "a course of study especially fitted for the training of young men who wish to enter business careers or branches of the public service in which a knowledge of business is essential." The practical utility of such a school to meet the demands of a commercial people requires no argument.

Under the head of immediate and special needs which will call for extra appropriations, the University authorities make most prominent a new building for the College of Agriculture, suitable equipment for the new building of the College of Engineering, and provision for the School of Commerce. I have no hesitancy in commending each of these proposed improvements as worthy your approval, but confess some doubt as to whether you will be able to honor all the worthy demands upon the taxing power without imposing an onerous burden upon the taxpaying power of the State. For reasons somewhat similar to those which prompt recommendations of State aid to country schools, I am inclined especially to favor every practical encouragement to the growth of the College of Agriculture without delay.

Perhaps it is as well to admit that the Executive may be influenced somewhat by a kindly prejudice in favor of the University of Wisconsin. But I am convinced that its friends will have no cause for disappointment if you deal with its requisitions and arguments with the most strict analysis of their merits.

The following suggestions from the report of the President of the Board of Regents to the Governor are submitted as the language of experience and wisdom:

"A great modern institution of learning demands a great and growing income. The problem is not merely how much to appropriate and expend, but how to make the use of the moneys received from the State, the Nation and individuals. While economy and care must always be exercised, the State will not have discharged its duty to the University, nor the University fulfilled its mission to the people, until adequate means have been furnished to every young man and woman in the State to acquire an education at home in every department of learning. . . ."

Trusts and Monopolies

The war on the great corporations, railroads, manufacturers, and distributors, as monopolists and destroyers of competition, was a hallmark of the Progressive Movement. La Follette, both in Wisconsin and in the United States Senate, led the fight against the abuse and misuse of economic power. This section from his message to the Legislature stated his views succinctly.

The evils to be reached by legislation on trusts and monopolies are such combinations and confederations as are organized to control prices, create monopolies and destroy competition, or which, in their practical working, have that effect.

It is not because a corporation has a large capital or transacts a large and profitable business that it is an injury to the community or a menace to its prosperity. On the contrary, the development and growth of modern business have made large aggregations of capital absolutely necessary, and such capital is fairly entitled to a reasonable and legitimate profit. The wrong is done and the injury inflicted when such combinations of capital are enabled, by means adopted for that purpose, to control prices, stifle competition and create a monopoly.

The decisions of the highest courts of the United States, and of the several States, leave no room to doubt that the power of the legislative branch of the government is ample to redress all wrongs so done to society. The decisions of the courts are practically uniform to the effect that no one has any right to enter into any agreement or combination when the purpose or the effect is to control prices or create a monopoly. Further, it is also apparent that the right to prohibit such contract or combination is clear, when the object is to control prices, even if it is not intended unreasonably to increase prices. It is along these lines that the anti-trust legislation of Congress known as the Sherman law was enacted, and also similar legislation by the several States. With only some unimportant exceptions, such legislation has been uniformly sustained by the courts. It is expected that during the present session the United States Senate will pass the House bill extending the scope of the Sherman law, increasing its penalties and making prosecutions under it mandatory on the part of the United States district attorneys of the country.

Evils of this kind exist and are in operation in every State. Their extent and harmful effect may or may not have been exaggerated in the public estimation, but all must agree that there is much that ought to receive the consideration of the legislative branch of the State government. The present law of this State on the subject is principally contained in chapter 357 of the General Laws of 1897. I regard it as entirely insufficient, either as a remedy or a restraint. In the first place it only applies to corporations. It is entirely plain, however, that partnerships and individuals may enter into agreements and combinations, which, in their results, will be just as disastrous to the public interests as can any confederation of corporations. It is not perceived that the corporate character of the party doing it makes the controlling prices, or the creating a monopoly, any more or less hurtful than if the same thing was done by a partnership or individual.

In the next place, it only denounces such combinations when entered into by corporations organized under the laws of this State. It is of course known that the whole subject of interstate commerce is under our system exclusively a matter of Federal cognizance; but surely the State has some control over the business transactions within its limits, even by foreign corporations. It is a large subject. The line where the power of the State ends and the power of the National government begins may be difficult to define, but, the State having some power in the matter, the duty of State government is exactly commensurate with the limits of its powers.

Furthermore, the only remedy provided or suggested by the present statute is a proceeding in the courts to vacate the charter and annul the existence of the offending corporation. Such a remedy is to a great extent illusory. Corporations must by necessity act by officers and agents, and it is submitted that the only efficacious way to control the corporation is to act upon the individuals who control its affairs and shape its policy. I recommend to the Legislature of this State an entire revision of the laws relating to this subject, and the enactment of such laws and shall promise an efficient remedy for the great evil, and which at the same time shall not hamper individual enterprise or take from capital the reasonable returns to which it is fairly entitled when invested in business enterprise.

I think legislation should be adopted providing that if a corporation organized under the laws of this or any other State or any partnership or association of individuals, or any individuals, shall enter into, or become a member of, or a party to, any trust, agreement, combination, confederation or understanding with any other corporation, partnership, person, or association of persons, to regulate or fix the price of any commodity or to limit the amount of any commodity to be manufactured, mined, sold, transported or placed on sale or disposed of, or to do, or to refrain from doing, any other thing with the intent to control and fix the price of any commodity to be manufactured, mined, sold or transported in this State, such corporation and the officers and agents thereof, and such partnerships, individuals and associations of persons, shall be deemed guilty of conspiracy to defraud, and shall be subject to such prosecution and punishment and such penalty or forfeiture as may in the judgment of the Legislature, be proper.

Such enactment should also contain suitable provisions making all such contracts and agreements void, and provide machinery for the collection of such penalties and forfeitures and for the annulment of the charter of such offender, if a domestic corporation, and for the forfeiture of the right to do business in this state if a foreign corporation, and imposing such penalties on the individuals convicted of violating the law, as may be appropriate.

2

Reform and the Senate[1]

When Robert La Follette took his seat in the United States Senate in January, 1906, he was already known throughout the country as a blazing reformer who had routed the old guard in his home state and had made Wisconsin one of the most progressive states in the union. His reception in the Senate was cool and his colleagues made it plain that they expected him to serve his apprenticeship in silence as did other freshmen senators. When La Follette had the audacity to make a major speech on the pending Hepburn bill only a few weeks after taking his seat, most senators rebuked him by absenting themselves from the floor. La Follette responded with the warning that unless the members faced this issue and solved it in the public interest ". . . seats now temporarily vacant may be permanently vacated by those who have the right to occupy them at this time." This speech illustrates "Fighting Bob's" determination to carry his crusade to the nation and to the Senate itself.

THE RELATION OF GOVERNMENT TO COMMERCE AND TRANSPORTATION

The commerce of a country is a measure of its material power. It is the product of all the labor and capital of the country—on the farms, in the mines, and factories, and shops, and every field of material production.

The labor and capital of a country employed in production upon a basis attaining to the upbuilding of any community is everywhere absolutely dependent on transportation.

The founders of this Government understood that commerce is vital to organized society; that the development of the country depends upon the ready exchange of commodities between its different communities and sections. And so they ordained that commerce should be free between the States.

[1] From the *Congressional Record,* 59th Congress, 1st sess. (April 23, 1906), Vol. 40, pp. 5684ff.

The founders of the Government and those who followed them understood that transportation is properly a function of government, and so they built highways, and turnpikes, and dug canals, and improved rivers and harbors, and finally built State railroads and aided in the building of interstate railroads. These highways by land and water were paid for wholly or in part out of the public treasury and the public domain.

The vital interest of organized society in commerce and the public nature of transportation imposes upon government the duty to maintain a control over transportation as a public service. Hence upon the broadest ground of public policy, wholly apart from any power to control, dependent upon charter grants, government must exercise, as a sovereign right, absolute authority over all persons and all property engaged in transportation.

The public character of the transportation service and the inherent right in sovereignty to exercise control over it, imposes upon the Government the obligation to require the common carrier to render the service upon reasonable terms and upon equal terms. For the Government to fail in this duty, for it to turn over to railroad corporations the uncontrolled right to dictate the terms of service and its character, is to abandon a function of government and place the common carrier in the control of the commerce of the country. To permit the railroads to control the commerce of the country is, in the final analysis, to permit the railroads to control the country.

I maintain, then, that the authority of government to control transportation, both as to the character of the service and the rate of the service, is inherent as a right of sovereignty and that the obligation rests upon government to exercise this power. . . .

The great bulk of commerce is interstate. The National Government has the exclusive power to regulate interstate commerce. It has the responsibility that goes with the power. Shall Congress use it freely, courageously, or timidly, cringingly, ineffectively?

The Supreme Court has decided that the Constitution fixes a limitation upon the power of Congress to establish rates. The fifth amendment provides that private property shall not be taken for public use without just compensation. The constitutionality of the orders of the Commission can always be tested on this ground, regardless of any express provision in the law to that effect.

Legally, it is as needless to provide that carriers may appeal to the courts to test the constitutionality of a law affecting their interests as it would be to add that provision to each and every law that passes Congress. The question of providing a so-called "broad court review" has resolved itself into one of public policy. Shall Congress expressly or impliedly extend to the carriers greater privileges of litigation than the Constitution guarantees them, or shall Congress limit their opportunity of litigation in so far as the Constitution permits?

Why should Congress provide that the railroads shall have the right to appeal from the rate established by the Commission on any other than constitutional grounds? Is not the provision that their property shall not be taken without just compensation sufficient protection? Does any man fear the precedent? Is it not the same test that the private citizen must abide when the railroad, by the authority conferred on it by the State, takes his home, without regard to its precious associations, and awards him only just compensation?

Does any man fear that limiting railroad companies to their constitutional rights will work them any wrong? Consider that Congress might itself fix a schedule of rates and prescribe specific regulations. What does it do instead? It creates a Commission. The Interstate Commerce Commission is appointed by the President. It is confirmed by the Senate. It is assumed that the President in appointing, and the Senate in confirming, will exercise great care. Their selection will be made with the same singleness of purpose with which the Supreme Court of the United States is chosen. Integrity, ability, fitness will be the consideration.

The members of the Commission, by the terms of the act, give all their time exclusively to the study of this single complex problem. They acquire expert knowledge. They reach definite well-grounded conclusions as to what constitutes reasonable rates and just practices in transportation. They are as conscientious as any court would be in the discharge of the duties assigned. Their judgment when finally reached is as deliberate, unbiased, and disinterested as that of any court. It is their duty to insure reasonable and just transportation rates to the public and to prevent unfair and discriminatory charges. That would be the duty of the court likewise. But the Commission presumably has a very much broader knowledge and deeper insight into the determining facts than any court could acquire in the course of a brief trial.

The Commission and the courts should complement each other. The Commission is the tribunal of the facts; the courts of the law. The Commission must always have consideration of the law in its application to facts. The courts must, of course, consider facts in the application of the law; but it is in the public interest that the judgment of the Commission on the facts should be final where possible.

There should be no unnecessary complexity in the solution of a great problem. There should be intelligent and economic division of work. The courts review the laws made by Congress to test their constitutionality. The Supreme Court has repeatedly said it does not pass upon the wisdom of laws.

The Commission may err. The judgment of the wisest, most conscientious, and most expert man is not always infallible. The conclusions of the court are not always infallible. But we must abide by them. For generations of time the judgment of juries as to facts has been accepted as final. How much more reliable the judgment of expert commissioners of the same high character and standing as the court. When the plain citizen must abide the verdict of the jury as to the facts, can it be seriously contended that the corporations should be accorded the privilege of having the facts adjudged by an expert commission tried over again in the courts? Is not their constitutional right a sufficient guaranty that they will not suffer serious wrong?

Does any man honestly believe the corporations are clamoring for a broad review in the interest of justice? Would they care for the privilege except as it gives opportunity for the endless delays of litigation that tend to defeat substantial justice? . . .

There is much less danger of railroad companies suffering from the decisions of the Commission than of the shippers being wronged by the action of the court that grants the preliminary injunction. The order of the Commission is reached after full consideration of all the facts; that of the court for preliminary injunction is the judgment of one judge upon affidavit by an interested party.

It would not, in dealing with corporations, establish any precedent that might not be safely applied to protect the property rights of any citizen. But I would not be more careful, more cautious, more timid in dealing with the corporations than in dealing with individuals. It has seemed to me that some who have spoken for this legislation have been too much on the defensive. They have been more eloquent and enthusiastic over their anxiety to defend the corporate interests from all harm than over their desire to frame a law that will bring railroad corporations back to their plain duties as common carriers, and protect the people from the existing intolerable abuses in transportation.

Prohibiting the use of preliminary injunction will enhance the value of this legislation beyond all computation. The operation of the law will be simplified and justice promoted.

To cut out this much abused process will not confer autocratic power upon the Commission. Indeed, it will not in anywise affect the power of the Commission. It will put upon the railroad companies the burden of hastening instead of delaying the final judgment of the court if they are sincerely seeking to secure justice.

Mr. President, I pause in my remarks to say this. I can not be wholly indifferent to the fact that Senators by their absence at this time indicate their want of interest in what I may have to say upon this subject. The public is interested. Unless this important question is rightly settled seats now temporarily vacant may be permanently vacated by those who have the right to occupy them at this time. . . .

Partisan politics should have no place in our discussion of this measure. It should influence no man's action. The question with which we are dealing goes too deeply into the life of the people of this country and the integrity of their Government to permit a single page of the record we are making to be stained with party strife for party advantage.

That this bill is before Congress to-day goes to the credit of no party, no platform, no man. It is here because the subject with which it purports to deal can no longer be suppressed. The principle back of this bill is not new. It was written in the Constitution in the beginning and asserted as a legislative power by four States in the upper Mississippi Valley more than thirty years ago. It is here to-day in the fullness of a generation of lusty growth, demanding not partial, but complete recognition.

Let us not mistake. This is no spasm of sentiment, no angry protest fired by agitation. It is the mature judgment of an enlightened public opinion, ripened by long experience and patient investigation. More than a score of years have passed since it became the settled conviction of the country—shippers, consumers, and producers alike—that the Federal Government had the absolute right and owed it as a duty to the public to regulate and control transportation charges on interstate commerce. . . .

And so, Mr. President, after all these years of legislative delay demoralizing private business and imposing grievous burdens upon the country, we are at last offered the Hepburn-Dolliver bill. Does it meet the requirements of the country's commerce? Does it promise a remedy? Let us examine its provisions.

Mr. President, this bill will not solve the transportation problem. Unless greatly strengthened, it will not meet the expectations of the country. It will not dispose of the question.

Why should we temporize? Why should we approach this subject on tiptoe, with apology to special interest and apostrophe to property rights? Honest wealth needs no guaranty of security in this country. Property rightfully acquired does not beget fear—it fosters independence, confidence, courage. Property which is the fruit of plunder feels insecure. It is timid. It is quick to cry for help. It is ever proclaiming the sacredness of vested rights. The thief can have no vested rights in stolen property. I resent the assumption that the great wealth of this country is only safe when the millionaires are on guard. Property rights are not the special charge of the owners of great fortune. Even the poor may be relied upon to protect property. They have so little —the little they possess is so precious—that they are easily enlisted to defend the rights of property.

No one here need offer himself as a martyr to protect the property of railway corporations against the results of popular clamor. Property rights are safe. The ample power of the Constitution is the everlasting bulwark of property rights. We can do nothing if we would to put the property of any corporation in the slightest jeopardy. We shall do well indeed if we prevent the railway company from wronging the citizen. If we will use all the power we have under the Constitution, we may compel the carrier to desist from acts which encroach upon the rights of the citizen and community. We shall not be able to do more than that. We ought to be willing to do that much.

Thirty years of experience, thirty years of struggle for legislation, thirty years of judicial decision plead with us, and yet we make no advance. The committees of Congress spend a decade listening to appeals, filing away petitions, taking testimony, hearing arguments, traveling over the same ground session after session. In the meantime individuals are wronged by extortionate rates and their business handed over to monopolies enjoying the favor of the railroads. Towns and cities, with natural advantages and locations to make them commercial centers, are discriminated against to build up great markets and railway terminals at the end of the long haul.

Men have grown gray in this protracted struggle to free the commercial highways from tyranny and bring the railroads of the country back to their legitimate business as common carriers. Weary and heartsore they accept this bill, not because it is fair and just and goes to the core of the trouble, but, as they declare, "Because it is all we can get now. It is as far as Congress will go."

I think it is demonstrated that every man charged with any official responsibility with respect to this legislation owes it as a public duty to go to the limit of constitutional power in clothing the Government with authority to regulate railway rates and railway services.

Mr. President, the bill before the Senate does not measure the importance of the subject to which it relates. The junior Senator from Iowa, whose share in the framing of this bill authorizes him to speak for its scope, directed attention in his eloquent address to "the three conspicuous propositions with which this measure is concerned."

First. Broadening the meaning of the word "transportation" to include independent car lines and refrigerator companies "by requiring that every charge incident to the service shall be reckoned as a part of the public rate."

Second. By authorizing the Commission "where complaint is made that a rate is unreasonable or unduly preferential to require the carrier to observe as a maximum in such a case the rate which, in its judgment, is in conformity with law."

Third. Requiring "a detailed report of the business of the railways compelling common carriers engaged in interstate commerce to conform their systems of accounts to the regulations made by the Commission and to keep them open to reasonable inspection under public authority."

Excepting, then, as this bill provides for the new device of the private car and refrigerator companies, it goes no further than to patch up the rents made by judicial decision and clarify and strengthen the section relating to the keeping of railway accounts, and reporting thereon. Hence it may be said that this bill is a measure to correct the blunders of 1887. . . .

I do not disparage this bill in its present form. I credit it with everything it can accomplish. It is fair to say that it will aid directly and indirectly to equalize rates; that it will afford opportunity for associations and municipal organizations representing communities where rates are higher than more favored localities to apply, on that ground, for relief. This will, in a limited way, result in some reductions. I say in a limited way, because only the larger, wealthier, more enterprising and aggressive communities will be represented by active organizations with the courage and the means to make a fight against the railroads for better rates. It will be further limited by the fundamental defect in the plan which provides no way of ascertaining the reasonable rate, but only the comparatively reasonable rate, as I shall presently show. . . .

I will present some of the more important recommendations for which this bill fails to make provision. I indulge the hope that the imperfections of the bill will be cured by amendment before it passes the Senate.

1. Valuation of Railway Property

The interstate commerce law declares all unreasonable rates unlawful. The Supreme Court declares reasonable rates to be such rates as shall afford just compensation to the carrier for the services performed. The Supreme Court has likewise held that "just compensation" is a fair return on the fair value of the railroad property.

The Commission has declared that—

No tribunal upon which the duty may be imposed, whether legislative, administrative, or judicial, can pass a satisfactory judgment upon the reasonableness of railway rates without taking into account the value of railroad property.

In its report for 1903 the Commission recommended Congress to authorize such a valuation to be made, and made an elaborate argument in support of such recommendation.

No such legislation has been enacted by Congress.

This bill makes no provision authorizing the Commission to ascertain the value of railway property.

I shall endeavor to discuss this most important branch of the subject with some thoroughness before I conclude.

2. The Power to Revise and Fix Rates, Fares, and Charges

The Commission has recommended year after year that it is necessary to the protection of the public that authority be conferred upon the Commission, acting either upon its own motion or upon complaint, to issue, and to enforce an order changing any rates, fares, or charges alleged to be unreasonable or otherwise unlawful after due notice and full hearing, upon a determination by the Commission that the rates, fares, and charges are unreasonable or otherwise unlawful.

The Commission informed Congress that these powers are "positively essential"; that until conferred upon the Commission its "best efforts at regulation must be feeble and disappointing"; that "knowledge of present conditions and tendencies increases rather than lessens the necessity for legislative action upon the lines indicated."

The pending bill does not confer upon the Commission the broad powers to revise rates, fares, and charges upon its own motion, or to fix absolute rates, fares, and charges under any circumstances whatever.

3. The Relation of Rates

For years extended discussions have been presented to Congress showing the necessity of considering the relation of rates in determining with respect to specific complaints. The reports are full of cases showing how vital this consideration is in the administration of justice.

The Commission has presented with great clearness and power its recommendations that this authority should be reposed in the Commission. Indeed, it is difficult to see how it can proceed to discharge the duties of its high office and dispense any measure of justice under the limitations of the proposed bill, which confers no power upon the Commission to issue orders upon its own motion, unless Congress shall vest it with full authority to pass upon the relation of rates.

This bill makes no provision granting such authority to the Commission.

4. The Control of Classification

The foundation of all rate making lies in classification. Sweeping changes are effected by a single order in classification, which the railroads make from time to time. The Commission has brought to the attention of Congress the fact that "many advances have been brought about by changes in classifications."

Changing the classification of an article of freight changes all the rates under which that article shall be shipped throughout the country. It is wholesale rate making. By comparison the powers proposed by this bill to be conferred on the Commission are only powers of retail rate revision to be exercised only on complaint and on the basis of comparisons with other rates fixed by the railroads.

The Commission has repeatedly recommended that when classifications are filed which the Commission finds on investigation and full hearing to be unreasonable, it shall determine what shall be a reasonable classification and prescribe the same, and shall order the carrier or carriers to file and publish, on or before a certain day, schedules in accordance with the decision of the Commission, subject to right of review thereon; that when such classification shall be so established it shall not be departed from without the consent of the Commission upon application of the carrier after due notice and full hearing.

This bill makes no provision conferring such authority upon the Commission.

5. The Power to Fix A Minimum Rate

During the ten years that the Commission exercised their supposed power with respect to rates they found that great injustice resulted in many cases because the railroad companies would readjust rates for competing towns to a common market, so as to defeat the orders of the Commission in securing to a city or community a reasonable opportunity to compete in such common market.

This defect in the law was many times reported to Congress by the Commission and numerous cases cited in support of a recommendation that the Commission be given authority to fix a minimum rate.

This bill makes no provision to correct the law in this important respect.

6. Long and Short Haul Discriminations Ignored

The long and short haul clause of the act of 1887 was designed to prevent a common form of most oppressive and unwarranted discriminations between places. The court has decided that this clause does not apply when the conditions are not alike at both points between which the discriminations exist. In practice there are no points at which conditions are alike. It lies in the power of the roads to make the conditions dissimilar whenever it suits their purposes. As a result this provision is without effect and there is no authority in the Commission to prevent any such unwarranted discriminations. Such discriminations prevail generally throughout all sections of the country.

Under the basing-point system a rate to a given point is computed by adding to the rate from the point of origin to the basing point the local rate from the basing point to the point of destination, or an arbitrary amount or percentage of the rate to the basing point. This is done for points between the point of origin and the basing point, thus making the rate to such points higher than the rate to the basing point beyond. For example, rates on some commodities from New York to Salt Lake are more than twice as high as to San Francisco, a thousand miles farther and over the same line. From New Orleans to Charlotte, N.C., the rates are twice as high as to Virginia cities twice as far distant, the Virginia traffic passing through Charlotte. Most absurd discriminations of this sort prevail against Danville, Va. Shippers in western Wisconsin wishing to ship grain and live stock to Chicago are actually forced, to get the best rates, to ship west to St. Paul and then reship to Chicago, the return shipment passing through the town from which it started.

The Commission has called attention to the defect in the law which permits these unwarranted discriminations. It has recommended that it be given the power to determine what conditions are dissimilar and what discriminations are warranted.

The proposed bill ignored these recommendations and the necessity of their enactment into law. It does worse than that; it reenacts the bad provisions of the old law.

7. The Trick of Withholding Testimony

It is a fact that railway companies have withheld important testimony upon the hearings before the Commission; that they have subsequently offered the testimony on the trial before the court, and have thereby succeeded in reversing and discrediting the Commission and in delaying the administration of justice; that this practice has been so prevalent as to call forth rebuke upon the railroad companies from the Supreme Court.

The Commission has reported these facts to Congress and recommended that legislation be enacted to correct this abuse.

This bill makes no provision to prevent the continuance of this wrongful practice on the part of the railway companies.

8. Imprisonment for Violations of Law

The Commission advised against exempting railroad officers and agents from imprisonment for violating the law. The railroads advised Congress to amend the law and grant immunity from imprisonment. Congress adopted the recommendations of the railroads and passed the Elkins law, exempting railroad officers and agents from imprisonment for violations.

In its report the Commission calls attention to violations of the Elkins law, and states that such violations are "liable to increase unless effectively restrained."

This bill contains no provision restoring the penalty of imprisonment and offers no remedy to "effectively restrain" such violations.

9. The Killed and Injured Employees and Passengers

For the fiscal year ending June 30, 1905, the railroads killed and injured 10,617 passengers and 48,487 employees. The list of killed and injured of both passengers and employees has steadily increased from year to year. The record is an appalling one.

We annually kill relatively three times and injure twenty-five times as many railway employees, and kill relatively six and one-half times and injure twenty-nine times as many passengers as do the Prussian railroads.

Day after day we place those who are dearer to us than life in the safekeeping of the men who run the railroad trains of the country. Patient, courteous, watchful, brave—there are no stronger, finer types of character and courage in American life. Out on the "iron trail" these men grimly meet death, day and night to save the trainload of humanity in their charge. The gruesome list of fatalities reveals the startling fact that more than one engineer out of every four dies upon his engine, his hand gripping the throttle and lever.

For seven years the trainmen of America have maintained a representative here to plead for legislation, giving a little measure of justice to their families, when the dark hour comes, for which they ever wait with dread anxiety. For seven years their bills have died in the committee rooms of Congress.

The Interstate Commerce Commission has each year urged legislation to reduce the long and increasing roll of this awful slaughter of employees and passengers.

This bill makes no provision for the adoption of the block system, or other well approved safety appliances, or for any other progressive legislation, for the preservation of life. . . .

I would not be unfair. This bill is not bad in its provisions, but weak because of its omissions. I do not believe that the bill is framed to meet the demands of "special interests." Nor has any broad consideration of public interest dominated its construction.

It has neither ill intent nor high purpose. Expediency seems to have been the controlling factor in framing it.

It seems a response to the impelling necessity for some legislation.

It is probably just to the members of the committee who joined in reporting this bill to the Senate to say that it is their measure of the willingness of Congress to legislate on the subject; that it is as strong a bill as they believe could pass the Senate. But if this bill is not amended to meet the public need, if it should pass without being strengthened and improved, so as to make it a basis upon which to build substantially in the future, then it may as well be understood now that it will not quiet public interest nor prevent further demands.

It will become the issue of a new campaign, more certain, more definite, and more specific than ever before.

This session of Congress will be but the preliminary skirmish of the great contest to follow. On the day that it is known that only the smallest possible measure of relief has been granted the movement will begin anew all over the country for a larger concession to public right. That movement will not stop until it is completely successful. The only basis upon which it can be settled finally in a free country is a control of the public service corporations broad enough, strong enough, and strict enough to insure justice and equality to all American citizens.

For the first time in many years a great measure is before this body for its final action. The subject with which it deals goes to the very heart of the whole question. Out of railroad combination with monopoly and its power over legislation comes the perilous relation which Mr. Justice Brewer says "lifts the corporation into a position of constant danger and menace to republican institutions."

Sir, we have the opportunity to meet the demands of the hour, or we may weakly temporize while the storm continues to gather.

On Plymouth Rock eighty-six years ago Daniel Webster, looking with prophetic vision into the century beyond, uttered these words, which fall upon this day and generation as a solemn mandate:

> As experience may show errors in our establishments we are bound to correct them, and if any practices exist contrary to the principles of justice and humanity within the reach of our laws or our influence, we are inexcusable if we do not exert ourselves to restrain and abolish them.

Mr. President, our responsibility is great; our duty is plain. If a true spirit of independent, patriotic service controls Congress, this bill will be reconstructed on the broad basis of public interest.

3

Editorials on the Role of the Minority and of Congress in the Making of Foreign Policy[1]

Far from being a negative obstructionist in the Senate when Woodrow Wilson and the Democrats came to power in 1913, La Follette believed that members of the minority party should play a positive and cooperative role wherever possible. He actively supported many of Wilson's domestic reforms and constantly urged the President to take even stronger measures to remain out of war. These two editorials from La Follette's Weekly Magazine *illustrate La Follette's independent stand on these major issues.*

THE MINORITY

It is announced that the Roosevelt-Perkins Party will, at the opening of the extra session, hold a caucus, nominate candidates for speaker, clerk and other House officers, and cast their votes for such candidates, when the House meets to effect its organization. This is a perfectly proper proceeding for the men nominated and elected by the Roosevelt-Perkins party. It will serve a very excellent purpose. It will be mentioned in the Washington dispatches of that day.

But when we come to the business of the session, there will be more important work in hand for the minority in both branches of Congress, than exploiting parties for political effect.

The policies of the party now dominant nationally are to be tried out. Centralized control of production and distribution, of capital and credit, began to be alarmingly manifest in the first years of the Roosevelt administration. Though greatly troubled, the people were led to believe, from day to day, that the "malefactors of great wealth" would be swept from power, and equal opportunity knock at every man's door. They waited in patience through the election of 1904 and the

[1] From Robert M. La Follette, "The Minority," *La Follette's Weekly Magazine* (Madison, Wisconsin), April 5, 1913, and "Congress Dodges Responsibility," *ibid.*, March, 1916.

"succession" in 1908. By 1912 the catch phrases and dazzling epigrams had worn threadbare. The burdens had become intolerable, and a Bryan-made platform and a Bryan-selected candidate were accepted willy-nilly.

The Democratic Party, under the conditions which prevailed, offered the only hope. Governor Wilson had given New Jersey a progressive administration. He comes to the Presidency of this nation with a limited experience in public life, but with the confidence of the American people that he will deal with the existing evils seriously and fearlessly in the public interest. He evinces a disposition to meet responsibilities. He is not waiting for them to be thrust upon him. He is not satisfied to sit in his place and distribute the spoils of office. He has entered at once upon the great task committed to him and his party. He has promptly called an extra session of Congress. He is ready to put forth a plan for tariff revision. It will be followed in good time with currency legislation, and later his administration will deal with trusts, conservation, and social wrongs, generally and specifically.

The responsibility for this program is upon the Democratic party. But the minority in the House and Senate must meet its responsibility, as well. It is no time for trifling or playing politics, or trying to put the Wilson administration in a hole. It is no time for the Roosevelt-Perkins Party or the Republican party to maneuver for 1916. The American people demand that money and credit and transportation, and the market place where labor and the products of labor are bought and sold, be freed from the control of powerful interests.

If the Wilson administration offers legislation which will best accomplish this result, it is the duty of the minority to support that legislation. If not, it will be the duty of the minority to offer better legislation instead. No greater opportunity was ever presented for patriotic statesmanship. The field is open to the minority as well as to the majority.

CONGRESS DODGES RESPONSIBILITY

President Wilson, in his work on "Constitutional Government in the United States," published in 1911, clearly defines his views as to the unlimited and exclusive prerogative of the Executive in dealing with foreign affairs. Beginning on page 77, second paragraph, he says:

> One of the greatest of the President's powers I have not yet spoken of at all: his control, which is very absolute, of the foreign relations of a nation. The initiative in foreign affairs, which the President possesses without any restriction whatever, is virtually the power to control them absolutely.

This statement of the views of Mr. Woodrow Wilson, writing on constitutional government in 1911, might be passed without concern. But if there is warrant to believe that President Wilson may, on the verge of a great world crisis, predicate vitally important and decisive action on that declaration, then it ought not to go unchallenged, unless we are compelled to accept it as correctly defining the power; then the President has authority to make war as absolutely as though he were Czar of Russia.

The President in the recent controversy as to the propriety of the introduction and consideration by Congress of the resolutions warning American citizens to keep off armed merchant-men evidently predicated his objection on the belief that the Executive should be left free to pursue any foreign policy whatever the issue, independent of any suggestion from either or both branches of Congress.

The peremptory manner in which President Wilson forced action upon the resolution in the Senate, the extraordinary proceedings by which the resolution was changed and tabled without opportunity for debate or explanation, warrants the belief that the President denies Congress the right to express its opinion upon a matter which lies within its constitutional authority quite as much as that of the Executive.

One Democratic member of high standing serving his seventh term in the House, brother of the ambassador to England, says:

> The President is not satisfied with an unreserved expression of confidence on the part of Congress, but demands a vote upon the warning of American citizens to refrain from using armed vessels of belligerent countries, asking that it be voted down.

In his letter to the Chairman of the Senate Foreign Relations Committee, Senator Stone, the President says:

> But in any event our duty is clear. No nation, no group of nations, has the right while war is in progress to alter or disregard the principles which all nations have agreed upon in mitigation of the horrors and sufferings of war; and if the clear rights of American citizens should very unhappily be abridged or denied by any such action, we should, it seems to me, have in honor no choice as to what our own course should be.

In view of this alternative which we are told we must face, Congress, if mindful of what happened at Vera Cruz, as well as the lessons of history and of the appalling consequences of the involvement of the United States in this European War, was bound to take action, to express its views, and to offer counsel which might avert the pending disaster.

So far as I have been able to discover, President Wilson's course is not only unusual but unprecedented in demanding that Congress keep silent in all that pertains to foreign affairs. The only justification for the President's interference was that in some way not obvious to Congress the warning resolutions might paralyze the negotiations which were being carried on. Even if this were true, it would seem that the President might have appealed to Congress in a message to defer action.

However, it is now reported apparently upon authority, that the State Department proposes to accomplish indirectly the object that the warning resolutions of Congress were intended directly to accomplish. If this is true, it serves to emphasize even more strongly that the only purpose of the President's remarkable course was to maintain a clear title in the Executive, to conduct foreign affairs without any suggestion from Congress.

He was enforcing to the letter, his views expressed in the paragraph which I have quoted from his work on Constitutional Government.

Up to the present time, so far as I have been able to investigate the matter, no President has held or attempted to enforce such extreme views. Congress has always exercised the privilege of expressing opinion, giving counsel and not infrequently has taken the initiative in suggestions as to conduct of foreign affairs.

Hinds' Precedents cites many instances where Congress has asserted its right to a voice in foreign affairs.

President Jackson in a message to Congress said:

> It will always be considered consistent with the spirit of the Constitution, and most safe, that it (the power to recognize new states) should be exercised, when probably leading to war, with a previous understanding with that body by whom all provisions for sustaining its perils must be furnished. Its submission to Congress which represents in one of its branches the States of this Union and in the other the people of the United States, where there may be reasonable ground to apprehend so grave a consequence, would certainly afford the fullest satisfaction to our own country and a perfect guaranty to all other nations of the justice and prudence of the measures which may be adopted.

Alexander Hamilton's argument and conclusions on this question are most illuminating. He says:

> The history of human conduct does not warrant that exalted opinion of human virtue which would make it wise in a nation to commit interests of so delicate and momentous a kind as those which concerns its intercourse with the rest of the world to the sole disposal of a magistrate created and circumstanced as would be a president of the United States.

President Wilson might have accepted the adoption of the resolution of warning as an endorsement of his policy in Mexico. He certainly did not regard it as an abject relinquishment of the sacred rights of American citizens to order them to abandon their property and to seek the shelter of the home country, in order to avoid the responsibility of protecting them in their rights in Mexico. I believe he was right in pursuing this course. It was a small sacrifice on the part of the few to preserve the peace of the nation. But how much less sacrifice it requires for our citizens to refrain from travel on armed belligerent ships! Or what is the difference in withholding a passport by Act of Congress and the letter of the Department of State, of October 4, 1914, which said:

> The Department does not deem it appropriate or advisable to issue passports to persons who contemplate visiting belligerent countries, merely for pleasure, recreation, touring or sight seeing.

It would hardly be practicable, if it were lawful, to inquire and distinguish as to all the varying motives which prompt the many thousand of people who travel. Moreover, whatever power the State Department exercises regarding this or any other matter is only such as is conferred by Act of Congress and can not exceed that possessed by Congress.

So far as the warning resolutions had any bearing upon the conduct of foreign affairs or rights of diplomacy, they were in no way an infringement upon Executive prerogative and were on other grounds entirely within the legislative power of Congress under the Constitution.

Clearly a law might be enacted prohibiting American citizens from traveling upon armed merchantmen that would come within the power of Congress to regulate commerce with foreign nations. Congress has enacted numerous laws in the interest of the safety of passengers. The Seaman's Law, for example, is in point, as well as the law that steamships carrying certain high explosives are required not to take passengers, and so a long list of other laws might be cited.

There is a larger international aspect of this question, with its accompanying responsibility, that can not be shirked or ignored. Across the water the nations of Europe are giving their lifeblood in a fratricidal struggle, which in its inception the people neither desired nor sanctioned.

And now the plain people, the saner people of the warring countries are organizing. For what? Why, to make sure that never again after this conflict has ceased shall the autocratic heads of European Governments have it in their power, through secret diplomacy, to bring on such another world catastrophe.

Democratic control of foreign policies is a basic principle of all organized effort looking for the future establishment of permanent world peace. To this end, throughout the world, leagues of earnest, determined men and women, animated by a common purpose, are formulating plans, based on the provisions by which, in this country, one or both of the legislative branches of Government have a share in the control of international affairs.

Shall we in this crisis of the world's history fail to assert our constitutional rights and by our negligence and default permit the establishment in this country of that exclusive executive control over foreign affairs that the people of Europe are now repenting amid the agonies of war?

If the Executive has exclusive authority to determine whether an American citizen in pursuit of his individual business or pleasure shall be permitted to jeopardize the peace of this country by traveling on an armed merchantman at this time, then he has the exclusive power to determine the conditions which may make war with a foreign country.

If the framers of the Constitution intended to give the President the power to make war, why did they not give him the power to declare war?

They gave the war power exclusively to Congress. The only power touching foreign affairs which they gave exclusively to the President was the authority to "receive" ambassadors.

Congress has no right even passively to evade its responsibility and its duty to assert at this time all the power conferred upon it under the Constitution. To be guilty of such action when it may even indirectly contribute to augment the danger of European complications, is little less than treason to the country.

The Constitution clothes Congress with a power which it holds in the United States for the people. Having the power, Congress cannot rightfully evade its responsibility. It is as much a betrayal of trust to surrender that power as it would be to abuse its exercise. The President in effect challenged the right of Congress to exercise its constitutional authority. Congress betrayed its trust when it dodged the issue raised by the President. It will be forced to meet the issue ultimately.

4

Neutrality[1]

Early in the fall of 1914 La Follette had established himself as a leader of the isolationists and was willing to adopt extreme measures to keep the United States out of the war. He supported the arms embargo, the travel-at-your-own-risk resolution, and a ban on loans and credits. He opposed the preparedness campaign and Wilson's hard line against Germany's submarine attacks. For his opposition to Wilson's armed ship proposal La Follette gained the designation of leader of "the little group of Willful Men." His speech to the Senate just before the War Declaration vote was taken on April 4, 1917, summed up his arguments why we should stay out of the conflict.

Mr. LA FOLLETTE. Mr. President, I had supposed until recently that it was the duty of Senators and Representatives in Congress to vote and act according to their convictions on all public matters that came before them for consideration and decision. Quite another doctrine has recently been promulgated by certain newspapers, which unfortunately seems to have found considerable support elsewhere, and that is the doctrine of "standing back of the President," without inquiring whether the President is right or wrong. For myself, I have never subscribed to that doctrine and never shall. I shall support the President in the measures he proposes when I believe them to be right. I shall oppose measures proposed by the President when I believe them to be wrong. The fact that the matter which the President submits for consideration is of the greatest importance is only an additional reason why we should be sure that we are right and not be swerved from that conviction or intimidated in its expression by any influence of power whatsoever. If it is important for us to speak and vote our convictions in matters of internal policy, though we may unfortunately be in disagreement with the President, it is infinitely more important for us to speak and vote our convictions when the question is one of peace or war, certain to involve the lives and fortunes of many of our people and, it may be, the destiny of all of them

[1] From the *Congressional Record,* 65th Cong., 1st sess. (April 4, 1917), Vol. 55, pp. 223ff.

and of the civilized world as well. If, unhappily, on such momentous questions the most patient research and conscientious consideration we could give to them leave us in disagreement with the President, I know of no course to take except to oppose, regretfully but not the less firmly, the demands of the Executive. . . .

Mr. President, many of my colleagues on both sides of this floor have from day to day offered for publication in the Record messages and letters received from their constituents. I have received some 15,000 letters and telegrams. They have come from 44 States in the Union. They have been assorted according to whether they speak in criticism or commendation of my course in opposing war.

Assorting the 15,000 letters and telegrams by States in that way, 9 out of 10 are an unqualified endorsement of my course in opposing war with Germany on the issue presented. I offer only a few selected hastily just before I came upon the floor which especially relate to public sentiment on the question of war.

Mr. President, let me say that the city of Monroe, Wis., is the county seat of Green County, which borders on the State of Illinois. I am not able to state exactly the percentage of the nationalities of the people, but I know that the foundation stock of that little city was of New England origin. In the last 10 or 15 or 20 years a great many Swiss have come into the county.

But, Mr. President, it is a good town, typical of any town of like size in any State in the Union. They held an election there on the 2d day of April, and the following vote was polled upon the question of declaring war against Germany. The telegram reporting the vote is as follows:

> Monroe election votes on referendum on war question. For peace, 954, for war, 95.

It is unfortunately true that a portion of the irresponsible and war-crazed press, feeling secure in the authority of the President's condemnation of the Senators who opposed the armed-ship bill, have published the most infamous and scurrilous libels on the honor of the Senators who opposed that bill. It was particularly unfortunate that such malicious falsehoods should fill the public press of the country at a time when every consideration for our country required that a spirit of fairness should be observed in the discussions of the momentous questions under consideration. . . .

Mr. President, let me make another suggestion. It is this: That a minority in one Congress—mayhap a small minority in one Congress—protesting, exercising the rights which the Constitution confers upon a minority, may really be representing the majority opinion of the country, and if, exercising the right that the Constitution gives them, they succeed in defeating for the time being the will of the majority, they are but carrying out what was in the mind of the framers of the Constitution; that you may have from time to time in a legislative body a majority in numbers that really does not represent the principle of democracy; and that if the question could be deferred and carried to the people it would be found that a minority was the real representative of the public opinion. So, Mr. President, it was that they wrote into the Constitution that a President—that one man—may put his judgment against the will of a majority not only in one branch of the Congress but in both branches of the Congress; that he may defeat the measure that they have agreed upon and may set his one single judgment above the majority judgment of the Congress. That seems when you look at it nakedly, to be in violation of the principle that the majority shall rule; and so it is. Why is that power given? It is one of those checks provided by the wisdom of the fathers to prevent the majority from abusing the power that they chance to have, when they do not reflect the real judgment, the opinion, the will of the majority of the people that constitute the sovereign power of the democracy. . . .

Just a word of comment more upon one of the points in the President's address. He says that this is a war "for the things which we have always carried nearest to our hearts—for democracy, for the right of those who submit to authority to have a voice in their own government." In many places throughout the address is this exalted sentiment given expression.

It is a sentiment peculiarly calculated to appeal to American hearts and, when accompanied by acts consistent with it, is certain to receive our support; but in this same connection, and strangely enough, the President says that we have become convinced that the German Government as it now exists—"Prussian autocracy" he calls it—can never again maintain friendly relations with us. His expression is that "Prussian autocracy was not and could never be our friend," and repeatedly throughout the address the suggestion is made that if the German people would overturn their Government it would probably be the way to peace. So true is this that the dispatches from London all hailed the message of the President as sounding the death knell of Germany's Government.

But the President proposes alliance with Great Britain, which, however liberty-loving its people, is a hereditary monarchy, with a hereditary ruler, with a hereditary House of Lords, with a hereditary landed system, with a limited and restricted suffrage from one class and multiplied suffrage power for another, and with grinding industrial conditions for all the wageworkers. The President has not suggested that we make our support of Great Britain conditional to her granting home rule to Ireland, or Egypt, or India. We rejoice in the establishment of a democracy in Russia, but it will hardly be contended that if Russia was still an autocratic Government, we would not be asked to enter this alliance with her just the same. Italy and the lesser powers of Europe, Japan in the Orient; in fact, all of the countries with whom we are to enter into alliance, except France and newly revolutionized Russia, are still of the old order—and it will be generally conceded that no one of them has done as much for its people in the solution of municipal problems and in securing social and industrial reforms as Germany.

Is it not a remarkable democracy which leagues itself with allies already far overmatching in strength the German nation and holds out to such beleaguered nation the hope of peace only at the price of giving up their Government? I am not talking now of the merits or demerits of any government, but I am speaking of a profession of democracy that is linked in action with the most brutal and domineering use of autocratic power. Are the people of this country being so well represented in this war movement that we need to go abroad to give other people control of their governments? Will the President and the supporters of this war bill submit it to a vote of the people before the declaration of war goes into effect? Until we are willing to do that, it illy becomes us to offer as an excuse for our entry into the war the unsupported claim that this war was forced upon the German people by their Government "without their previous knowledge or approval."

Who has registered the knowledge or approval of the American people of the course this Congress is called upon to take in declaring war upon Germany? Submit the question to the people, you who support it. You who support it dare not do it, for you know that by a vote of more than ten to one the American people as a body would register their declaration against it. . . .

Jefferson asserted that we could not permit one warring nation to curtail our neutral rights if we were not ready to allow her enemy the same privileges, and that any other course entailed the sacrifice of our neutrality.

That is the sensible, that is the logical position. No neutrality could ever have commanded respect if it was not based on that equitable and just proposition; and we from early in the war threw our neutrality to the winds by permitting England to make a mockery of it to her advantage against her chief enemy. Then we expect to say to that enemy, "You have got to respect my rights as a neutral." What is the answer? I say Germany has been patient with us. Standing strictly on her rights, her answer would be, "Maintain your neutrality; treat these other Governments warring against me as you treat me if you want your neutral rights respected."

I say again that when two nations are at war any neutral nation, in order to preserve its character as a neutral nation, must exact the same conduct from both warring nations; both must equally obey the principles of international law. If a neutral nation fails in that, then its rights upon the high seas—to adopt the President's phrase—are relative and not absolute. There can be no greater violation of our neutrality than the requirement that one of two belligerents shall adhere to settled principles of law and that the other shall have the advantage of not doing so. The respect that German naval authorities were required to pay to the rights of our people upon the high seas would depend upon the question whether we had exacted the same rights from Germany's enemies. If we had not done so we lost our character as a neutral nation, and our people unfortunately had lost the protection that belongs to neutrals. Our responsibility was joint in the sense that we must exact the same conduct from both belligerents. No principle of international law is better settled than that which is stated by Oppenheim, the great English authority on international law, in volume 2, second edition, page 365. He says:

> Neutrality as an attitude of impartiality involves the duty of abstaining from assisting either belligerent either actively or passively.

Had the plain principle of international law announced by Jefferson been followed by us, we would not be called on to-day to declare war upon any of the belligerents. The failure to treat the belligerent nations of Europe alike, the failure to reject unlawful "war zones" of both Germany and Great Britain, is wholly accountable for our present dilemma. We should not seek to hide our blunder behind the smoke of battle, to inflame the mind of our people by half truths into the frenzy of war, in order that they may never appreciate the real cause of it until it is too late. I do not believe that our national honor is served by such a course. The right way is the honorable way.

One alternative is to admit our initial blunder to enforce our rights against Great Britain as we have enforced our rights against Germany; demand that both those nations shall respect our neutral rights upon the high seas to the letter; and give notice that we will enforce those rights from that time forth against both belligerents and then live up to that notice.

The other alternative is to withdraw our commerce from both. The mere suggestion that food supplies would be withheld from both sides impartially would compel belligerents to observe the principle of freedom of the seas for neutral commerce.

5

The Versailles Treaty[1]

In the fight against the Versailles Treaty and the adherence of the United States to the Covenant of the League of Nations, La Follette displayed a consistent opposition which was critical and fearful of the treaty in any form. He also showed a detailed and sophisticated knowledge of minority groups in Europe and the issues involved in drawing the "new map of Europe." In the complete speech he provided charts and maps to demonstrate the imperialistic character of the treaty and lashed at Great Britain's "share of the spoils." In this excerpt, La Follette displays a strong bias in favor of "self-determination of peoples" which should be applied to the smaller and weaker nations of Europe as well as to the victorious Allies.

THE SECRET TREATIES—THE NEW MAP OF EUROPE AND OUR OBLIGATIONS UNDER ARTICLE 10

Mr. LA FOLLETTE. Mr. President, I propose to state as briefly as possible some of the obligations, in so far as we are permitted to know them, which the United States is called upon to assume under the terms of this treaty and the league compact, and particularly article 10, which is before the Senate at this time. I shall limit myself at this time to a discussion of those obligations alone which are imposed by so much of the treaty as deals with the distribution of spoils to allied powers other than Great Britain.

We have already paid a fearful price for our participation in the late war. It has cost us the lives of more than 50,000 of our finest young men slain in battle, and over 200,000 maimed and wounded, and many thousands of others who lost their lives through disease growing out of the war. It has cost us some thirty billions of dollars, most of which still remains to be wrung from our people—principal and interest—by heartbreaking taxes which must be paid by this and succeeding generations. It has cost us the friendship of great nations, with whose people our national desires, as well as our national interests, require close

[1] From the *Congressional Record,* 66th Cong., 1st sess. (November 13, 1919), Vol. 58, pp. 8427ff.

and friendly association. I do not refer here merely to the people of Germany and Austria, but to those of Russia and possibly China as well.

One of the first results of the President's policy in attempting to form alliances with European Governments has been to make us a party either active or passive to the robbery of China under the much-discussed Shantung provisions of this treaty.

Another result of the President's policy, as foolish as it is illegal, by which our Government has sent soldiers and munitions into Russia to be used in assisting one of the warring factions there against another, is that whichever faction eventually wins, we will have earned the hatred and contempt of both.

As a result of this war also our domestic concerns are in as sorry a plight as our foreign affairs. On the pretense that they were necessary as war measures, the forces of reaction have succeeded in passing one law after another destroying freedom of speech and of the press and immunity from unlawful search and seizure, until at this hour the substance of civil liberty is destroyed in this country. While most of the legislation of which I speak was confined by its terms to the period of the war, bills have been prepared and are now pending in Congress by which these same repressive measures are to be made applicable to times of peace as well as war.

I shall show before I get through that if we ever become a member of this proposed league of nations we will be perpetually in a state of war, so that no new principle will need to be invoked in order to suppress any publication offensive to the administration, or to imprison any citizen whose criticism of the Government is offensive to Federal officeholders.

We have as a result of this war aroused in this country bitternesses and class hatred which threaten at any time to break out into disorder and violence. By this war, as by all wars, a favored few profited immensely, while the great mass of the people suffered immeasurably. Available reports seem to indicate that 20,000 new millionaires were made in the United States as a result of this war. That is just about one millionaire created for every three boys who lost their lives in France. While the evermounting cost of the necessaries of life brings home to the common man as never before the problem of making a decent living, the profiteers of the war brazenly flaunt before the public their new-made wealth. Is it any wonder that labor is dissatisfied and discontented; that strikes, the most extensive in all the history of our country, are existing and impending; that discontent is everywhere; that even our form of government as ordained and established by the Constitution is perhaps threatened? . . .

Every Senator when he cast his vote for war knew that it meant the things I have mentioned. This much we contracted for when we entered the war. And, sir, these are the burdens which the mass of people of this country must bear, and a part of which must be passed on to succeeding generations. No one doubts that we are strong enough and resourceful enough to pay in full our war debts; and if we go our way in peace, we will in time be able to restore our country to normal conditions. We can never bring back the lives that were sacrificed; we can never restore the maimed and wounded to health. The hearts broken through this war we can never heal; the suffering it has entailed we can never recall; and all that we knew we bargained for when we entered the war.

But, sir, there is one thing which is now demanded of us that we did not bargain for when we entered this war, and that is the surrender of our right to control our own destiny as a Nation.

After all, Mr. President, that is what membership in this proposed league of nations is to cost us. Up until the present time we are still free to travel the road which the founders of our Government intended us to travel. We are still free to fulfill the destiny for which we are fitted by the genius of our people, the character of our institutions, our great resources, and our fortunate geographical position. All this we are asked to surrender in order to become a member of this league of nations. We are asked to emasculate, if not destroy, our form of government by recognizing the right of some assembly or council of nations, in which we have small voice, to interfere with our most vital concerns. We are asked to place our resources, not only our wealth, but the lives of our people, at the disposal of Governments and peoples in the remote sections of the earth and to uphold there policies foreign to the purposes and desires of our own people. We are asked to depart from the traditional policy which our position on the American Continent has enabled us to pursue of keeping free from entangling alliances of European politics, and to become a party to every political scheme that may be hatched in the capitals of Europe or elsewhere in this world of ours.

This, Mr. President, is something that no one contemplated when we entered the war, and I do not believe that one vote in favor of the war would have been cast in the Congress of the United States if it had been understood that such a result would follow our participation in the war.

Now, let us examine more closely and somewhat in detail the obligations we are called upon to assume if we vote ourselves into this league of nations. Everyone understands and concedes that by article 10 of the covenant we undertake, when we become a member of the league, to protect and preserve the political and territorial status quo of all members of the league of nations as against any external aggression.

By article 11, as I shall attempt to show, we undertake substantially the same obligation where the status quo is threatened by revolution.

For the present, however, it is sufficient to consider our obligations under article 10. I am not going to stop to quibble about reservations, mild or drastic, or the methods by which our obligations are to be enforced. If we enter this league we must assume the responsibility that goes with membership in it. If we are not going to be bound by the obligations which go with membership in the league, then the only honest thing to do is to keep out of it. The language of article 10 leaves nothing to construction. It is at least one thing about this league that is perfectly clear. That article provides:

> The members of the league undertake to respect and preserve as against external aggression the territorial integrity and existing political independence of all members of the league.

Now, either we are going to do that, specifically that thing, or we are not going to do it. If we are not going to do it, we have no business in the league. We can not promise to preserve political independence and territorial integrity of some members and not of others. We can not promise to preserve the territorial integrity and political independence of the members of the league on some occasions and refuse to do it on other occasions. We can not be permitted to preserve the political independence and territorial integrity of a member of the league when it is to our interest to do so and seek to destroy the political independence or territorial integrity of a member of the league when it is to our interest to take that course. Such action on the part of the members of the league would destroy the whole plan and purpose of the league. It would at once reduce it to a mere aggregation of warring factions and petty alliances, in which every dispute submitted to the league would beget as many others as there are members of the league. I assume that if we go into the league we go into it with the honest intention of fulfilling our obligation to preserve the political and territorial status quo created by the peace conference at Paris.

Austria

Now, let us see what that obligation involves. We will consider the simplest situation first, which is that presented by Austria.

I recall to your mind in this connection the language of the President on December 4, 1918, in an address to the Congress. He then said:

We owe it, however, to ourselves to say that we do not wish in any way to impair or rearrange the Austro-Hungarian Empire.

I have no doubt that the President used this language in the utmost good faith. At that time he had not been to Paris, where he has told us he first learned of the secret treaties, and he says when he arrived in Paris he was still ignorant of the designs and purposes of the Allies.

I pause at this time to direct attention to the fact that this is the most remarkable statement made to the Committee on Foreign Relations when it visited the White House at the request of the President. The secret treaties had been published broadcast in November, 1917. They had been published in full in pamphlet form and distributed by the New York Evening Post. Columns upon columns on the front page of the Post and other great newspapers in America had carried all of the covenants of those secret treaties shortly after they were published in Russia by the Lenin government. . . .

Why, Mr. President, it was not only generally known in the United States, it was not only spread at large upon the front pages of all the great papers of this country, but it was discussed in all the parliaments of the world. It was discussed day after day. There were more than 40 allusions to it in the British Parliament during that time. The ministry was put to answer questions respecting these secret treaties day after day, and it is a matter of record in the parliamentary debates of Great Britain that Balfour said that the President was fully informed regarding them.

I pass that, Mr. President, because he said to the Committee on Foreign Relations that he did not know anything about them until he arrived in Paris in December, 1918, or January, 1919. But, sir, for more than two years the public prints of the country and the parliamentary debates of the world had teemed with discussion and publication regarding the secret treaties made between the allied powers for the distribution of the territory of Europe and Asia and Africa that we are asked to ratify in the treaty which is now pending before the Senate.

Let me say this, further, that a study of the terms of those secret treaties and of the treaty that is pending here now and of such other information as we have been able to secure with regard to other treaties shows that the work of the Paris conference, held behind closed doors at Versailles, pursued not the terms of the armistice but utterly disregarded the terms of the armistice and followed line by line the boundaries fixed in the secret treaties that had been made in 1916 and 1917.

If he was ignorant, he was the only man connected in any way with public life in the United States who was ignorant of the terms and purposes of the secret treaties.

Prior to the war the Austro-Hungarian Empire contained 251,000 square miles and a population of 51,000,000 people. The Paris conference has divided it into five separate and independent States, to wit, Austria, Hungary, Czechoslovakia, Jugo-Slavia, sometimes called the Serb-Croat-Slovene State, and Poland.

Austria, as whittled down by the Paris conference, now has a population of about 5,500,000, and an area of about 45,000 square miles, Hungary an area of about 55,000 square miles and a population of about 8,000,000, Czechoslovakia an area of about 60,000 square miles and a population of about 13,000,000—10,500,000 are Czechoslovakians and 2,500,000 are Germans—the Serb-Croat-Slovene State has about 90,000 square miles and a population of from 12,000,000 to 13,000,000. Its boundaries are still in dispute. To Poland is allotted an area containing about 125,000 square miles and a population of 36,000,000.

That this grotesque partition of the Austro-Hungarian Empire was not made on the principles of nationality is obvious. For example, Poland, before her partition in 1772, had an area of 274,000 square miles. She is allotted under the Paris conference one-half of this territory. Czechoslovakia is given control over 2,500,000 Germans, while the Tyrol, inhabited by pure German stock, is taken from Austria and given to Italy.

Roumania also comes in for her share of the former Austrian Empire, and, not satisfied with the amount of spoils awarded her by the Paris conference, has marched her armies into the capital of Budapest, which she holds now in defiance of the Allies and the league of nations.

Lord Bryce, one of the most learned and distinguished living Englishmen, in an article in the Manchester Guardian, which was copied by the Literary Digest of July 6, 1919, said:

> What appears to be now demanded is the cession to Italy of more than 200,000 Tyrolese (as a matter of fact, it is about 300,000) who have never been Italian in any sense, and who do not wish to be transferred to Italian rule. What is to be said of this demand for the annexation of more than 200,000 Tyrolese, an honest, simple, industrious race of peasants, as those of us who have climbed their cliffs and peaks know them to be? It was their misfortune and not their fault that they were dragged into a wicked war by a group of unscrupulous politicians surrounding an imbecile monarch. How can such a demand be reconciled with the principles of nationality and self-determination of peoples which the Allies proclaimed as the principles for which they were fighting? . . .

And in an interview published in the press of this country on November 1, 1919, Lord Bryce discussed the same subject. I quote from the interview, as follows:

> Under the treaty signed with the little bit of Austria which remained, he said 280,000 Tyrolese were taken and handed over to Italy. He said he had searched in vain for the reason for this action, but could find none, although it was totally opposed to the doctrine of nationality. The Italian Government said it wanted the Tyrolese territory for strategic purposes, Lord Bryce said; but, he declared, they could not want it for that purpose against a virtually bankrupt State of only 6,000,000 persons.

Now, I am citing these outrageous violations of every principle of ethnology and racial alignment because they bear upon the obligations that we are to assume under article 10. What this league decrees done, we must enforce by armies, by soldiers, by the boys raised in South Dakota, in Wisconsin, in Pennsylvania, in New Jersey, and elsewhere; and if the Paris conference violated every principle upon which nationalities are aligned, if they violated every obligation of the principles laid down as we fought this war step by step, shall we not, if we vote to enter this league, have an accounting with our constituents that ought to give us pause and make us hesitate to take this step?

There is, of course, no pretense of supporting the award of Transylvania to Roumania—a territory substantially as large as Roumania itself—on any principle of nationality. The explanation of all this, of course, lies—here we come to it—in the secret treaties. . . .

Italy was induced to violate her treaty with the Central Powers and go in with the Allies by the secret treaty which was made and which is known as the treaty of London. The treaty of peace consummated at Versailles, in which we are asked to concur, has no regard for nationality; no regard for the will of subject peoples; no regard for ethnological lines; no regard for racial attractions or racial repulsions. It is made on the hard-and-fast lines of the secret treaties entered into for the purposes of the war in the period 1915 to 1918. . . .

The explanation of all this, of course, lies in the secret treaties by which the Allies bribed Roumania and Italy to join them in the war, while Serbia, of course, is also given a choice bit of Hungarian territory. It is well to recall, while speaking of Hungary, that her repeated and heroic attempts to free herself from the domination of the Hapsburg monarchy, including that of 1848 under the leadership of Kossuth, were only defeated by the action of those countries, or some of them, who were allies in the late war. The testimony taken before the Foreign Relations Committee of the Senate established the absolute falsity of any claim that the principle of nationality or self-determination controlled in the partition of the Austro-Hungarian Empire.

Dr. Sekely, one of our most distinguished citizens of Austro-Hungarian descent, in his testimony before that committee—that is, the Committee on Foreign Relations—on September 2, which I venture to say, few, if any, Members of the Senate have read, after pointing out that the action of the Paris peace conference violated and outraged every principle of self-determination and nationality of the people abroad, said:

> This "league of injustice" intends to build an impregnable and indestructible Chinese wall around the subjugated races, a wall so high as to shut out all rays of hope for liberation, a wall so strong through the united cooperation of the mightiest nations of the earth as to imbue the peoples which had been caught in the diplomatic net of

> the Paris peace conference, as the Hungarians—or else had been ignored by it, as the Irish—with the paralyzing knowledge of their utter impotency to escape and to be free again. Instead of joy it brings sorrow, instead of light it sheds darkness, instead of righting wrongs it commits new ones, instead of developing international law it makes the law of egotism international, instead of heralding the dawn of a new world it means the doom of all the highest aspirations of mankind toward universal justice, fairness and a square deal.

It does all that with a deceiving smile and with an abundance of hypocritically sweet words.

We must remember, Mr. President, that it is this condition we undertake to uphold and perpetuate when we become a member of this league. This situation is well stated by the celebrated newspaper writer, Mr. Frank H. Simonds, in the London Times of June 2 last. I quote from that interview:

> In sum it is essential for Americans to recognize that, so far as the peace of the world is concerned, the Austrian settlement is even more important than the German, and that the possibilities of permanent adjustment are far less numerous. Actually the war, by destroying the central authority of the Hapsburg monarchy, has released races whose rivalries are at least a thousand years old. These races are as unwilling to submit their claims to the final decision of the league of nations as were the Balkans to subordinate theirs to the will of the concert of Europe. However the boundaries may be drawn, hundreds of thousands of people will, in the nature of things, be subjected to a rule they will not recognize. Germans will be placed under Slavs, Slavs under Italians, Hungarians under Roumanians, Poles under Ukranians, and Ukranians under Poles, and such a situation can only lead to new crisis.

We, sir, if we become a member of this league of nations, assume the obligation of standing guard over this territory, with all its rivalries and hatreds and its petty and artificial governments brought into existence by the mere word of the two or three men who controlled the Paris conference.

I have spoken of the secret treaties and their effect upon the dismemberment and destruction of the Austro-Hungarian Empire, but even after Roumania, Italy and Serbia have been satiated with new territory there was left an area extensive enough and a population sufficiently large to have made up a substantial State.

Great Britain's interests in the Far East, however, required this territory should be made into buffer States, and this was done in the manner stated. We all recall, as one of the causes of the war, the rivalry between Germany and Great Britain for trade in the Far East, and the efforts of Germany through the Bagdad Railway to tap the great resources of the vast country, and how she has been thwarted in her purpose temporarily at least at the time the war began in 1914.

President Wilson very frankly stated the truth in his St. Louis speech on September 5 last when he said:

> What was the old formula of Pan Germanism? From Bremen to Bagdad, wasn't it? Well, look at the map. What lies between Bremen and Bagdad? After you get past the German territory there is Poland, there is Bohemia, which we have made into Czechoslovakia; there is Hungary, which is now divided from Austria and does not share Austria's strength; there is Roumania; there is Jugo-Slavia; there is broken Turkey; and then Persia and Bagdad. We have undertaken to say this route is closed.

There you have the second of the causes of Austria's dismemberment and destruction. It was that the road leading to England's vast possessions in the Far East might be closed to any other country. To accomplish this purpose these petty and arbitrary States have been raised up, and we are going to underwrite their political independence and territorial integrity for the benefit of Great Britain. . . .

I have dwelt at some length on the destruction and dismemberment of Austria, because it is characteristic of everything done at the Paris conference. Starting out with the declaration of President Wilson that the Austrian Empire was not going to be impaired or even rearranged, we find that it is utterly destroyed for the most sordid and selfish purposes, and that a condition has been created which is absolutely certain to keep central Europe in turmoil and war for years to come.

While the Austrian treaty has never been placed before the Senate, it has been printed, and we can speak with some degree of certainty of its provisions. It is a remarkable fact, Mr. President, that the treaty with Germany which we are now considering is only a fragment of the settlement concluded at Paris. Five major treaties were drafted by the Paris conference—that with Germany, and the treaties with Austria-Hungary, Bulgaria, and Turkey. The treaty with Turkey is not yet completed. Each, I understand, is interwoven with the other.

These treaties have been described by President Wilson as intertwining. As Secretary Lansing said before the Committee on Foreign Relations of the Senate—I should like to have the Senators think of this for a moment—as Secretary Lansing said, the full engagements in which the United States may be involved can not be determined until we get full texts of the treaties.

Does the Senate realize that it has not the full texts of these treaties, and that we are asked to subscribe to an obligation incorporated within the league of nations that binds us to carry out all of the provisions of all the treaties that have been made? We do not know what is in the other treaties, aside from the one that has been presented, the treaty with Germany. We have an unofficial copy of the treaty with Austria.

I can not quite understand, Mr. President, the standards of the present Senate. I do not believe that there is a man here who is a lawyer who, if employed by a client to advise him with regard to the making of a contract, would permit his client to sign his name to a contract only a part of the obligations of which were stated in the document which he signed; and yet that is exactly what we are asked to do and what we are proceeding to do. We know nothing about these other treaties, or the obligations which the league of nations compels us to carry out with respect to them. They have not been submitted to us. We know nothing about the mandatories, or the arrangements that are being made, day by day and hour by hour, by the representatives of the different Governments at Paris, now in session, that impose obligations which we must carry out and back up with troops and money, and send soldiers to fight and die to preserve. And yet we go on complacently, ready to set our hands to a document that shall bind the people of this Government with regard to covenants about which we can know absolutely nothing. Not one of us, as a responsible lawyer dealing with a client, would do a thing of that kind any more than he would cut off his arm.

What does it mean? It means that the Senate of the United States has been recreant to its traditions. You may smile, but if we could turn the clock back a generation of time the President of the United States, when he sent down the German treaty and covenant, withholding the other treaties, would have been informed that it would not be considered for a moment until the Senate of the United States had on the table all of the obligations that the league of nations carried with it, that they might know about them, and that they might in their trust capacity in binding the American people, act intelligently.

I say that the present Senate is derelict in its duty, and has failed to discharge its responsibility to the American people by permitting itself to be coerced into the consideration of a contract more than one-half of which is blank, and is being forced to sign that contract without knowing the obligations that will be written into the blank places when the other treaties, the mandatories, and the protectorates are worked out by those who are engaged in that business in Paris now.

Why is it that these things have been held back from us? Why is it that the President of the United States did not transmit with these treaties the minutes of the Paris conference? They have been asked for. They have been denied. Neither the Committee on Foreign Relations nor the Senate has been permitted to know the discussion that took place when the different provisions in the German treaty and the league of nations were set down and agreed upon. That discussion would help to enlighten us. We have had days and days of debate here to determine what certain provisions of this covenant mean. If we could have had the debate that took place behind the doors of the conference at Versailles, it would have shed some light upon the meaning of these obscure provisions. Every Senator knows that, as to the Constitution of the United States, when the Madison papers, the minutes that were kept of the proceedings of the Constitutional Convention, were published they threw a flood of light upon the provisions of the Constitution; and we all of us go back, in obscure passages of the Constitution, in conflicting or doubtful meanings there, to the debates and to the minutes of the Constitutional Convention.

In God's name, Mr. President, what sort of a body has this become? I undertake to say that if Webster, or Thurman, or Edmunds, men of that stamp and that generation, were Members of this body to-day, they would have said to the President of the United States, "Take this treaty back. It is only a part of the obligation you ask us to assume, and we will not bind ourselves by it. We will not even consider it until we know all about it. Bring in everything that relates to it."

But, Mr. President, we have been trained for two years during the war, we have been taught, as a part of the Congress, to jump through the hoop and to perform other circus acrobatics. . . .

The proposal that we shall ratify the German peace treaty without knowing what is in the other four, with which it is "intertwined," illustrates the manner in which our Government has been led deeper and deeper into the morass of European affairs, until it is now proposed that we not only guarantee the peace of Europe but that we shall be the guardian of those peoples and territories over which the European Governments do not care to accept the mandates. If they have any job over there that is particularly hard they turn it over to us.

Italy's Share of the Spoils

I pass now to Italy's share in the spoils of the war, in the possession of which we undertake to protect her by signing this league agreement. . . .

The simplest way to arrive at the facts is to turn to the secret treaty of London, signed April 26, 1915, and published by the Lenin government after it came into power in Russia. The terms of this treaty are fairly well known, thanks to the publication of the secret treaties to which Russia was a party by the revolutionary Russian Government when it came into power.

You know we would have never known anything about these secret treaties if it had not been for that much-denounced Government in Russia. They got possession of the infamous documents and gave them to the world.

Under article 4 of the treaty of London it was agreed by Great Britain, France, and Russia, parties to the treaty, that Italy should receive that part of Austria known as the Trentino, the entire southern Tyrol, the city and suburbs of Trieste and various other parts of Austria, the Istrian Islands along her eastern coast, and the Province of Dalmatia and various islands adjacent thereto. Furthermore, it was agreed to by this precious quartet of nations that Italy, in consideration of the foregoing spoils, was not to object to or oppose a desire on the part of France, Great Britain, and Russia to redistribute among Montenegro, Serbia, and Greece the northern and southern districts of Albania.

Such a thing as an agreement to dismember a friendly, though weak, power would hardly shock the countries that later agreed with Japan to carve up and distribute the territory of their ally, China.

But there are other provisions of this treaty which, if we are to guarantee it, we should scan with care.

By article 9 of this treaty it is provided that France, Great Britain, and Russia recognize in Italy her "right to receive on the division of Turkey an equal share with them in the basin of the Mediterranean, and more specifically in that part of it contiguous to the Province of Adalia.* * * The zone subject to transfer to the sovereignty of Italy will be more specifically defined in due time, and in correspondence with the vital interests of France and Great Britain."

Article 13 of this precious document provides as follows:

> In the event of expansion of French and English colonial domains in Africa at the expense of Germany, France and Great Britain recognize in principle the Italian right to demand for herself certain compensations in the sense of expansions of her lands in Erithria, Somaliland, in Libya, and colonial districts lying on the boundary, with the colonies of France and England.

By article 17 it is provided:

> This treaty must be kept secret.

That seemed to be an important provision.

Now, the significance of all this is that no one knows up to date, or at least the Senate of the United States does not know it, what Italy's share is to be on the division of Turkey, nor what her share is to be on the division of the German colonies, nor, indeed, what her share is to be in the much more specific matter of division of territory taken from Austria.

It seems that the city of Fiume was not mentioned specifically as part of Italy's share of the spoils, but she is in possession of it, and Mr. Wilson and all the league of nations do not seem to be able to dispossess her. When we undertake, as we do, by becoming a member of this league to guarantee the territorial integrity of Italy, do we guarantee her the possession of Fiume, or do we guarantee its possession to Czechoslovakia,[2] whose claims the President seems to support?

Are you going to arrive at a settlement of the division of the world by becoming a party to that dispute? Do you think you are doing the best you can to take one side or the other of that proposition? You have to take one side or the other of it. Or will you better represent the people of your State by washing your hands of the entire affair and saying we have done our part in this business and we will get back on to our own soil, we will take care of the problems that are pressing upon us from the States. With strikes everywhere, the very earth under our feet quaking with unrest, we, with eyes uplifted and following voices in the air, troop after Woodrow Wilson to look after the affairs of the world.

What is the territory in Africa and in the Mediterranean which we undertake to defend for Italy? As far as we know, it has not yet been determined. Italy, France, and Great Britain either have not settled it among themselves or if they have we have not been officially advised of the settlement. We have to answer these questions some time; we might as well ask them now. Suppose they quarrel about it. We will have to take a hand in that quarrel.

Yet, sir, it is proposed that we shall defend Italy in the possession of whatever lands may be allotted to her and uphold her rule over whatever people are made subject to her will.

Mr. President, I can not understand why the Senate will even consider so mad a proposition as this. We do not know what Italy is to receive, but we propose to guarantee it to her anyway. That is what this means. Vote it if you dare. We do not know but what the award made to her by the Paris conference—or which, in the case of Fiume, she may seize and hold in spite of that conference, finally compelling acquiescence—will violate every principle of justice and self-determination; but we sign the bond. That is what it means to go into this business. It is proposed that we shall bind this Government.

We are to bind the people of this country to defend Italy's possessions as determined by the peace conference, right or wrong, to uphold her rule, and the decision and decree of the peace conference, however shocking it may be to us as individuals.

It is a strange thing, Mr. President, that we have been debating for months whether we would pledge the United States to uphold and defend the revolutionary, territorial, and political changes made by the Paris conference; but we have not inquired, and we do not to-day know, as we are proceeding to vote upon this treaty, what is involved in those territorial and political changes brought about in Paris.

I do not know how any member of the Committee on Foreign

[2] [The reference intended is, of course, to Yugoslavia.]

Relations can defend the course that has been pursued. I think all of us have an obligation. I think Members of the Senate ought to have risen in their places here and protested against the consideration of this treaty at all until all the treaties and all the documents and all the papers were before us. Why not? I shall be glad to yield to another Senator here who will answer.

I know that the chairman of the Committee on Foreign Relations has asked for these documents; I know that the Senate has passed resolutions requesting that the various documents should be sent to us; but when they were not sent there was another answer to make the imperious power at the other end of the Avenue. What was it? "Very well, if you decline to put us in possession of all of the facts which will enable us to know what obligation we are incurring as a Government and imposing upon our people, by giving us all the treaties that are a part of and intertwine with this compact of the league of nations, then we refuse to move one inch in the consideration of it, and we refuse to take it up for consideration at all."

Then it would have been the old Senate, it would have been a Senate that stood for its rights under the Constitution, that was willing to go back to the people of the country on the issue of whether it was abiding by the Constitution or whether the President was violating the Constitution.

Three or four old men over there within the last few months have assumed to rewrite the map of the world and to change the Governments under which hundreds of millions of people are living, and we are asked to accept their work on faith and to declare that it is good in advance, without knowing anything about it, and to pledge the money and the lives of our citizens to uphold and defend it.

I say, sir, that what we know of the work of the Paris conference as revealed in the German treaty and as revealed in what we suppose in the Austrian treaty gives us no reason to believe that selfish ambitions, greed, and the desire of revenge will not be manifest in the settlements made by that conference, of which as yet we know practically nothing.

I think it is safe to say that the Senate is not going to ratify the German treaty with the Shantung provision. Even the mildest of the mild reservationists can not stand for that. Yet how do we know how many Shantungs we will find in the Austrian treaty and in the Bulgarian treaty and in the Turkish treaty when we see them?

Am I consuming the time of the Senate here needlessly? Am I asking questions that have no significance and no meaning? If so, I should like to be told of it. I would not prolong this session by this address a minute. But if we now concur in the German treaty and subscribe to this covenant it will be too late when we see the other treaties to strike out or refuse to be bound by such shameful provisions as the Shantung provision of this treaty. When we have undertaken by becoming party to this covenant to preserve the territorial integrity and political independence of the members of the league in all that has been allotted to them by the Paris conference, we have ratified all the treaties in substance and effect. The rest is mere detail, after this first job is over.

There is another thought in this connection worthy of consideration. Italy, in common with the other allies, as a result of their victory in this war has become imperialistic to an extent hardly conceived of before the war.

I wonder how many Senators on this floor have been studying the emanations from the Italian writers since the war spirit fired that emotional nationality? The powerful Nationalist Party in Italy is preaching the doctrine, which is received by the Italians with enthusiasm, that Italy must once more play the part of ancient Rome. Prof. Corradini, a member of this party and one of the most influential men in Italy, recently expressed it thus—and I want to say that this is not an isolated case. I could fill a dozen pages with quotations from the writings of eminent writers of Italy who are now seeking to stir this spirit, to fire with enthusiasm the people of Italy into a movement that is to make them sweep on and on in conquest until they are the foremost power of the world. Here is what Prof. Corradini says:

> Italy must become once more the first nation of the world.* * * All our efforts will tend toward making the Italian a warlike race. We will give it a new will; we will instill into it the appetite for power, the need of mighty hopes. We will create a religion—the religion of the fatherland victorious over the other nations. (From article in the Forum, September, 1915, by T. L. Stoddard.)

The Italian literature of to-day, its press, and even its schools and colleges are teaching this doctrine of Italian domination. The manner in which a picturesque Italian character has taken possession with a volunteer army of the city of Fiume and its holding it from Jugoslavia, in spite of the league of nations and the Paris conference and their combined authority, is merely a concrete manifestation of the spirit in which Italy is going forward to collect the balance of her claims in the spoils of this war. Who shall say what bloody conflicts will arise in the course of that adjustment and to what distant lands our soldiers must be sent to sacrifice their lives in the settlement of selfish quarrels wherein we have no interest and feel no sympathy with either side?

It is becoming more obvious every day that the so-called economic and moral power of this league will amount to little or nothing. The Allies know this. They know that this so-called league is merely an alliance in which the United States is to become a party and bind itself to defend the possessions and dominions which the imperialistic Governments of the league claim for themselves as a result of the war. . . .

This is but a brief and imperfect survey of the shocking conditions which await us upon our entrance into this league.

No rational man can doubt but the United States will be the Nation relied upon to furnish the men and the money to enforce the decrees and mandates of the league throughout central Europe and parts of Asia and Africa.

Who can doubt that the self-interest of Italy, Roumania, Greece, and Serbia, when they find their ambitions thwarted by the more powerful members of the league, particularly by the United States, will come together in a union of self-interest, and what we start to do in the first instance with a few thousand men we shall soon find requires a vast army? All this and vastly more is involved in the obligations we will assume under article 10 of this treaty.

Mr. President, the little group of men who sat in secret conclave for months at Versailles were not peacemakers. They were war makers. They cut and slashed the map of the Old World in violation of the terms of the armistice. They patched up a new map of the Old World in consummation of the terms of the secret treaties the existence of which they had denied because they feared to expose the sordid aims and purposes for which men were sent to death by the tens of thousands daily. They betrayed China. They locked the chains on the subject peoples of Ireland, Egypt, and India. They partitioned territory and traded off peoples in mockery of that sanctified formula of 14 points, and made it our Nation's shame. Then, fearing the wrath of outraged peoples, knowing that their new map would be torn to rags and tatters by the conflicting warring elements which they had bound together in wanton disregard of racial animosities, they made a league of nations to stand guard over the swag!

The Old World armies were exhausted. Their treasuries were empty. It was imperative that they should be able to draw upon the lusty man power and the rich material resources of the United States to build a military cordon around the new boundaries of the new States of the Old World.

Senators, if we go into this thing, it means a great standing Army; it means conscription to fight in foreign wars, a blighting curse upon the family life of every American home, every hour. It means higher taxes, higher prices, harder times for the poor. It means greater discontent; a deeper, more menacing unrest.

Mr. President, whatever course other Senators take, I shall never vote to bind my country to the monstrous undertaking which this covenant would impose.

6

Issues of the Twenties: Speeches During the Presidential Campaign of 1924[1]

When both the Republican and Democratic conventions of 1924 nominated conservative candidates for President and adopted rather reactionary platforms, La Follette felt that they had betrayed the people. Somewhat reluctantly, for he was now sixty-nine, "Fighting Bob" agreed to make the campaign for President as an Independent Progressive candidate. The Progressive convention (CPPA) in Cleveland nominated him by acclamation, with Senator Burton K. Wheeler of Montana as his running mate. Urging an "honest realignment" of American parties, La Follette hoped to present a program that would meet the problems of the day and "build a hope" for tomorrow. This would attract the progressives of both old parties throughout the country as well as the liberal-minded independents. In his campaign, La Follette put together a coherent and positive platform to reform and remedy the abuses which were apparent in the administrations of Harding and Coolidge. In retrospect it is probable that such a pattern of reforms would have prevented or mitigated the Great Depression of 1929.

At Rochester, New York, Oct. 6.—Declaring that "the Progressive campaign is just beginning," Senator La Follette, at Convention Hall here tonight, in the first speech of his cross-country tour, explained the executive and legislative program which he would seek to put into effect if he were elected President.

Nearly 5,000 men and women crowded into Convention Hall and gave Senator La Follette a noisy greeting. An overflow meeting was held outside the Auditorium. Departing from his prepared text, Senator La Follette said:

"There will be no Daughertys or Falls in my Administration, nor will there be any Jesse Smiths or Howard Mannings."

[1] *The New York Times,* October 7–15, 1924. Copyright 1924 by The New York Times Company. Reprinted by permission.

There was great applause when the speaker pledged that if he were elected there would be "no Daugherty and Palmer. Injunctions and Federal troops will not be degraded into the shameful condition of strike-breakers."

Dividing his hoped-for term of office into two parts, Senator La Follette said the first would embrace "the house-cleaning period, which would occupy the eighteen months prior to the Congressional elections of 1926." The second would be "the constructive period, occupying the balance of my first term."

Saying that he was making his program public, "an unprecedented step on the part of the Presidential candidates," because he believed the American people had a right to know what their public servants would do if elected, the Wisconsin Senator described in detail how he would essay to carry out his plans. The house-cleaning period would apply to men as well as to measures. He proposed "not only to renovate the executive departments but also to wipe off the statute books the reactionary laws which are used as the instruments of exploitation and oppression."

The "house cleaning" would include "the appointment of a cabinet selected without regard to party or political obligation," and composed of men pledged to rid their departments of every special interest representative and to enforce the law without fear or favor.

In the appointment of his Cabinet he would give due recognition to agriculture, labor and the independent business men. The house cleaning would remove "the henchmen of special interests" as well as "the incompetents and time servers," and restore the merit system.

HIS LEGISLATIVE PROGRAM

"If I am elected to the Presidency of the United States, I shall call Congress into special session immediately after the 5th of March, and in my first message recommend substantially the following immediate legislative program:

"Enactment of emergency legislation for the relief of agriculture. This is not class legislation, but in the highest sense legislation for the public welfare to remedy the disastrous results of the unwise policies of the last two Administrations. I believe that a clear, nonpartisan majority favoring the enactment of sound legislation for this purpose already exists in the present Congress and will act speedily when the obstructions hitherto placed in the way of such legislation by President Coolidge and the reactionary leaders of Congress have been removed."

"Revision or repeal of the two great charters of special privilege enacted by the reactionaries during their recent control of Congress: The Esch-Cummins Railroad law and the Fordney-McCumber Tariff Act.

"These two laws are now imposing upon all classes of the American people burdens which total in the aggregate billions of dollars. It is certain that a large majority of both the House and Senate are ready to repeal these measures at the earliest opportunity and to substitute for them legislation drafted in the interest of the American People.

"Repeal of the veterans' 'tombstone' bonus, enacted by the last Congress and the substitution of legislation to provide genuine adjusted compensation for veterans of the great war. This question will not be settled until the nation's obligations have been fairly and squarely discharged. An overwhelming majority of the present Congress have demonstrated their readiness to support such a measure.

"Enactment of the Howell-Barkley bill. This bill proposes to abolish the present discredited Railroad Labor Board and substitute a plan for the adjustment of controversies between the railroads and their employees, every feature of which has been tested and proved by past experiences. A clear majority favoring this bill now exists in both houses of Congress and it will pass at the next session if there is no interference by the Administration.

"Revision of salaries of postal employees and of pensions of Civil and Spanish War veterans to conform to the increased cost of living. These bills were passed by the last Congress and were defeated only by the veto of President Coolidge.

"I submit that all the items in this immediate legislative program already command overwhelming support in Congress and are not dependent upon partisan majorities. They would already have been passed except for opposition by the Harding-Coolidge Administrations, or obstruction by reactionary leaders of the two old parties in Congress.

"If these measures, or any of them, should not be enacted, we would go to the country in the Congressional elections of 1926 confident that upon these issues the American people would express their will in unmistakable terms.

CONSTRUCTIVE PROPOSALS

"While this immediate legislative program is being enacted during the house cleaning period I propose to direct the appropriate executive departments, with the advice and counsel of the progressives in Congress and the best experts available in the United States, to prepare a detailed constructive program covering the following subjects.

"Reconstruction of the Federal Reserve and Federal Farm Loan Systems, so as to make the nation's credit available on fair terms and without discrimination to business men, farmers and home builders.

"A permanent transportation policy including a comprehensive study and analysis of methods of providing for public ownership of railroads, with adequate safeguards against bureaucratic control, and political manipulation.

"A national superpower system to develop the water powers now in the possession of the Federal Government and make the resulting electric power available to the people at cost.

"Development of cooperative marketing to eliminate profiteering and reduce the enormous spread that now exists between the primary producer upon the farms and the ultimate consumer in the cities. This would supplement the emergency legislation for the relief of agriculture, for which I should demand immediate consideration upon the convening of an extra session of Congress.

"Control of trusts and combinations to fortify and supplement such weaknesses in existing legislation as may be disclosed by the honest and vigorous attempt to enforce the present anti-trust laws, which we should initiate as one of the first acts of the Progressive Administration.

"There is one other important matter upon which I have not yet touched, and which I can at this time cover only in the barest outline. That is the foreign policy which I would expect to pursue if elected President of the United States.

"As a preface to this discussion, it is my opinion that the Congress, composed of the elected representatives of the people, is entitled to a voice in the determination of the foreign policy of the Government. I have expressed this view repeatedly upon the floor of the Senate, and I should expect to uphold it if I were elected President. I do not believe that the President or the State Department should have the power, without the knowledge and consent of the Congress or the people, to involve the nation in such a way as to lead to inextricable entanglements, unfavorable commitments or to war. I believe in the democratic control of foreign policy and am unalterably opposed to secret diplomacy.

"The great war which began ten years ago is now generally admitted to have been an imperialistic war, born of the greed of financiers, exploiters of foreign lands, imperialists who conquered defenseless peoples in order to protect their usurious loans and destructive concessions. They made war on foreign peoples as they profiteered and made war on the liberties of the people at home. They used diplomacy, the office, battleships and the country's youth to promote and protect their imperialistic possessions and in time brought the whole world to the cataclysm which caused ten million of its youth to be slain on the field of battle and twenty millions to be invalided by wounds and disease.

FOREIGN POLICY

"We will end invisible government and American imperialism. We will keep out of other people's lands. We will extend to those peoples the same freedom that we seek for ourselves. Our State Department shall not be the agent of bankers, investors and imperialists. Your sons shall not be conscripted as a collection agency of private debts.

"And as an evidence of our good faith in this program of peace we propose:

"1. A referendum on the declaration of war except in case of actual invasion.

"2. To end our imperialistic attitude toward Central and South America. We will withdraw our Marines from Haiti, Santo Domingo and every other place where they are now being used to coerce local governments for the benefit of American financiers and special interests.

"3. We will give the Philippines their independence. We will fulfill the solemn pledge made to them by the American Congress.

"4. We will end the partnership between our State Department and imperialistic interests, and we will divorce it from Standard Oil and international financiers.

"5. We will use every peaceful influence to bring about a revision of the Treaty of Versailles, not in terms of hate and punishment, but in accordance with the more generous terms of the armistice.

"6. Finally, we will use the influence of this Government to outlaw war, to abolish conscription, to drastically reduce air, land and naval armaments, and to guarantee referendums on peace and war. We can then hope to secure for these purposes the cooperation of the new Governments of Europe, the democratic Governments of Europe, the Governments which are sprung from the people themselves, and which, for the first time in a century are seeking to end war by ending the causes of war.

"I intend to win the election on Nov. 4. On that day I believe the people of the country will take the control of the Government back into their own hands, where it rightfully belongs.

"If I wanted the election to be thrown into Congress, I would stay in Washington and take it easy for the rest of the campaign.

"Our reactionary opponents in both the old party camps are charging that my sole purpose is to have the election thrown into Congress. This is utterly ridiculous.

"The election is now in Congress. I mean that if the election were held today no candidate would receive a majority of the votes in the

Electoral College. Certainly neither Coolidge nor Davis could win a majority.

"I want the election decided by the people in a voice that brooks no misinterpretation. Reports from every part of the country lead me to believe that the Progressive tide is rising at a tremendous rate. It has not reached its crest. The reports lead me to believe that we can increase the power of this movement to the point of a clean-cut election in November. That is why I am on this trip. I believe the people want to hear the message I have to give. I intend to do everything in my power to see that it reaches them.

"When our opponents say, as they have been saying for the last five weeks, that our power has passed its peak, they are merely whistling to keep up their courage.

"We are in this fight to win and we will not be content with anything except victory."

At Cincinnati, Ohio, Oct. 10.—Senator La Follette devoted practically his entire speech tonight at the Music Hall to an outline of the foreign policy of the Progressives. He declared that his was a policy of cooperation with other nations to end conscription, for disarmament, and for the release of subject peoples. He would "end all secret diplomacy, end all profit from war, and in the event of a defensive war he would pay for the war as we go" and "leave no heritage of debt on subsequent generations."

Eight thousand men and women heard Senator La Follette. Five thousand crowded into Music Hall and 3,000 listened in front of the hall, where amplifiers carried his voice to the outermost edge of the crowd.

Asserting that he was not an advocate of "peace at any price," Senator La Follette said he would repel invasion or the aggressive acts of any power "that would seize our territory or imperil our national life or institutions."

In his address in a community which has a large German element, Mr. La Follette gave it as his opinion that "secret treaties" and "crooked diplomacy" were responsible for the World War, and that it was "not a war of unprovoked aggression by one nation."

"It was a war which had its birth in secret diplomacy, in national fears kept alive by military castes, and, most of all, by private munition makers and a capitalistic press in all of the great powers," he said.

After remarking that the diplomacy of the last four years "may involve us in another war," the speaker enumerated the principles which he said the Progressives would invoke to end war "and at the same time to make permanent our liberties at home."

ATTACKS SECRET DIPLOMACY

The Senator attacked secret diplomacy and said that, in effect, it made it possible for the State Department "to involve us in commitments and obligations, in acts of aggression and in entanglements which involve the honor of the nation." War, he added, became an accomplished fact "before the nation was aware of even the possibility of such a contingency."

Senator La Follette criticized the State Department, which, he asserted, had adopted the diplomatic secrecy of Europe.

"Even the United States Senate is not advised of its acts. When a demand is made from the Senate for information regarding relations with foreign Governments, the stereotyped refusal of the State Department is: 'It is incompatible with the public interest that such information should be published.' " So sacred is this secrecy in foreign relations that a President may involve 110,000,000 people in a foreign war without the consent of Congress and in defiance of the will of the American people.

"We would bring all diplomacy out into the open. We would publish our engagements, if such there were, with foreign nations. In carrying out our pledge for the democratic control of foreign policy we would at all times keep Congress fully advised and concede to it its constitutional share in the conduct of foreign relations."

The second plank in his foreign policy was summed up in the sentence, "We will end profit in war." "Ending the expectations of profits from war, would end the hysteria, the activity of fearmongers and the promotion of international rivalries in armaments."

The Senator's third plank called for a "pay-as-you-go policy" in the event of a defensive war.

"If war is forced upon us, we shall leave no heritage of debt on subsequent generations. We shall pay for war as we go. We shall not permit your Government again to force billions of war securities onto the workers, the farmers and the poor, with guarantees that they should always be worth the dollars that bought them and then permit a conspiracy of bankers to hammer down the value of such Liberty bonds and shake out millions of patriotic investors in the interest of the banking syndicates which acquired them at their depreciated value and then raised their value to par."

PROMISES NO ANNEXATION OF TERRITORY

No annexation of the territory of any other nation was the fourth plank enunciated by Senator La Follette.

"We will not menace the integrity of Mexico," he added. "We will withdraw our Marines from Haiti, from Santo Domingo and from the Central American States. We will not join in the dismemberment of China or seek to coerce China, or any other dependent people, to permit us to share with other powers in their spoliation.

"We will give self-government to the Philippines, thus fulfilling the solemn promises of our Congress."

The Senator's fifth plank called for a referendum on war; "except in cases of emergency arising from armed invasion, an emergency which I cannot conceive to arise.

"We will make no war until those who are to offer their lives and who are to make the sacrifices vote their approval of war. Such a war would not require the subversion of the Constitution, the trampling under foot of civil liberties, and the denial of the rights of free opinions."

"We will seek the whole-hearted co-operation of the nations of the world to reduce armaments to a defensive basis," is the sixth plank.

Coming to the seventh plank, to which he invited close attention, Senator La Follette discussed "dollar diplomacy," "financial imperialism," and "the doctrine that the flag followed the investor." In the latter doctrine, he asserted, was to be found the explanation of almost every war of the last generation.

America had become the credit reservoir of the world, he said, and since the war eight billions of dollars had been invested abroad. The speaker said:

"It has gone to Europe and Asia, to Africa and to South and Central America. J. P. Morgan & Co. has become the dictator of the destiny of a great part of Europe. It fixes the terms upon which Governments may endure. It determines whether Ministries shall rise or fall. It dictates the terms of peace, and holds the fate of European democracy in its hands."

ASSAILS "THE BANKERS' DOCTRINE"

"The doctrine that the flag follows the investor is a bankers' doctrine. It was conceived in the British Foreign Office seventy years ago. It was this wicked doctrine that destroyed the liberties of a great part of the world. It led to the bombardment of Alexandria and the invasion of Egypt. It made Tunis, Algiers and Morocco subject to France. It laid its hands on all of Africa. It inspired the Boer war. It lay back of the conflict over the Bagdad Railway and the conquest of the Mediterranean.

"Dollar diplomacy, financial imperialism, the doctrine that the flag follows the investor, is responsible for the great war itself."

He denounced the Treaty of Versailles as "a treaty of financial imperialists, of exploiters, of bankers, of all monopolists, who sought through mandates to sanctify and make permanent a redistribution of the spoils of the world and to cement forever the stranglehold of the power of gold on the defenseless peoples of the earth."

"The Progressives propose to end financial imperialism. They will divorce the State Department from imperialistic financial agencies. They will repudiate the doctrine that the American flag shall follow the investor. American youth shall no longer be sent to the tropics, to Mexico, to Santo Domingo, or Haiti. They shall not be used in Europe or in other continents as a collection agency for private debts.

"This is the foreign policy of the Progressives. It is a policy of avowed peace to the world. It is a policy of non-aggression. It is a policy of cooperation with other nations for the ending of conscription, for disarmament, for the release of subject peoples. It is a conservative policy. A policy of peace on earth and good-will to all mankind, a policy that would mobilize the world for peace, that would free the world from conquests and release its workers for the production of wealth and for its enjoyment unpoisoned by fear.

"We believe that the people of all nations are war-weary and that they will force their governments to join with us to promote peace and banish war forever from the world."

At Chicago, Oct. 11.—"You cannot convict a hundred million dollars in the United States," declared Senator La Follette, Progressive candidate for President, tonight before an audience of 10,000 in the Thirty-fifth Street Armory.

"You cannot punish a millionaire as a poor man would be punished, no matter how revolting or inhuman his crime may be."

The program of the Progressives will be to "restore economic equality before the law," he told the audience, in whose minds the Loeb-Leopold case is still fresh. The Progressives, said the Wisconsin Senator, were fighting "to restore Government to the broad basis of the popular will."

Equality before the law does not exist in the United States today, he asserted, adding "the Chief Justice of the United States Supreme Court has admitted it. There is one law for the rich, another for the poor."

It was then that the speaker made his allegation concerning the alleged impossibility of punishing a millionaire, and said: "It is this fact that gives this nation, to its shame, a crime record without parallel in the civilized world."

SAYS PROGRESSIVE TIDE SWEEPS NATION

Senator La Follette received an ovation when he was introduced by Jane Addams, head of Hull House. The Armory was filled shortly after the doors were opened and 2,000 were unable to gain admission. His attack on "the economic oligarchy" was applauded and another outburst greeted his assertion that "corruption and greed have penetrated even to the doors of the White House."

"The people of America are aroused," he told the audience.

"I have seen people of New York, Pennsylvania, New Jersey, Michigan, Ohio, and Illinois. Everywhere it is the same story. The people are flocking to the Progressive standard.

"They are in revolt against the decadence and corruption of the two old parties. But that is not the cause of their enthusiasm. It is far deeper. They see in the Progressive movement a new hope. They find a new spirit. They know that it voices their aspirations for justice, liberty and peace.

"The Progressive tide is rising from the Atlantic to the Pacific. It cannot be restrained. Today the Democratic and Republican candidates are defeated; they cannot win. We can. We are not going to throw this election into the House of Representatives. This election will be settled, like every other Presidential election in the last hundred years, by the people of the United States at the polls."

Deviating from his prepared address, the Senator thanked the newspapers for their fairness in reporting his speeches, saying:

"There was a day when my name was not permitted to appear in the press. But a new day has come and I stand here speaking for millions who will cast their votes for me in November."

This statement evoked wild applause and cheers. Hisses and boos greeted his attack on the Department of Justice and "injunction judges," and his statement that the Supreme Court by a 5-to-4 decision had upheld the ruling of Judge Van Orsdel of the District of Columbia, who declared the minimum wage act unconstitutional.

SAYS PROPERTY RIGHTS ARE PUT FIRST

No intelligent citizen believed the assertion that the courts were the defenders of the liberties of the people, Senator La Follette continued. While he knew many judges who had rendered signal service to the people yet in recent years, he declared, the courts have more and more "exalted the rights of property above the rights of man." He added:

"The climax was reached in the decision of Justice Van Orsdel of the Court of Appeals of the District of Columbia in the minimum-wage case when he declared: 'It should be remembered that of the three fundamental principles which underlie Government and for which Government exists, the protection of life, liberty and property, the chief of these is property.' "

"And that Justice, my friends, who dared proclaim such un-American doctrine is on the bench for life, and his decision holding the minimum wage law unconstitutional was sustained by the Supreme Court of the United States by a vote of 5 to 4. Moreover, that decision destroys the power of the Federal Government and perhaps of the State Governments to enact legislation for the protection of the wages of women workers no matter how helpless they may be until by the slow process of Constitutional amendment the will of the people can at last be asserted.

"Thus property rights are made supreme over human rights. Thus capital is exalted above labor.

"I offer this challenge to all those who regard judges as the sole defenders of our liberties: Show me one case in which the courts have protected human rights and I will show you twenty in which they have disregarded human rights to protect property."

In discussing the question of equality before the law, the candidate asserted that the Republican and Democratic parties were powerless to deal with that problem, "not that they condone crime, but that their political organizations are subject to and controlled by those who profit by this disregard of equal and exact justice."

The Progressives would not go into office with such limitations, because their campaign contributions came in large measure in driblets from the people, and we have no bosses and have made no pledges or promises to any man or group of men which are not contained in our public declaration."

INVASION OF INDIVIDUAL FREEDOM

Mr. La Follette then charged the invasion of the freedom of the individual, the freedom of speech, religion and the press, "particularly in the epoch of postwar hysteria and orgy of greed."

"Those offenses against constitutional liberties have not been limited to individuals and organizations. Government officials from the lowest to the highest have been the greatest offenders.

"We need legislation in this country making it a crime for any individual whether an official or a private citizen, or for any organization, to interfere with the exercise of the rights of free speech, free press and freedom of assembly.

"I believe that all true Americans will join with me in this demand. The preservation of these fundamental rights depends upon the maintenance of genuine representative government. The people themselves, through their elected representatives, must guard their liberties. No one else will protect them."

At Kansas City, Oct. 13.—Opening his campaign in the corn and wheat belt at a meeting in the Grand Theatre here tonight Senator La Follette appealed to the farmers, the workers and the businessmen to send him to the White House because the Republican and Democratic Parties had failed to stop "the deflation plans of the great bankers," as a result of which agriculture four years ago "was prostrated by the most sudden price decline in the history of the world."

Asserting that the decline in farm prices in 1920 was caused "by a conspiracy of bankers and government officials," the candidate declared that the action of the Federal Reserve Board four years ago "wiped out" $20,000,000,000 of farm land values; that $19,000,000,000 more were lost in the values of farm products and that "more than 1,500 banks failed, more than 60,000 business houses were thrown into bankruptcy and 4,000,000 wage earners were thrown out of employment."

REFERS TO "WHITE HOUSE SILENCE"

"There has been a conspiracy of silence," he said. Then, interrupting himself, he laid a finger on his lips and lowering his voice, exclaimed dramatically, "Sh-h-h! I think it originated in the White House." When the laughter subsided he added, "To keep the facts from the American people."

In a digression he paid a tribute to Senator Sherman, author of the Sherman Anti-Trust law, and asserted that the law "has never had one hour of honest enforcement. From the hour it was written to this, the interests that were named in that statute have named the Attorney General of the United States," he asserted.

The audience applauded enthusiastically when he said:

"If the combined nations of the earth moved on our coast defenses, I have the highest military authority for saying that men manned with pitchforks could dispose of them."

He called on the nations of the world to revise the Treaty of Versailles. The treaty differed from the terms of the armistice, he said, and he did not think it fair.

Senator La Follette drew a picture of a vast conspiracy aimed at the farmer, railroads being "the chief offenders" because of their freight rate increases. Bankers, too, were criticized as being responsible in a large measure for the farmers' plight. He jumped "exploiters" in a statement that "The railroads of the country are interlaced with the packers, with the millers, with the commission men, with the grain pits and together they form an economic system ruled from Wall Street."

"The economic life of 8,000,000 American farmers is determined by a handful of men," he continued. "It is determined by the banking, railroad and exploiting agencies owned by J. P. Morgan and the Standard Oil Company. These are the masters of America. These men have changed this great empire from the hope, the comfort and prosperity of 1890 to the despair of today."

CALLS RAILROADS WORST OFFENDERS

"There are few political crimes, for they are political crimes, that arouse me as does the neglect, if not the direct participation, of this government of ours in the destruction of the farmer, for the recent history of American agriculture has been one of neglect on the one hand and exploitation on the other. The farmer has been neglected by both parties. Neither the President nor Congress was concerned over his necessities.

"In time neglect became exploitation. This exploitation became an orgy during the years that followed the war. The farmer produced from $10,000,000,000 to $20,000,000,000 of wealth, yet the price he received for his produce was fixed for him by the packing monopoly, by commission men and millers, by the grain pits and the gamblers, and by the transportation agencies of the nation. These were the farmers' only buyers and they [paid] as little as possible. Unable to meet production costs from sales, the farmer had to go to the banks to make up the deficiency. This is why we have farm mortgages. Monopoly would not even pay the labor cost on the farm. The farmer had to borrow to keep alive. He did not get his own living from the farms."

ATTACKS DEFLATION OF 1920

"One million men left the countryside in a single year. Six hundred thousand farmers have become bankrupt and given up their farms since 1920. They did not leave the farms because of the lure of the city. They were driven from the farms by foreclosures and went to the city, not because of its lure, but because the struggle became hopeless. How quickly that change came about may be seen in the neighboring State of Oklahoma. It was born into the Union only seventeen years ago. Its rolling prairies lured to itself the best stock of America. The Government endowed each settler with a homestead, but along with the homesteader came the money lender.

"And the money lender of Oklahoma was often a usurer. The wreckage that followed the usurer in Oklahoma and Texas can hardly be paralleled in any nation."

Referring to the deflation period of 1920, the Progressive nominee said:

"More than 1,500 banks failed. More than 60,000 business houses were thrown out of employment, business life was stagnated in the great cities of the West whose commerce depended upon the prosperity of agriculture.

"Kansas City was harder hit than any other city. Its bank clearings fell from $12,000,000,000 in 1920 to $7,000,000,000 in 1923. $5,000,-000,000 less business a year for this one city.

"This was the greatest destruction of prosperity and property values in the history of the nation. The loss in farm values alone in the United States was $20,000,000,000. The total losses claimed by the French for destruction during the World War was only $13,000,000,-000. The total property damage claims of the Belgians was only $7,-500,000,000.

"This colossal destruction of property and prosperity did not happen, my friends, under a Communistic Government. It did not happen under a Socialistic Government. It did not happen under a Progressive Government. It occurred under Democratic and Republican Party Governments. It happened when the reactionaries of those parties were in full control of all branches of the government."

PLEDGES PROGRAM OF RELIEF

He pledged the Progressive Party to the enactment of the following measures for farm relief:

"Emergency legislation embodying the principle of agricultural equity which underlies both the McNary-Haugen and the Norris-Sinclair bills.

"Genuine farmer representation in the Cabinet and on the Federal Reserve Board, Federal Farm Loan Board, Tariff Board, Interstate Commerce Commission and other governmental bodies.

"Repeal of the Esch-Cummins Railroad law and immediate freight reductions to approximately pre-war levels on agricultural products, including live stock, and upon materials and implements required upon American farms.

"Revision of the Federal Reserve system so as to remove its control from the hands of private monopoly and insure an effective voice in the management for the users of credit—the farmers, merchants, manufacturers and employees—on an equal footing with the bankers who sell the people's credit.

"Reduction of the price of fertilizer by the governmental development of the Muscle Shoals project and similar water power resources now under the control of the Federal Government.

"Immediate downward revision of the present excessive manufacturers' tariff schedules, which place an unwarranted burden of at least $3,000,000,000 upon the American people.

"Sweeping investigation within the Department of Agriculture and other executive departments to locate and remove every employee who owes his position to the influence of the packers, the railroads, and other privileged groups."

At St. Louis, Mo., Oct. 14.—Addressing a gathering of 10,000 men and women at the coliseum tonight, Senator La Follette, independent candidate for President, assailed the foreign policy of the Wilson and Harding-Coolidge Administrations and, with many Germans in the audience, he denounced President Wilson for not adhering to his 1914 policy of "absolute neutrality."

Senator La Follette declared he was convinced that America's foreign policy today was being dictated by the same forces that were responsible for the abandonment of American neutrality during the World War. He summed up these forces in the phrase "private monopoly system," said he was convinced that American neutrality was abandoned through the influence of J. P. Morgan & Co. and cited a statement of former Assistant Secretary of the Treasury Oscar T. Crosby to support his assertion.

In addition to a bitter denunciation of President Wilson's policy, Mr. La Follette attacked the present Administration's foreign policy, especially the four-power treaty negotiated at the Washington disarmament conference.

Elected upon a pledge to avoid entangling alliances, "the Republican Party had involved this country in a compact with the three great imperialistic nations of the world, England, France, and Japan," and he asserted that the compact committed the United States to support those nations "in the exploitation of Asia."

ATTACKS FOUR-POWER COMPACT

"This compact—the four-power treaty—was negotiated under cover of the so-called disarmament conference. It is a peril to the American people and a direct threat to the world peace. The international bankers, oil companies, and other exploiting interests alone will profit from it."

After declaring that it was time to return to the fundamental American traditions in the conduct of foreign affairs as well as domestic policy, Senator La Follette reviewed the doctrine of Neutrality as formulated under Washington, Webster, Clay, and Lincoln.

"Today, there is not one of these fundamental principles that has not been ignored, violated or utterly rejected. Those who have controlled our foreign policy during the last ten years have departed entirely from American traditions and American principles and permitted our policy to be shaped by the imperialistic maxims and precepts of European diplomacy."

He thought it true that our departure from traditional American policy began with William McKinley, following the Spanish War, and the breach was broadened under Roosevelt and Taft. Nevertheless, he said, it was his opinion "that the complete abandonment of the true American foreign policy came under the Administration of Woodrow Wilson and has been continued and expanded under the present Harding-Coolidge Administrations."

Crediting Wilson with having tried in the first two years of his term to live up to his anti-imperialistic platform the speaker pointed to the late President's "absolute neutrality policy" in 1914 as "a true American policy," which, had it been adhered to, would never have drawn this country into the war.

TELLS WHAT WE COULD HAVE SAVED

"We would be free from every form of foreign entanglement. Sixty thousand American boys would still be alive, we would not have a colossal war debt. We would be free from our heavy burden of taxation. We would have no problem of caring for hundreds of thousands of wounded, diseased and shell-shocked veterans. We would not have American agriculture prostrate and demanding speedy relief.

"We would have no such concentration of wealth in the hands of a few, as we have witnessed in recent years. Above all, we should have preserved our proud distinction of a nation steadfastly devoted to peace. Had the plain principles of international law announced by Washington and Jefferson been followed, we would not have been called upon to declare war upon any of the belligerent nations of Europe. The fatal error came in the failure of President Wilson to treat the belligerent nations of Europe alike—the failure to reject the unlawful "war zones" of both Germany and Great Britain.

"I do not doubt that President Wilson was sincere when he declared for absolute neutrality. I know the influences which surrounded him and which, day after day, month after month, brought the heaviest imaginable pressure to induce him to abandon his position of neutrality and throw the strength of the United States openly on the side of the allied Governments."

PART TWO

LA FOLLETTE VIEWED BY HIS CONTEMPORARIES

7

Lincoln Steffens, "The Story of Governor La Follette"[1]

By 1904 Lincoln Steffens was famous as a political reporter and as a muckraking journalist. His articles in McClure's Magazine *on the "Shame of the Cities" had attracted nationwide attention and he then turned to do a similar series of articles on the states. By his own admission, Steffens went to Wisconsin certain that La Follette was a "charlatan and a crook." His article would expose the Wisconsin governor for what he was. When the story appeared, in the midst of the desperate gubernatorial campaign of 1904, it won hundreds if not thousands of votes for La Follette and made the two men warm friends. This article did much to make "Fighting Bob" a national figure.*

The story of the State of Wisconsin is the story of Governor La-Follette. He is the head of the state. Not many governors are that. In all the time I spent studying the government of Missouri, I never once had to see or name the Governor of Missouri, and I doubt if many of my readers know who he is. They need not. He is only the head of the paper government described in the Constitution, and most governors are simply "safe men" set up as figureheads by the System, which is the actual government that is growing up in the United States in place of the "government of the people, by the people, and for the people, which shall not perish from the earth." The System, as we have found it, is a reorganization of the political and financial powers of the state by which, for boodle of one sort or another, the leading

[1] From Lincoln Steffens, "Enemies of the Republic, Wisconsin: A State Where the People Have Restored Representative Government—The Story of Governor La Follette," *McClure's Magazine,* XXIII, 6 (October, 1904), 563–579.

politicians of both parties conduct the government in the interest of those leading businesses which seek special privileges and pay for them with bribes and the "moral" support of graft. And a "safe man" is a man who takes ease, honors and orders, lets the boss reign, and makes no trouble for the System.

There is trouble in Wisconsin. Bounded on the east by Lake Michigan, on the north by Lake Superior, on the west by the Mississippi River, Wisconsin is a convenient, rich and beautiful state. New England lumbermen stripped fortunes of forest off it, and uncovering a fat soil watered by a thousand lakes and streams, settlers poured in from Northwestern Europe and made this new Northwest ripen into dairy farms and counties of golden wheat. From the beginning Wisconsin has paid, nor is there now any material depression or financial distress in the state. Yet there is trouble in Wisconsin. What is the matter? I asked a few hundred people out there to explain it, and though some of them smiled and others frowned, all gave substantially one answer: "LaFolletteism." They blame one man.

THE STORY OF "BOB" LAFOLLETTE

Robert Marion LaFollette was born on a farm in Dane County, Wisconsin, June 14th, 1855. His father was a Kentucky bred French Huguenot; his mother was Scotch-Irish. When the boy was eight months old the father died, leaving the mother and four children, and, at the age of fourteen, "Little Bob," as his followers still call him, became the head of the family. He worked the farm till he was nineteen years old, then sold it and moved the family to Madison, the county-seat and capital of the state. If, with this humble start, LaFollette had gone into business, his talents might have made him a captain of industry; and then, no matter how he won it, his success would have made him an inspiration for youth. But he made a mistake. He entered the state university with the class of '79. Even so, he might have got over his college education, but his father's French blood (perhaps) stirred to sentiment and the boy thrilled for glory. He had a bent for oratory. In those days debates ranked in the Western colleges where football does now, and "Bob" LaFollette won, in his senior year, all the oratorical contests, home, state, and interstate. His interstate oration was on Iago, and his round actor's head was turned to the stage, till John McCullough advised him that his short stature was against that career. Also, he says, his debts chained him to the earth. He had to go to work, and he went to work in a law office. In five months he was admitted to the bar, and in February, 1880, he opened an office and began to practice. A year or so later the young lawyer was running for an office.

"They" say in Wisconsin that LaFollette is ambitious; that he cannot be happy in private life; that, an actor born, he has to be on stage. I should say that a man who can move men, as LaFollette can, would seek a career where he could enjoy the visible effect of his eloquence. But suppose "they" are right and the man is vain;—I don't care. Do you? I have noticed that a public official who steals, or, like Lieutenant-Governor Lee, of Missouri, betrays his constituents, may propose to be governor, without being accused of ambition. "They" seem to think a boodler's aspirations are natural. He may have a hundred notorious vices; they do not matter. But a "reformer," a man who wants to serve his people, he must be a white-robed, spotless angel, or "they" will whisper that he is—what? A thief? Oh, no; that is nothing; but that he is ambitious. This is the System at work. It was the System in Missouri that, after spending in vain thousands of dollars to "get something on Folk," passed about the damning rumor that he was ambitious. And so in Wisconsin, "they" will take you into a back room and warn you that LaFollette is ambitious. I asked if he was dishonest. Oh dear, no. Not that. Not a man in the state, not the bitterest foe of his that I saw, questioned LaFollette's personal integrity. So I answered that we wanted men of ambition; that if we could get men to serve us in public life, not for graft, not for money, but for ambition's sake, we should make a great step forward.

Mr. LaFollette has ambition. He confessed as much to me, but he is after a job not an office; Governor LaFollette's ambition is higher and harder to achieve than any office in the land.

A Politician and His First Office

The first office he sought was that of District Attorney of Dane County, and, though his enemies declare that the man is a radical and was from the start a radical, I gathered from this same source that his only idea at this time was to "pose" before juries "and win cases." Mr. LaFollette married in this year (a classmate) and he says he thought of the small but regular salary of the district attorney. However this may be, he won the office and he won his cases, so he earned his salary. District Attorney LaFollette made an excellent record. That is freely admitted, but my attention was called to the manner of his entrance into politics, as proof of another charge that is made against him in Wisconsin. "They" say LaFollette is a politician.

"They" say in Missouri that Folk is a politician. "They" say in Illinois that Deneen is a politician. "They" say in the United States that President Roosevelt is a politician. "They" are right. These men are politicians. But what of it? We have blamed our politicians so long for the corruption of our politics that they themselves seem to have been convinced that a politician is necessarily and inherently bad, and we have been discovering in our studies of graft that a bad business man is worse. To succeed in reform, a man has to understand politics and play the game, or the bad business man will catch him and then what will he be? He will be an "impracticable reformer," and that, we all know, is awful.

Running Around the Ring

"Bob" LaFollette is a politician. Irish, as well as French, he was born a master of the game and he did indeed prove his genius in that first campaign. Single-handed he beat the System. Not that he realized then that there was such a thing. All the young candidate knew when he began was that E. W. Keyes, the postmaster at Madison, was the Republican state boss, and, of course, absolute master of Dane County, where he lived. LaFollette was a Republican, but he had no claim of machine service to the office he wanted, and he felt that Boss Keyes and Philip L. Spooner, the local leader, would be against him, so he went to work quietly. He made an issue; LaFollette always has an issue. It had been the practice of district attorneys to have assistants at the county's expense, and LaFollette promised, if elected, to do all his own work. With this promise he and his friends canvassed the county, house by house, farm by farm, and, partly because they were busy by day, partly because they had to proceed secretly, much of this politics was done at night. The scandal of such "underhand methods" is an offense to this day to the men who were beaten by them. Mr. "Phil" Spooner (the Senator's brother) speaks with contempt of LaFollette's "night riders." He says the LaFollette workers went about on horseback after dark and that he used to hear them gallop up to their leader's house late at night. Of course he knows now that they were coming to report and plot, but he didn't know it then. And Boss Keyes, who is still postmaster at Madison, told me he had no inkling of the conspiracy till the convention turned up with the delegates nearly all instructed for LaFollette for District Attorney. Then it was too late to do anything.

Boss Keyes thought this showed another defect in the character of LaFollette. "They" say in Wisconsin that the Governor is "selfish, dictatorial, and will not consult." "They" said that about Folk in Missouri, when he refused to appoint assistants dictated by Boss Butler. Wall Street said it about Roosevelt when he refused to counsel with Morgan upon the advisability of bringing the Northern Securities case, but the West likes that in Roosevelt. The West said it about Parker when he sent his gold telegram to the Democratic National Convention, but the East likes that in Parker. There must be something back of this charge, and a boss should be able to explain it. Boss Keyes cleared it up for me. He said that at the time "Bob" was running for district attorney, "a few of us here were—well, we were managing the party and we were usually consulted about—about things generally. But LaFollette, he went ahead on his own hook, and never said a word to—well, to me or any of us." So it's not a matter of dictation, but of who dictates, and what. In the case of LaFollette, his dictatorial selfishness consisted in this, that he "saw" the people of the county and the delegates, not "us," not the System. No wonder he was elected. What is more, he was reëlected; he kept his promises, and, the second time he ran, LaFollette was the only Republican elected on the county ticket.

During the two terms of District Attorney LaFollette, important changes were occurring in the Wisconsin state system beyond his ken. Boss Keyes was deposed and Philetus Sawyer became the head of the state. This does not mean that Sawyer was elected Governor; we have nothing to do with governors yet. Sawyer was a United States Senator. While Keyes was boss, the head of the state was in the post-office at Madison, and it represented, not the people, but the big business interests of the state, principally lumber and the railways, which worked well together and with Keyes. There were several scandals during this "good fellow's" long reign, but big business had no complaint to make against him. The big graft in the Northwestern state, however, was lumber, and the typical way of getting hold of it wholesale, was for the United States to make to the state grants which the state passed on to railway companies to help "develop the resources of the state." Railroad men were in lumber companies, just as lumber men were in the railway companies, so the railway companies sold cheap to the lumber companies, which cleared the land—for the settlers. This was business, and while it was necessary to "take care" of the legislature, the original source of business was the Congress, and that was the place for the head of the System. Keyes had wished to go to the Senate, but Sawyer thought he might as well go himself. He had gone, and now, when Keyes was willing to take the second seat, the business men decided that, since it was all a matter of business, they might as well take it out of politics. Thus Senator Sawyer became boss, and, since he was a lumberman, it was no more than fair that the other seat should go to the railroads. So the big business men got together and they bought the junior United States Senatorship for the Honorable John C. Spooner.

Spooner's Senatorship Bought for Him

At Marinette, Wisconsin, lives to-day a rich old lumberman, Isaac Stephenson. He was associated for years with Senator Sawyer and the other enemies of the republic in Wisconsin, and he left them because they balked an ambition of his. Having gone over, however, he began to see things as they are, and no man to-day is more concerned over the dangers to business of the commercial corruption of government than this veteran who confesses that he spent a quarter of a million in politics.

Once he and Senator Sawyer were comparing notes on the cost to them of United States Senatorships.

"Isaac," said Sawyer, "how much did you put in to get the legislature for Spooner that time?"

"It cost me about twenty-two thousand, Philetus. How much did you put in?"

"Why," said Sawyer, surprised, "it cost me thirty thousand. I thought it cost you thirty."

"No, it cost me thirty to get it for you when you ran."

Friends of mine who are friends of Senator Spooner in Washington, besought me, when they heard I was going to Wisconsin, to "remember that Spooner is a most useful man in the Senate," and I know and shall not forget that. Able, deliberate, resourceful, wise, I believe Senator Spooner comes about as near as any man we have in that august chamber to-day to statemanship, and I understand he loathes many of the practices of politics. But the question to ask about a representative is, what does he represent?

Senator Spooner, at home, represented the railroads of his state. He served a term in the Wisconsin assembly, and he served the railroads there. After that he served them as a lobbyist. I do not mean that he went to Madison now and then to make arguments for his client. Mr. Spooner spent the session there. Nor do I mean to say that he paid bribes to legislators; there are honest lobbyists. But I do say that Mr. Spooner peddled passes, and any railroad man or any grafter will tell you that this is a cheap but most effective form of legislative corruption. United States Senator Spooner, then, is a product, a flower, perhaps, but none the less he is a growth out of the System, the System which is fighting Governor LaFollette.

The System was fighting LaFollette 'way back in those days, but the young orator did not know it. He was running for Congress. So far as I can make out, he was seeking only more glory for his French blood and a wider field to shine in, but he went after his French satisfaction in a Scotch-Irish fashion. Boss Keyes told me about it. Keyes had been reduced to the control only of his congressional district, and, as he said, "We had it arranged to nominate another man. The place did not belong to Dane County. It was another county's turn, but Bob didn't consult us." Bob was consulting his constituents again, and his night riders were out. The System heard of it earlier than in the district attorney campaign, and Keyes and Phil Spooner and the other leaders were angry. Keyes did want to rule that congressional district; it was all he had, and Phil Spooner (who now is the head of the street railway system of Madison) sensed the danger in this self-reliant young candidate.

"What's this I hear about you being a candidate for Congress?" he said to LaFollette one day. "Don't you know nobody can go to Congress without our approval? You're a fool."

But LaFollette's men were working, and they carried all except three caucuses (primaries that are something like town meetings) against the ring. The ring bolted, but the people elected him; the people sent LaFollette to Congress at the same time they elected the legislators that sent John C. Spooner to the United States Senate.

The System at Washington

When LaFollette had been in Washington a few weeks, Senator Sawyer found him out and became "like a father" to him. "Our boy" he called him, for LaFollette was the "youngest member." The genial old lumberman took him about and introduced him to the heads of departments and finally, one day, asked him what committee he would like to go on. LaFollette said he would prefer some committee where his practice in the law might make him useful, and Sawyer thought "Public Lands" would about do. He would "fix it." Thus the System was coming after him, but it held back; there must have been a second thought. For the Speaker put LaFollette not on "Public Lands," but on "Indian Affairs."

The Governor to-day will tell you with a relish that he was so green then that he began to "read upon Indians": he read especially Boston literature on that subject, and he thought of the speeches he could make on Indian wrongs and rights. But there was no chance for an orator. The committee worked and "our boy" read bills. Most of these bills were hard reading and didn't mean much when read. But by and by one came along that was "so full of holes that," as the Governor says, "even I could see through it." It provided for a sale of pine on the Menominee reservation in Wisconsin. Mr. LaFollette took it to the (Cleveland's) Commissioner of Indian Affairs, and this official said he thought it "a little the worst bill of the kind that I have ever seen. Where did it come from?" They looked and they saw that it had been introduced by the member from Oshkosh (Sawyer's home district). None the less, Mr. LaFollette wanted a report and the Commissioner said he could have one if he would sit down and write for it. The report so riddled the bill that it lay dead in the committee. One day the congressman who introduced it asked about it.

"Bob, why don't you report my bill?" he said.

"Bill," said Bob, "did you write that bill?"

"Why?"

"It's a steal."

"Let it die then. Don't report it. I introduced it because Sawyer asked me to. He introduced it in the Senate and it is through their committee."

Sawyer never mentioned the bill, and the incident was dropped with the bill. Some time after, however, a similar incident occurred, and this time Sawyer did mention it. The Indian Affairs committee was having read, at the rate of two hours a day, a long bill to open the big Sioux Indian reservation in Dakota, by selling some eleven million acres right through the center. It was said to be a measure most important to South Dakota, and no one objected to anything till the clerk droned out a provision to ratify an agreement between the Indians and certain railroads about a right of way and some most liberal grants of land for terminal town sites. LaFollette interrupted and he began to talk about United States statutes which provided not so generously, yet amply, for land grants to railways, when a congressman from a neighboring state leaned over and said:

"Bob, don't you see that those are your home corporations?"

Bob said he saw, and he was willing to grant all the land needed for railway purposes, but none for town site schemes. When the committee rose, and LaFollette returned to his seat in the house, a page told him Senator Sawyer wanted to see him. He went out and the Senator talked to him for an hour in a most fatherly way, with not a word concerning the Sioux bill till they were about to separate. Then quite by the way, he said:

"Oh, say, when that Sioux Injun bill comes up there's a little provision in it for our folks which I wish you to look after."

LaFollette said the bill was up then, they had just reached the "little provision for our folks," and that he was opposing it.

"Why, is that so?" said Sawyer. "Let's sit down and—" they had another hour, on town sites. It was no use, however. LaFollette "wouldn't consult." Sawyer gave up reasoning with him, but he didn't give up "the little provision." Political force was applied, but not by the senior Senator. The System had other agents for such work.

Henry C. Payne's Part in the System

Henry C. Payne arrived on the scene. Payne was chairman of the Republican State Central Committee of Wisconsin, and we have seen in other states what the legislative functions of that office are. Payne reached Washington forty-eight hours after LaFollette's balk, and he went at him hard. All sorts of influence was brought to bear, and when LaFollette held out, Payne became so angry that he expressed himself the spirit of the System—in public. To a group in the Ebbitt House he said:

"LaFollette is a damned fool. If he thinks he can buck a railroad with five thousand miles of continuous line, he'll find he's mistaken. We'll take care of him when the time comes."

The state machine fought the congressman in his own district, and so did Keyes and the "old regency" at Madison, but LaFollette, the politician, had insisted upon a congressman's patronage, all of it, and he had used it to strengthen himself at home. LaFollette served three terms in Congress, and when he was defeated in 1890, for the fourth, he went down with the whole party in Wisconsin. This complete overthrow of the Republicans was due to two causes, the McKinley tariff (which LaFollette on the Ways and Means Committee helped to frame) and a piece of state school legislation which angered the foreign and Catholic voters. We need not go into this, and the Democratic administration which resulted bears only indirectly on our story.

One of the great grafts of Wisconsin (and of many another state) was the public funds in the keeping of the state treasurer. The Republicans, for years, had deposited these moneys in banks that stood in with the System, and the treasurer shared with these institutions the interest and profits. He, in turn, "divided up" with the campaign fund and the party leaders. The Democrats were pledged to break up this practice and sue the ex-treasurers. Now these treasurers were not all "good" for the money, and when the suits were brought, as they were in earnest, the treasurers' bondsmen were the real defendants. Chief among these was Senator Sawyer, the boss who had chosen the treasurers and backed them and the practice for years. Sawyer was alarmed. It was estimated that there had been $30,000 a year in the graft alone, and the Attorney-General was going back twenty years, and his suits were for the recovery of all the back interest. Several hundred thousand dollars was at stake. And the judge before whom the cases were to be tried was Robert J. Siebecker, brother-in-law and former law partner of Robert M. LaFollette.

One day in September, 1891, LaFollette received from Sawyer a letter asking for a meeting in the Plankington Hotel, Milwaukee. The letter had been folded first with the letter head on, then this was cut off and the sheet refolded; and, as if secrecy was important, the answer suggested by Sawyer was to be one word "yes" by wire. LaFollette wired "yes," and the two men met. There are two accounts of what occurred. LaFollette said Sawyer began the interview with the remark that "nobody knows that I'm to meet you to-day"; he spoke of the treasury cases and pulled out and held before the young lawyer a thick roll of bills. Sawyer's subsequent explanation was that he proposed only to retain LaFollette, who, however, insists that Sawyer offered him a cash bribe for his influence with Judge Siebecker.

Since Sawyer is dead now, we would better not try to decide between the two men on this particular case, but there is no doubt of one general truth: that Philetus Sawyer was the typical captain of industry in politics; he debauched the politics of state with money. Old Boss Keyes was bad enough, but his methods were political—patronage, deals, etc., and he made the government represent special interests. But when the millionaire lumberman took charge, he came with money; with money he beat Keyes; and money, his and his friends', was the power in the politics of his régime.

His known methods caused no great scandal so long as they were confined to conventions and the legislature, but the courts of Wisconsin had the confidence of the state, and the approach of money to them made people angry. And the story was out. LaFollette, after consultation with his friends, told Judge Siebecker what had happened, and the Judge declined to hear the case. His withdrawal aroused curiosity and rather sensational conjectures. Sawyer denied one of these, and his account seeming to call for a statement from LaFollette, the young lawyer told his story. Sawyer denied it and everybody took sides. The cases were tried, the state won, but the Republican legislature, pledged though it was to recover in full, compromised. So the System saved its boss.

But the System had raised up an enemy worthy of all its power. LaFollette was against it. "They" say in Wisconsin that he is against the railroads, that he "hates" corporate wealth. It is true the bitterest fights he has led have been for so-called anti-railroad laws, but "they" forget that his original quarrel was with Sawyer and that, if hatred was his impulse, it probably grew out of the treasury case "insult." My understanding of the state of his mind is that before that incident, LaFollette thought only of continuing his congressional career. After it, he was for anything to break up the old Sawyer machine. Anyhow, he told me that, after the Sawyer meeting, he made up his mind to stay home and break up the System in Wisconsin. And, LaFollette did not originate all that legislation. Wisconsin was one of the four original Granger States. There seems to have been always some discontent with the abuse of the power of the railways, their corrupting influence, and their escape from just taxation. So far as I can make out, however, some of the modern measures labeled LaFolletteism, sprang from the head of a certain lean, clean Vermont farmer, who came to the legislature from Knapp, Wisconsin. I went to Knapp. It was a long way around for me, but it paid, for now I can say that I know A. R. Hall. He is a man. I have seen in my day some seventeen men, real men, and none of them is simpler, truer, braver than this ex-leader of the Wisconsin assembly; none thinks he is more of a failure and none is more of a success.

A. R. Hall's a Man

Hall knows that there is a System in control of the land. Sometimes I doubt my own eyes but Hall knows it in his heart, which is sore and tired from the struggle. He went to the legislature in 1891. He had lived in Minnesota and had served as an assemblyman there. When he went to the legislature in Wisconsin, one of the first demands upon him was from a constituent who wanted not a pass, but several passes for himself and others. Hall laughed at the extravagance of the request, but when he showed it to a colleague, the older assemblyman took it as a matter of course and told him he could get all the passes he cared to ask for from the railroad lobbyists. "I had taken passes myself in Minnesota," Hall told me, "but I was a legislator, it was the custom and I thought nothing of it." A little inquiry showed him that the custom in Wisconsin was an abuse of tremendous dimensions. Legislators took "mileage" for themselves, their families and for their constituents till it appeared that no man in the state was compelled to pay his fare. Hall had not come there as a reformer; like the best reformers I have known, experience of the facts started him going, and his reforms developed as if by accident along empirical lines. Hall says he realized that the legislators had to deliver votes—legislation—for these pass privileges, and he drew an anti-pass resolution which was offered as an amendment to the Constitution. It was beaten. Not only the politicians, the railroads also fought it, and together they won in that session. But Hall, mild spoken and gentle, is a fighter, so the anti-pass measure became an issue.

One day Assemblyman Hall happened to see the statement of earnings of a railroad to its stockholders. Railroads in Wisconsin paid by way of taxes a percentage on their gross receipts, and, as Hall looked idly over the report, he wondered how the gross receipts item would compare with that in the statement to the state treasurer. He went quietly about his investigation, and he came to the conclusion that, counting illegal rebates, the state reports were from two to five millions short. So he asked for a committee to investigate and he introduced also a bill for a state railroad commission to regulate railroad rates. This was beaten, and a committee which was sent to Chicago to look up earnings reported for the railways. But this was not enough. Hall was "unsafe" and he must be kept out of the legislature. So, in 1894, "they" sent down into Dunn County men and money to beat Hall for the renomination. They got the shippers out against him (the very men who were at the mercy of the roads), and one of these business men handled the "barrel" which, as he said himself, he "opened at both ends." Hall had no money and no organization, but he knew a way to fight. The caucuses were held in different places at different times, and Hall posted bills asking the voters to assemble one hour before time and listen to him. At these preliminary meetings he explained just what was being done and why; he said that he might not be right, but he had some facts, which he gave, and then he declared he was not against the railroads, that he only wished to make sure that they were fulfilling their obligations and not abusing their power. "I had only been trying to serve honorably the people I represented, and it was hard to be made to fight for your political life, just for doing that. But we won out. Those voters went into those caucuses and Dunn County beat the bribery. They then tried to buy my delegates."

Mr. Hall was leaning against the railroad station as he said this. We had gone over the night before, his twelve years' fight, up to his retirement the year before, and we were repeating now. He was looking back over it all, and a hint of moisture in his eyes and the deep lines in his good face made me ask:

"Does it pay, Mr. Hall?"

"Sometimes I think it does, sometimes I think it doesn't. Yes, it does, Dunn County—" He stopped. "Yes, it does," he added. "They used to cartoon me. They lampooned and they ridiculed, they abused and vilified. They called me a demagogue; said I was ambitious; asked what I was after, just as they do LaFollette. But he is a fighter. He will never stop fighting. And if I had served them, I could have had anything, just as he could now. It is hard and it hurts, when you're only trying to do your duty and be fair. But it does pay. They don't question my motives now, any more."

And they don't question Hall's motives any more. When "they" became most heated in their denunciations of the Governor and all his followers, I would ask them, the worst haters, "What about A. R. Hall?" and the change was instantaneous.

"Now, there's a man," they would say; not one, but everybody to whom I mentioned A. R. Hall.

When LaFollette began his open fight against the System in 1894, he took up the issues of inequalities in taxation, machine politics and primary elections. Hall and LaFollette were friends and they had talked over these issues together in LaFollette's law office in Madison, during the session. "They" say in Wisconsin that LaFollette is an opportunist. They say true. But so is Folk an opportunist, and so are the Chicago reformers—as to specified issues. So are the regular politicians who, in Wisconsin, for example, adopted later these same issues in their platform. The difference is this: the regulars wanted only to keep in power so as to continue the profitable business of representing the railroads and other special interests; Hall and LaFollette really wanted certain abuses corrected, and LaFollette was, and is, for any sound issue that will arouse the people of Wisconsin to restore representative government.

In 1894 LaFollette carried his issues to the state convention with a candidate for governor, Nils P. Haugen, a Norse-American who had served in Congress and as a state railroad commissioner. LaFollette and his followers turned up with one-third of the delegates. The regulars, or "Stalwarts," as they afterwards were called, were divided, but Sawyer, declaring it was anybody to beat LaFollette, managed a combination on W. H. Upham, a lumberman, and Haugen was beaten. Hall was there, by the way, with an anti-pass plank, and Hall also was beaten.

Appealing to the Voters Direct

The contest served only to draw a line between the LaFollette "Halfbreeds" and the "Stalwarts," and both factions went to work on their organizations. Upham was elected, and the Stalwarts, who had been living on federal patronage, now had the state. They rebuilt their state machine. LaFollette, with no patronage, continued to organize, and his method was that which he had applied so successfully in his early independent fights for district attorney and congressman. He went straight to the voters.

"They" say in Wisconsin that LaFollette is a demagogue and if it is demagogy to go thus straight to the voters, then "they" are right. But then Folk also is a demagogue and so are all thorough-going reformers. LaFollette from the beginning has asked, not the bosses, but the people for what he wanted, and after 1894 he simply broadened his field and redoubled his efforts. He circularized the state, he made speeches every chance he got, and if the test of demagogy is the tone and style of a man's speeches, LaFollette is the opposite of a demagogue. Capable of fierce invective, his oratory is impersonal; passionate and emotional himself, his speeches are temperate. Some of them are so loaded with facts and such closely knit arguments, that they demand careful reading, and their effect is traced to his delivery, which is forceful, emphatic, and fascinating. His earnestness carries the conviction of sincerity, and the conviction of his honesty of purpose he has planted all over the state by his Halfbreed methods.

What were the methods of the Sawyer-Payne-Spooner Republicans? In 1896 the next governor of Wisconsin had to be chosen. The Stalwarts could not run Governor Upham again. As often happens to "safe men," the System had used him up; his appointments had built up the machine, his approval had sealed the compromise of the treasury cases. Some one else must run. To pick out his successor, the Stalwart leaders held a meeting at St. Louis, where they were attending a national convention, and they chose for governor Edward W. Scofield. There was no demagogy about that.

LaFollette Beaten with Money

LaFollette wished to run himself; he hoped to run and win while Sawyer lived, and he was holding meetings, too. But his meetings were all over the state, with voters and delegates, and he was making headway. Lest he might fall short, however, LaFollette made a political bargain. He confesses it, and calls it a political sin, but he thinks the retribution which came swift and hard was expiation. He made a deal with Emil Baensch, by which both should canvass the state for delegates, with the understanding that which ever of the two should develop the greater strength was to have both delegations. LaFollette says he came into convention with enough delegates of his own to nominate him, and Baensch had 75 or so besides. The convention adjourned over night without nominating and the next morning LaFollette was beaten. He had lost some of his own delegates, and Baensch's went to Scofield.

LaFollette's lost delegates were bought. How the Baensch delegates were secured, I don't know, but Baensch was not a man to sell for money. It was reported to LaFollette during the night that Baensch was going over, and LaFollette wrestled with and thought he had won him back, till the morning balloting showed. As for the rest, the facts are ample to make plain the methods of the old ring. Sawyer was there; and there was a "barrel." I saw men who saw money on a table in the room in the Pfister Hotel, where delegates went in and out, and newspaper men present at the time told me the story in great detail. But there is better evidence than this. Men to whom bribes were offered reported to their leader that night. The first warning came from Captain John T. Rice, of Racine, who (as Governor LaFollette recalls) said: "I have been with the old crowd all my life and I thought I knew the worst, but they have no right to ask me to do what they did to-night. I won't tell you who, but the head of the whole business asked me to name my price for turning over the Union Grove delegation from you to Scofield." There are many such personal statements, some of them giving prices—cash, and federal and state offices—and some giving the names of the bribery agents. The Halfbreed leaders tried to catch the bribers with witnesses, but failed, and at midnight Charles F. Pfister, a Milwaukee Stalwart leader, called on LaFollette, who repeated to me what he said:

"LaFollette, we've got you beaten. We've got your delegates. It won't do you any good to squeal, and if you'll behave yourself we'll take care of you."

So LaFollette had to go on with his fight. He would not "behave." His followers wanted him to lead an independent movement for governor; he wouldn't do that, but he made up his mind to lead a movement for reform within the party, and his experience with corrupted delegates set him to thinking about methods of nomination. The System loomed large with the growth of corporate wealth, the power of huge consolidations over the individual and the unscrupulous use of both money and power. Democracy was passing, and yet the people were sound. Their delegates at home were representatives, but shipped on passes to Milwaukee, treated, "entertained" and bribed, they ceased to represent. The most important reform was to get the nomination back among the voters themselves. Thus LaFollette out of his own experience, took up this issue—direct primary nominations by the Australian ballot.

Stalwarts Take LaFollette's Platform

During the next two years LaFollette made a propaganda with this issue and railroad taxation, the taxation of other corporations—express and sleeping car companies which paid nothing—and the evils of corrupt machines that stood for corrupting capital. He sent out circulars and literature, some of it the careful writings of scientific authors, but, most effective of all, were the speeches he made at the county fairs. When the time for the next Republican state convention came around in 1898, he held a conference with some thirty of his leaders in Milwaukee, and he urged a campaign for their platform alone, with no candidate. The others insisted that LaFollette run, and they were right in principle. As the event proved, the Stalwarts were not afraid of a platform, if they could be in office to make and carry out the laws. LaFollette ran for the nomination and was beaten—by the same methods that were employed against him in '96; cost (insider's estimate), $8,000. Scofield was renominated.

But the LaFollette-Hall platform was adopted—anti-pass, corporation taxation, primary election reform, and all. "They" say now in Wisconsin that Lafollette is too practical; that he has adopted machine methods, etc. During 1896, 1897, and 1898 they were saying he was an impracticable reformer, and yet here they were adopting his impracticable theories. And they enacted some of these reforms. The agitation (for LaFollette is indeed an "agitator") made necessary some compliance with public demand and platform promises, so Hall got his anti-pass law at last; a commission to investigate taxation was appointed, and there was some other good legislation. Yet, as Mr. Hall says, "In effect, that platform was repudiated." The railway commission reported that the larger companies, the Chicago, Milwaukee & St. Paul and the Northwestern, respectively, did not pay their proportionate share of the taxes, and a bill was introduced by Hall to raise the assessment. It passed the house, but the senate had and has a "combine" like the senates of Missouri and Illinois, and the combine beat the bill.

The failures of the legislature left all questions open and LaFollette and his followers continued their agitation. Meanwhile Senator Sawyer died, and when the next governmental election (1900) approached, all hope of beating LaFollette was gone. The Stalwarts began to come to him with offers of support. One of the first to surrender was J. W. Babcock, congressman and national politician. Others followed, but not John C. Spooner, Payne and Pfister, not yet. They brought out for the nomination John M. Whitehead, a state senator with a clean reputation and a good record. But in May (1900) LaFollette announced his candidacy on a ringing platform, and he went campaigning down into the strongest Stalwart counties. He carried enough of them to take the heart out of the old ring. All other candidates withdrew and Senator Spooner, who is a timid man, wrote a letter which, in view of his subsequent stand for reëlection, is a remarkable document; it declared that he was unalterably determined not to run again for the Senate. LaFollette was nominated unanimously, and his own platform adopted. The victory was complete. Though the implacable Stalwarts supported the Democratic candidate, LaFollette was elected by 102,000 plurality.

Victory, the Beginning of War

Victory for reform is often defeat, and this triumph of LaFollette, apparently so complete, was but the beginning of the greatest fight of all in Wisconsin, the fight that is being waged out there now. Governor LaFollette was inaugurated January 7, 1901. The legislature was overwhelmingly Republican and apparently there was perfect harmony in the party. The Governor believed there was. The Stalwart-Halfbreed lines were not sharply drawn. The Halfbreeds counted a majority, especially in the house, and A. R. Hall was the "logical" candidate for Speaker. It was understood that he coveted the honor, but he proposed and it was decided that, in the interest of peace and fair play, a Stalwart should take the chair. The Governor says that the first sign he had of trouble was in the newspapers which, the day after the organization of the legislature, reported that the Stalwarts controlled and that there would be no primary election or tax legislation. The Governor, undaunted, sent in a firm message calling for the performance of all campaign promises, and bills to carry out campaign pledges were introduced under the direction of the LaFollette leaders, Hall and Judge E. Ray Stevens, the author of the primary election bill. These developed the opposition. There were two (alternative) railway tax bills; others to tax other corporations; and, later, a primary election bill—nothing that was not promised by a harmonious party, yet the outcry was startling and the fight that followed was furious. Why?

LAFOLLETTE AND THE RAILROADS

I have seen enough of the System to believe that that is the way it works. I believe just such opposition, with just such cries of "boss," "dictator," etc., will arise against Folk when he is governor, and possibly against Deneen. And I believe they will find their legislatures organized and corrupted against them. But in the case of LaFollette there was a "misunderstanding." In the year (1900) when everything was LaFollette, Congressman Babcock, Postmaster-General Payne and others sought to bring together the great ruling special interests and inevitable governor. Governor LaFollette said, like President Roosevelt, that he would represent the corporations of his state, just as he would represent all other interests and persons; but no more. He would be "fair." Well, that was "all we want," they said, and the way seemed smooth. It was like the incident in St. Louis where Folk told the boodlers he would "do his duty," and the boodlers answered, "Of course, old man."

But some railroad men say LaFollette promised in writing to consult with them before bringing in railroad bills; there was a certain famous letter written in the spring of 1900 to Thomas H. Gill, an old friend of the Governor, who is counsel to the Wisconsin Central Railroad; this letter put the Governor on record. Everywhere I went I heard of this document, and though the noise of it had resounded through the state for four years, it had never been produced. Here it is:

> Madison, Wis., May 12th, 1900
>
> Dear Tom:
>
> You have been my personal and political friend for twenty years. Should I become a candidate for the nomination for Governor, I want your continued support, if you can consistently accord it to me. But you are the attorney for the Wisconsin Central R.R. Co., and I am not willing that you should be placed in any position where you could be subjected to any criticism or embarrassment with your employers upon my account. For this reason, I desire to state to you in so far as I am able my position in relation to the question of railway taxation, which has now become one of public interest, and is likely to so continue until rightly settled. This I can do in a very few words.
>
> Railroad corporations should pay neither more nor less than a justly proportionate share of taxes with the other taxable property of the state. If I were in a position to pass officially upon a bill to change existing law, it would be my first care to know whether the rate therein proposed was just in proportion to the property of other corporations and individuals as then taxed, or as therein proposed to be taxed. The determination of that question would be controlling. If such rate was less than the justly proportionate share which should be borne by the railroads, then I should favor increasing it to make it justly proportionate. If the proposed rate was more than the justly proportionate share, in comparison with the property of other corporations, and of individuals taxed under the law, then I should favor decreasing to make it justly proportionate.
>
> In other words, I would favor equal and exact justice to each individual and to every interest, yielding neither to clamor on the one hand, nor being swerved from the straight course by any interest upon the other. This position, I am sure, is the only one which could com-

mend itself to you, and cannot be criticised by any legitimate business honestly managed.

Sincerely yours,

The Mr. Gill to whom this letter was addressed is one of the most enlightened and fair-minded corporation lawyers that I ever met, even in the West, where corporation men also are enlightened. He convinced me that he and the other railroad men really did expect more consideration than the Governor gave them, and so there may have been a genuine misunderstanding. But after what I have seen in Chicago, St. Louis, and Pittsburgh, and in Missouri and Illinois and the United States, I almost am persuaded that no honest official in power can meet the expectations of great corporations; they have been spoiled, like bad American children, and are ever ready to resort to corruption and force. That was their recourse now.

Governor LaFollette says he learned afterward that during the campaign, the old, corrupt ring went about in the legislative districts, picking and "fixing" legislators, and that the plan was to discredit him with defeat by organizing the legislature against him. However this may be, it is certain that when his bills were under way, there was a rush to the lobby at Madison. The regular lobbyists were reinforced with special agents; local Stalwart leaders were sent for, and federal patronage, force, and vice were employed to defeat bills promised in the platform. Here is a statement by Irvine L. Lenroot, now the Speaker of the Assembly. He says:

OFFICIAL DESCRIPTION OF THE LOBBY

"From the first day of the session the railroad lobbyists were on the ground in force, offering courtesies and entertainments of various kinds to the members. Bribery is a hard word, a charge, which never should be made unless it can be substantiated. The writer has no personal knowledge of money being actually offered or received for votes against the bill. It was, however, generally understood in the Assembly that any member favoring the bill could better his financial condition if he was willing to vote against it. Members were approached by representatives of the companies and offered lucrative positions. This may not have been done with any idea of influencing votes. The reader will draw his own conclusions. It was a matter of common knowledge that railroad mileage could be procured if a member was 'right.' Railroad lands could be purchased very cheaply by members of the legislature. It was said if a member would get into a poker game with a lobbyist, the member was sure to win. Members opposed to Governor LaFollette were urged to vote against the bill, because he wanted it to pass. A prominent member stated that he did not dare to vote for the bill, because he was at the mercy of the railroad companies, and he was afraid they would ruin his business by advancing his rates, if he voted for it."

I went to Superior and saw Mr. Lenroot, and he told me that one of the "members approached by representatives of the companies and offered positions," was himself. He gave his bribery stories in detail, and enabled me to run down and verify others; but the sentence that interested me most in his statement was the last. The member who did not dare vote for the railway tax bill, lest the railways raise the freight on his goods and ruin his business, confessed to Governor LaFollette and others. Another member stated that in return for his treason to his constituents, a railroad quoted him a rate that would give him an advantage over his competitors.

Well, these methods succeeded. The policy of the administration was not carried out. Some good bills passed, but the session was a failure. Not content with this triumph, however, the System went to work to beat LaFollette, and to accomplish this end, LaFollette's methods were adopted, or, rather, adapted. A systematic appeal was to be made to public opinion. A meeting of the leading Stalwarts was held in the eleventh story of an office building in Milwaukee, and a Permanent Republican League of the State of Wisconsin was organized. This became known as the "Eleventh Story League." A manifesto was put out "viewing with alarm" the encroachments of the executive upon the legislative branch of the government," etc., etc. (The encroachments of boodle business upon all branches of the government is all right.) An army of canvassers was dispatched over the state to interview personally every voter in the state and leave with him books and pamphlets. Now this was democratic and fair, but that League did one thing which is enough alone to condemn the whole movement. It corrupted part of the country press. This is not hearsay. The charge was made at the time these papers swung around suddenly, and the League said it did not bribe the editors; it "paid for space for League editorial matter, and for copies of the paper to be circulated." This is bribery, as any newspaper man knows. But there was also what even the League business man would call bribery; newspaper men all over the state told me about direct purchase—and cheap, too. It is sickening, but, for final evidence, I saw affidavits, published in Wisconsin, by newspaper men, who were approached with offers which they refused, and by others who sold out, then threw up their contracts and returned the bribes, for shame or other reasons.

These "democratic" methods failed. When the time arrived for the next Republican state convention, the Stalwarts found that the people had sent up delegates instructed for LaFollette, and he was nominated for a second term. What could the Stalwarts do? They weren't even "regular" now. LaFollette had the party, they had only the federal patronage and the Big Business System. But the System had resources. Wherever a municipal reform movement has hewed to the line, the leaders of it, like Folk and the Chicago reformers, have seen the forces of corruption retire from one party to the other and from the city to the state. This Wisconsin movement for state reform now had a similar experience. The Wisconsin System, driven out of the Republican, went over to the Democratic party; that had not been reformed; beaten out of power in the state, it retreated to the towns; they had not been reformed.

THE SYSTEM IN THE TOWNS

The System in many of the Wisconsin municipalities was intact. There had been no serious municipal reform movements anywhere, and the citizens of Milwaukee, Oshkosh, Green Bay, etc., were pretty well satisfied, and they are still, apparently. "We're nothing like Minneapolis, St. Louis, and the rest," they told me with American complacency. Green Bay was exactly like Minneapolis; we know it because the wretched little place has been exposed since. And Marinette and Oshkosh, unexposed, are said by insiders to be "just like Green Bay." As for Milwaukee, that is St. Louis all over again.

District Attorney Bennett has had grand juries at work in Milwaukee since 1901, and he has some 42 persons indicted—12 aldermen, 10 supervisors, 9 other officials, 1 state senator, and 10 citizens; four convictions and three pleas of guilty. The grafting so far exposed is petty, but the evidence in hand indicates a highly perfected boodle system. The Republicans had the county, the Democrats the city, and both the council and the board of supervisors had combines which grafted on contracts, public institutions, franchises, and other business privileges. The corrupt connection of business and politics was shown; the informants were merchants and contractors, mostly small men, who confessed to bribery. The biggest caught so far is Colonel Pabst, the brewer, who paid a check of $1,500 for leave to break a building law. But all signs point higher than beer, to more "legitimate" political business. As in Chicago, a bank is the center of this graft, and public utility companies are back of it. The politicians in the boards of management, now or formerly, show that. It is a bi-partizan system all through. Henry C. Payne, while chairman of the Republican State Central Committee, and E. C. Wall (the man the Wisconsin Democracy offered the National Democratic Convention for President of the United States), while chairman of the Democratic State Central Committee, engineered a consolidation of Milwaukee street railway and electric lighting companies, and, when the job was done, Payne became manager of the street railway, Wall of the light company. But this was "business." There was no scandal about it.

The great scandal of Milwaukee was the extension of street railway franchises, and the men who put that through were Charles F. Pfister, the Stalwart Republican boss, and David S. Rose, the Stalwart Democratic mayor. Money was paid; the extension was boodled through. The Milwaukee *Sentinel* reprinted a paragraph saying Pfister, among others, did the bribing, and thus it happened that the Stalwarts got that paper. Pfister sued for libel, but when the editors (now on the Milwaukee *Free Press*) made answer that their defense would be proof of the charge, the millionaire traction man bought the paper and its evidence too. It is no more than fair to add—as Milwaukee newspaper men always do (with delight)—that the paper had very little evidence, not nearly so much as Pfister seemed to think it had. As for Mayor Rose, his friends declare that he has told them, personally and convincingly, that he got not one cent for his service. But that is not the point. Mayor Rose fought to secure for special interests a concession which sacrificed the common interests of his city. I am aware that he defends the terms of the grants as fair, and they would seem so in the East, but the West is intelligent on special privileges, and Mayor Rose lost to Milwaukee the chance Chicago seized to settle the public utility problem. Moreover, Rose knew that his council was corrupt before it was proven so; he told two business men that they couldn't get a privilege they sought honestly from him, without bribing aldermen. Yet he ridiculed as "hot air" an investigation which nevertheless produced evidence enough to defeat at the polls, in a self-respecting city, the head of an administration so besmirched. Milwaukee reëlected Rose; good citizens say they gave the man the benefit of the doubt—the man, not the city.

But this is not the only explanation. The System was on trial with Mayor Rose in that election, and the System saved its own. The Republicans, with the Rose administration exposed, had a chance to win, and they nominated a good man, Mr. Guy D. Goff. Pfister, the Stalwart Republican boss, seemed to support Goff; certainly the young candidate had no suspicion to the contrary. He has now, however. When the returns came in showing that he was beaten, Mr. Goff hunted up Mr. Pfister, and he found him. Mr. Goff, the Republican candidate for mayor, found Charles F. Pfister, the Stalwart Republican boss, rejoicing over the drinks with the elected Democratic mayor, David S. Rose.

BOTH RINGS AGAINST LAFOLLETTE

I guess Mr. Goff knows that a bi-partizan System rules Milwaukee, and, by the same token, Governor LaFollette knows that there is a bi-partizan System in Wisconsin. For when Governor LaFollette beat the Stalwarts in the Republican state convention of 1902, those same Stalwarts combined with the Democrats. Democrats told me that the Republican Stalwarts dictated the "Democratic" anti-LaFollette platform and that Pfister, the "Republican" boss, named the "safe man" chosen for the "Democratic" candidate for governor to run against LaFollette—said David S. Rose.

"They" say in Wisconsin that LaFollette is a Democrat; that "he appeals to Democratic voters." He does. He admits it, but he adds that it is indeed to the Democratic voters that he appeals—not to the Democratic machine. And he gets Democratic votes. "They" complain that he has split the Republican party; he has, and he has split the Democratic party too. When "they" united the two party rings of the bi-partizan System against LaFollette in 1902, he went out after the voters of both parties, and those voters combine; they beat Rose, the two rings, and the System. The people of Wisconsin reëlected LaFollette, the "unsafe," and that is why the trouble is so great in Wisconsin. The System there is down.

There is a machine, but it is LaFollette's. When he was reëlected, the Governor organized his party, and I think no other of his offenses is quite so heinous in Stalwart eyes. They wanted me to expose him as a boss who had used state patronage to build up an organization. I reminded "them" that their federal patronage is greater than LaFollette's in the state, and I explained that my prejudice was not against organization; their kind everywhere had been urging me so long to believe that organization was necessary in politics, that I was disposed to denounce only those machines that sold out the party and the people. And as for the "boss"—it is not the boss in an elective office where he is responsible that is so bad, but the irresponsible boss back of a state figurehead; this is the man that is really dangerous. Then they declared that Governor LaFollette had sacrificed good service to the upbuilding of his machine. This is a serious charge. I did not get thoroughly into it. Cases which I investigated at Stalwart behest, held, with one exception very little water, and I put no faith in the rest. But, for the sake of argument, let us admit that the departments are not all they should be. What then? As in Chicago, the fight in Wisconsin is for self-government, not "good" government; it is a fight to reëstablish a government representative of all the people. Given that; remove from control the Big Business and the Bad Politics that corrupt all branches of the government, and "good" government will come easily enough. But Big Business and Bad Politics are hard to beat.

The defeat of Rose did not beat them. The Stalwarts still had the Senate, and they manned the lobby to beat the railroad tax and the primary election bills. But Governor LaFollette outplayed them at the great game. He long had been studying the scheme for a state commission to regulate railway freight rates. It was logical. If their taxes were increased the roads could take the difference out of the people by raising freight rates. Other states had such commissions, and in some of them, notably Iowa and Illinois, the rates were lower than in Wisconsin. Moreover, we all know railroads give secret rebates and otherwise discriminate in favor of individuals and localities.

When then, the battle lines were drawn on the old bills in the legislature of 1903, the Governor threw into the fight a bristling message calling for a commission to regulate railway rates. The effect was startling. "Populism," "Socialism," "they" cried, and they turned to rend this new bill. They let the tax bill go through to fight this fresh menace to "business." They held out against the primary election bill also, for, if that passed they feared the people might keep LaFollette in power forever. Even that, however, they let pass finally, with an amendment for referendum. Concentrating upon the rate commission bill, Big Business organized business men's mass meetings throughout the state, and with the help of favored or timid shippers, sent committees to Madison to protest to the legislature. Thus this bill was beaten by Business and, with the primary election referendum, is an issue in this year's campaign.

As I have tried to show, however, the fundamental issue lies deeper. The people of Wisconsin understand this. The Stalwarts dread the test at the polls. But what other appeal was there? They knew one. When the Republican state convention met this year, the Stalwarts bolted; whatever the result might have been of a fight in the convention, they avoided it and held a separate convention in another hall, hired in advance. The Halfbreeds renominated LaFollette; the Stalwarts put up another ticket. To the Stalwart convention came Postmaster-General Payne, United States Senators Spooner and Quarles, Stalwart congressman and federal office holders—the Federal System. The broken State System was appealing to the United States System, and the Republican National Convention at Chicago was to decide the case. And it did decide—for the System. I attended that convention, and heard what was said privately and honestly. The Republicans who decided for Payne-Spooner-Pfister-Babcock, etc., said "LaFollette isn't really a Republican anyhow."

Isn't he? That is a most important question. True, he is very democratic essentially. He helped to draw the McKinley tariff law and he is standing now on the national Republican platform; his democracy consists only in the belief that the citizens elected to represent the people should represent the people, not the corrupt special interests. Both parties should be democratic in that sense. But they aren't. Too often we have found both parties representing graft—big business graft. The people, especially in the West, are waking to a realization of the state of things and (taking a hint from the Big Grafters) they are following leaders who see that the way to restore government representative of the common interests of the city or state, is to restore to public opinion the control of the dominant party. The Democrats of Missouri have made their party democratic. The next to answer should be the people of Wisconsin. The Stalwarts hope the courts will decide. They hope their courts will uphold the decision of the National Republican Party, that they, who represent all that is big and bad in business and politics, are the regular "Republicans." This isn't right. The people of Wisconsin are not radicals; they are law-abiding, conservative, and fair. They will lay great store by what their courts shall rule, but this is a question that should be left wholly to the people themselves. And they are to be trusted, for, no matter how men may differ about Governor LaFollette otherwise, his long, hard fight has developed citizenship in Wisconsin—honest, reasonable, intelligent citizenship. And that is better than "business"; that is what business and government are for—men.

8
The Progressive Campaign of 1912

HENRY A. COOPER, THE PERIODICAL PUBLISHERS BANQUET [1]

Henry Allen Cooper represented the First District, Wisconsin, in Congress from 1893 to 1919, and from 1921 to his death in 1931. He was a long-time progressive Republican and a close personal friend of La Follette. It was Cooper who offered La Follette's reform program as a minority platform committee report to the 1908 Republican convention. Again in 1924 it would be Cooper who presented the La Follette platform to the Republican convention that shouted it down and nominated Calvin Coolidge. In the years between Cooper had supported La Follette's progressive program at every turn and also backed his anti-war stand in 1917. For his own opposition to the war, Cooper suffered defeat in 1918 but successfully won re-election two years later.

During the heat of the Presidential campaign of 1912, La Follette, overworked and ill, accepted an invitation to speak at the Periodical Publishers Banquet in Philadelphia. Probably because of his friendship with the Wisconsin Senator, Cooper was also invited to attend the dinner. His penciled memorandum on the back of his invitation reveals in stark fashion the scene at the banquet. To Cooper this debacle was the critical episode in the scuttling of La Follette's campaign for the Presidency in 1912.

I accepted and was present. La Follette killed himself politically, by his most unfortunate (worse than that) speech. It was a shocking scene. He lost his temper repeatedly—shook his fist—at listeners who had started to walk out too tired to listen longer,—was abusive, ugly in manner.—Stopped many times to shout at men walking out. From

[1] From Memorandum of Henry Allen Cooper with letter, Mark Sullivan to Henry A. Cooper, January 23, 1912, in the Cooper Papers, State Historical Society of Wisconsin, Madison, Wisconsin. Reprinted with the permission of the State Historical Society of Wisconsin.

the very outset his speech was tedious, inappropriate (for a banquet occasion like that), stereotyped; like too many others of his was extreme in matter and especially in manner. The editor of both bureau[s] (Philadelphia) said to me: "Mr. Cooper, this is shocking—too bad. What ails him?" John Hannan, La Follette's secretary, came over to me after I had moved into the center of the room and with a dejected, disgusted look said softly to me—"This is terrible—he is making a d________d fool of himself." It ends him for the Presidency.

WILLIAM ALLEN WHITE, "LETTER TO CHARLES VAN HISE," UNIVERSITY OF WISCONSIN, MAY 24, 1912 [2]

William Allen White, the famous editor of The Emporia Gazette, *was a friend of both La Follette and Theodore Roosevelt. Through 1911 White supported La Follette and helped to organize local committees in Kansas in his behalf. After the debacle of the Periodical Publishers Banquet White shifted his support to Roosevelt. As he said, "we stopped insisting on La Follette delegates to the national convention and let nature take its course." This letter to La Follette's classmate and close friend, the President of the University of Wisconsin, attempted to explain the situation.*

My Dear Mr. Van Hise:

I hope that our mutual friendship for Senator LaFollette will be sufficient excuse for writing this letter to you. I am deeply pained and in great anxiety at the conduct of Senator LaFollette in the campaign at this time. I feel that he is acting under a sad misapprehension of the facts. I feel that he is exhibiting animus against Colonel Roosevelt which, even if based upon facts that LaFollette presupposed, would be unmanly, undignified and politically suicidal to him, and absolutely disastrous to the cause for which we are all working. I see by the papers that in Ohio Senator LaFollette devoted most of his time to abusing Colonel Roosevelt. Colonel Roosevelt is a very human person. He has done a number of things which I cannot agree with. I feel very strongly about some of his faults. But, on the other hand, I believe that his faults are entirely secondary faults, temperamental rather than fundamental. I think he has done great service to the progressive cause as a preacher. I have not regarded him as a great

[2] From William Allen White to Charles Van Hise, May 24, 1912, in *The Selected Letters of William Allen White,* edited by Walter Johnson (New York, Henry Holt and Company, 1947), 133–35. Reprinted with the permission of W. L. White for the Estate of William Allen White, holder of the copyright.

constructive statesman, and I think in the past he has been prone to compromise in things that I have regarded as vital. But he has learned in the bitter school of experience much in the last four years that will make him a sounder, safer man and more aggressive president than he ever was. He knows whom to appoint for federal judge, he understands the state boss system, he would never tie up with a Payne or a Spooner [Congressman S. E. Payne, coauthor of the Payne-Aldrich Tariff, and conservative Senator Spooner of Wisconsin], he knows how the railroads and insurance companies and brewers form an autocracy in state government. He knows it because that autocracy has opposed him in this fight in every American state. He does not know it as LaFollette knew it, as a lifelong struggle, but nevertheless Roosevelt has got the idea of what the autocracy of politics means thoroughly into his head.

Moreover, he did not crowd LaFollette out of the race. I thought in November and December that LaFollette could win against Taft. I became thoroughly convinced in January and February that LaFollette could not carry Kansas, and if he could not carry Kansas he could not make a very strong race. I went over our community thoroughly when I found that LaFollette was not holding his own. I studied the men from one end of our town and county to the other carefully. I did not want Roosevelt to run. The files of my letterbook will show that I wrote letter after letter telling him that I thought his candidacy would be a mistake. When he got in, it was all one way in Kansas. In the counties wherein we put LaFollette's name on the ballot, LaFollette did not receive to exceed thirty or forty votes to a county. It has been the same all over the United States. If LaFollette had been pitted against Taft, Taft would have won. It was not that LaFollette is not in many ways better equipped than Roosevelt. The whole thing lies in the fact that the prestige of the ex-Presidency was a powerful weapon in this contest.

I am writing to you in the hope that you may say some word or will have some influence upon Senator LaFollette that will make him see things as they are. It would be a serious mistake for him to tie up with the Taft forces in the organs of the National Convention. Moreover, it would be a calamity if he should vote alone and allow the Taft forces to organize that convention. If he would tie up the nomination, that is his fair play, but to tie up the organization of the convention, to give the reactionary forces in that convention the immense advantages of organization, so that by force and violence and cheating they might force the progressive delegates into a bolt and leave the reactionary forces in control of the party organization for the next ten years, would put an immense machinery and weapon for righteousness into their hands, and I hope he may not do that. I am not writing this letter at the suggestion, direct or indirect, of Colonel Roosevelt or any friend of Colonel Roosevelt's. I have talked only to Mrs. White. But it does seem to me if you have any influence with Senator La-Follette, as a patriot and as a friend, it is your opportunity to use it for good. I have been accused of deserting Senator LaFollette. I did not desert him at all. In forming our "Roosevelt for President" league in Kansas, I made part of the platform declaration a message of congratulation to Senator LaFollette for his North Dakota victory and a specific declaration of him as a pioneer leader in the progressive movement. In our Republican state platform, which I largely wrote, I inserted an endorsement of Senator LaFollette and a specific instruction for our delegates to vote with his delegates upon the organization of the convention. Moreover, so far as it was within my power, I saw to it that no man was named by the Kansas progressives for delegate to Chicago who would not, if it ever became wise or expedient, vote for LaFollette for President. This last I did under a definite promise from Mr. McKenzie at the LaFollette headquarters in Washington last March that I would do so. So that whatever suspicion lurks in La-Follette's mind that I have deserted him is without warrant or foundation. If I had put the name of Senator LaFollette on the ballot in Kansas, it would have resulted in a defeat for him and possibly a victory for Taft. I set these things down to let you know my attitude toward the Senator and to make it plain why I turn to you rather than to him personally at this time. If you know of anybody in Wisconsin to whom this letter may be turned over in confidence, you have my permission to use it as you will, except that I do not want it made a public document or printed in any newspaper at this time.

Kindly remember me to Mrs. Van Hise and your family and to my acquaintances about the University.

9
The War and Its Aftermath

SENATOR JOSEPH T. ROBINSON ATTACKS LA FOLLETTE [1]

After La Follette's vote against the Declaration of War, his opposition to the draft, and especially after his St. Paul speech in September 1917, he was widely denounced as pro-German. Even in the Senate, erstwhile friends and companions now vied with each other to attack him, evidently certain that the Committee on Privileges and Elections would soon expel him from the upper house. Especially virulent were the remarks of the Southern Democratic senators who made loyalty to the President an article of faith. Although not necessarily the most violent, the speech by Senator Joseph T. Robinson of Arkansas was representative of these attacks, through which La Follette sat stoically—not deigning to reply.

Mr. President and Senators, I regret that the address of the Senator from Wisconsin has been made in the closing hours of this session of Congress, so that the minds and labors of Senators are diverted from matters of important public interest to a consideration of the questions which are involved in the views which he has expressed. The greater portion of his address was directed toward the vindication of the constitutional privilege and right of freedom of the press and freedom of speech and to the quotation of mere platitudinous utterances by great men of the past.

Mr. President, the Senator from Wisconsin seems to me strangely inconsistent in insisting upon his right, under the constitutional guaranty of free speech, to declare in substance that this Government has entered upon war for no just cause, and to assail the Executive Department of the Government for its manner of conducting this conflict, to assail the legislative branch of the Government for a failure to perform its alleged duty, and even to attack the courts of the United States for their failure to protect the citizens of this country in the enjoyment of their constitutional rights. If it is the right of a Senator of the United States to speak freely upon topics of this character, why

[1] From the *Congressional Record,* 65th Cong., 1st sess. (October 6, 1917), Vol. 55, 7888–7893.

should the Senator from Wisconsin or any other Senator entertaining those views denounce newspaper men and other citizens of this country who, in the exercise of the same right of free thought and free speech, have declared that the Senator ought to abandon his seat in the United States Senate and seek membership in the German Bundesrath?

Mr. President, the Senator from Wisconsin has sought to justify his attitude in this debate upon the record of Abraham Lincoln and Daniel Webster. It may be recalled that Mr. Lincoln, who introduced the resolution denouncing and criticizing his government for engaging in the Mexican War and for its manner of conducting that conflict, was defeated for reelection by an Illinois constituency. Daniel Webster is not remembered for the speech the Senator quotes; his name does not linger in the memory of millions of American citizens because of the act of which the Senator from Wisconsin has spoken to-day—that is, because of this criticism of his Government for entering the Mexican War—but Daniel Webster will live in the hearts of the American people as long as men love liberty because he stood in this sacred presence and declared for the preservation of this country and the maintenance of its flag.

It is a singular thing to me, Senators, that a Senator of the United States should consume two and a half hours in denouncing his Government and have not one word for its flag, not one word for the Commander in Chief of the Armies of the United States, not one word for the encouragement of the men who have already been sent to the far-stretched battle fronts of Europe, and who are now upholding with their lives the honor, the dignity, and the safety of this great Nation. If it is a privilege of free speech for Senators to test the patience of their colleagues and the patience of the citizens of this Nation, it is equally a right of other citizens, in the exercise of free speech, to criticize the conduct of Senators.

If I entertained the sentiments which the Senator from Wisconsin has expressed in this presence this morning, I would not wait for the United States Senate to pass upon the question of my loyalty or disloyalty; I would seek the companionship of those whom my discussion and my sentiments are calculated to support. . . .

The Senator, during the course of his address, referred to the failure of the courts to protect citizens of the United States in the exercise of their rights as citizens. I was astounded when, in the beginning of his address, he made the statement that Government agencies, acting under the authority of the Executive, are invading the private homes of loyal citizens, are arresting and confining innocent and loyal American citizens in jail, without warrant and without cause; that Government officers are violating every private and sacred right of the people of this Government. Passing over the references made by the Senator from Minnesota, taking the speech just made as the basis of my address, I say to you that while I can not find language within the rules of the Senate to appropriately characterize the sentiments uttered on this floor this morning by the Senator from Wisconsin, if I entertained those sentiments I would not think I had the right to retain a seat on the floor of the United States Senate. I would apply to the Kaiser for a seat in the Bundesrath. . . .

Mr. President, the Senator from Wisconsin has characterized as diabolical the acts of the executive department of this Government in making investigations of those who were suspected of being disloyal to the country. He has said that every private right guaranteed to the citizen by the Constitution is being invaded by the agents of the Government of the United States. Mr. President, the expenditure of millions of dollars by the German Government in the United States, the hiring of countless agents, the placing throughout this land of numerous spies, has made necessary activity upon the part of the Department of Justice and other agencies of this Government in order to protect our country and our people against the iniquitous schemes and devices of those German hirelings. It may be true, Mr. President, that in some instances unnecessary investigations have been made; but I suspect that if the Senator from Wisconsin would produce his evidence here, it would be found that those who made the affidavits to which he has referred in condemnation of his Government are German sympathizers, and some of them German spies. . . .

I love peace as much as any man on this earth, but who wants a German peace save a German? In the name of God, is all the blood that has been shed by valiant men and women, and children, is all the blood that France has poured out on her battle fields, are all the sacrifices of Britain, Italy, and Russia to be wasted? Is Germany to be established "over all"?

If the Senator from Wisconsin had his will, if the Kaiser had his will, liberty would become a memory, honor a tradition, and tyranny the ruling power throughout this world. We pray for peace. We will make peace. When? When the army of the Kaiser is rolled back toward Berlin; when from the fields and homes of France and Italy arises the shout of victory, when bleeding Belgium arises from her desolation and cries, "Glory, glory, liberty, liberty, through the combined efforts of the forces of civilization; liberty through the power and wrath of the American people!" God pity the man who comes in the way of this wrath. God have mercy on the men who would paralyze the arm of American power in this great conflict. The American people will show him no mercy. . . .

The hour has come for loyal Americans to assert their manhood. We do not want any half-hearted support of this flag. You had the right to question the wisdom of the war, if in your honest judgment you doubted it, but when Congress passed the declaration of war, then, instead of going about the country and leaving your place on the floor of the Senate, where duty calls you, instead of going over the country, stirring up sedition, and gathering together the discontented elements of the country and seeking to inflame them against your flag, your country, and your President; by God, you ought to stand here and support the flag and the President and help bring victory to American arms!

Mr. President, let no mistake be made. The Congress and the people are loyal to this Government. They do not regard the President of the United States as an usurper, who is trying to take over to himself the prerogatives of Congress and the courts, and as a partner in the house of Morgan and of the munition makers. If that question were left to the people of the United States for a vote to-day they would say that Woodrow Wilson, by his courage, his capacity for leadership, his calm demeanor, his fearless conduct in the hour of peril, is entitled to a place with Washington, with Jefferson, and with Lincoln.

Do not deceive yourselves with the thought that you can organize the disgruntled, semidisloyal elements of the United States and run for the Presidency on a platform of disloyalty. It can not be done. You can not even start the running, much less win. That flag stands for justice—justice at home and liberty abroad. That flag never was lifted in a nobler cause than in the present conflict with Germany. If you can not agree with this statement, for God's sake so familiarize yourselves with current events as to escape the fearful responsibility of misrepresenting your country and its leadership before the American people.

A day of judgment is coming. The duty of every citizen, whether he is an officer or a private citizen, is to support his Government. He has the right to lead a revolution—the God-given right. If I believed, as the Senator from Wisconsin has asserted, that this war was inspired for the benefit of the house of Morgan and by the munition makers, and to guarantee the right of an American citizen to sail on vessels bearing munitions, I would not support the Government. But I can not comprehend how any man, much less a Senator, can make that statement or seek to justify his questionable action on theories of that kind. History belies his statement; every circumstance known to students of current events shows that that declaration is a libel upon the Government which he misrepresents.

We have some duty, my fellow Senators, besides the duty of talking. Some Senators seem to think that there is a paramount obligation to exercise the speaking power, but there come times when men of judgment remain silent. Perhaps I have already talked longer than I am justified, but I have done my duty as I see it. I have no malice toward the Senator from Wisconsin. I am a loyal American citizen and the fact that I happen for a short time to occupy a seat in the United

States Senate has not so inflated my opinion of myself that I conceive I am entitled to disregard my duty and obligations to the people who have sent me here and to the people of this great Republic. With me the first consideration is the honor of our flag and the safety of our Nation. We are fighting in the noblest cause that can inspire human hearts with courage. . . .

POLITICS, PROFITS AND PATRIOTISM IN WISCONSIN [2]

La Follette's stubborn opposition to the Declaration of War in 1917 and to many of Wilson's war policies brought a violent split at the University of Wisconsin among his former friends and supporters. A majority of the faculty signed a round-robin letter condemning the senator's war stand, and others cut him off from their acquaintance. In this short essay in The Nation *Horace M. Kallen, of the Wisconsin Philosophy Department, defends La Follette against the charge of being "pro-German," and notes that this charge "in these times is an excellent stick to beat a dog with." Frederic L. Paxson and Carl Russell Fish, both prominent American historians, responded in a strongly worded letter which appeared in the next issue of* The Nation. *This exchange was representative of the controversy that raged within the university and the state.*

Wisconsin's record for political decency, called significantly "progressivism," is one which was attained by bitter struggle and maintained by constant vigilance and battle. The leader of the "progressive" movement has been and is Senator La Follette. Because of him, the people of the State have been divided, regardless of party lines, into two irreconcilable factions, and towards him there has been directed an extraordinary devotion and an equally extraordinary rancor. In temperament a combination of Puritan and prima donna, he is to-day the chief preoccupation of interests and politicians in the State of Wisconsin, and all issues, remote as they may seem, end ultimately in pro or anti-La Follettism. The reasons are not far to seek. Mr. La Follette has made certain principles of government peculiarly his own; indeed, he appears to be temperamentally incapable of separating principles from personalities, and this incapacity has cost him the Presidency, has destroyed the unity of the "progressive" movement in the State, and has earned for La Follette the bitter and relentless enmities that beset him. The advantage accruing from this essential vanity is a

[2] From H. M. Kallen, "Politics, Profits, and Patriotism in Wisconsin," *The Nation,* 106 (March 7, 1918), 257.

readiness to fight for a principle as for life; the history of "progressivism" in Wisconsin is largely the history of La Follette's personal fight with "the interests."

In the course of that fight the citizens of the State were awakened to "progressive" principles of government, and they have remained awake to those principles ever since. The victory over "the interests" relaxed the attention of the public from government, but did not alter its disposition towards good government: Mr. Emanuel Phillip's [*sic*] first election to the Governorship was due entirely to La Follette's vindictiveness, which destroyed the unity of the political liberals in the State. Governor Phillip's second election was due to the fact that he was a Republican candidate who had won his nomination in the primaries over a split "progressive" ticket. It is significant, however, that the two measures about which this ex-railroad lobbyist was most concerned failed to pass the Legislature. One would have "denatured" the Tax Commission and seriously weakened the income tax; the other would have given much satisfaction to the water-power "interests." The voters of Wisconsin are essentially "progressive."

The voters of Wisconsin are also essentially loyal Americans. Certain citizens of the State, zealous about her reputation for patriotism, have taken care to give her a bad name. La Follette's reputed position on the war, particularly his obsession that our going in was engineered by "the interests," has been used to reinforce this defamation. His circulation of his pre-war speeches, evidently designed to clarify his position to his constituents, served only to enhance this defamation, and to give his enemies the chance they wanted. The existence of a strong Socialist faction in Milwaukee and of a certain amount of German sympathy as well have been made much of. The State's record, however, for voluntary enlistments, in which men with German names bulk largely, and for all the other forms of service to the nation in its need, indicate what a libel, malicious or accidental, the whole thing has been and is. In point of fact, patriotism has been made a cover for politics and profits. "Pro-German," in these times, is an excellent stick to beat a dog with.

It is true that prior to our participation in the war the citizens of Wisconsin of German blood and the press that addressed itself to them were of German sympathy. Blood is thicker than water, and cousins and uncles and fathers were fighting in the German armies. After our declaration of war, the sons and nephews and cousins of these same citizens volunteered for the militia and the regular army and were drafted into the National Army. Sympathy followed affection. This thirty per cent. of the population of the State is today as loyal as any thirty per cent. of any State in the Union.

As for the doctrinaire Socialists, they were and have remained intransigent with respect to the war. But they maintain that position with respect to all wars. They have the blindness and stupidity of all religionists regardful of dogmas rather than of events. But to call them "pro-German" is as absurd as to call Lenine [*sic*] and Trotzky [*sic*] pro-German.

There remains La Follette. His position on war issues is in bad repute throughout the country, and his motives have been declared to be regardful of the "German vote" in his State. In view of the fact that the "German" population of the State is but thirty per cent. of the whole, the charge that he had his eye on the "German vote" is not without its irony. Readers of the Congressional Record will know what the evidence in libel suits he has initiated is making clear—that there has been wilful misrepresentation of his position and his votes. Out of forty-five or more votes connected with the war, he failed to vote on the declaration against Austria, he voted against our going to war with Germany, against conscription, against the conscription of aviators. In all other matters he appears to have voted with the Administration. His speeches lend more color to the opinion created concerning him. But nobody who knows the prima-donna type of rhetorician, with its play of ego and of vindictiveness towards disagreement, will lay much stress on phrases arising out of such qualities. It is these that have helped to give La Follette and Wisconsin a bad name in the present crisis, and have been capitalized on by the "stalwarts" of the State in their attempt to win complete control.

For the war brought what seemed a golden opportunity. State machinery, created by national legislation to assist the national Government in the task of effective organization for war, offered a convenient means of operation. This machinery is the State Council of Defence, with its subordinate county councils. The chairman of the State Council is one Magnus Swenson, identified with water-power interests, so hating La Follette that he required the immediate resignation (which was refused) of one member of a county council who had been reported as approving something the Senator had done. On the county councils appeared officers of corporations whose excess profits La Follette's taxation bill would have considerably reduced. A passion and a hysteria spread over the State. Newspapers that had been "progressive" suddenly became anti-La Follette. A new paper, reputed to be of "progressive" proclivities, was denounced as pro-German. "Loyalty legions" sprang up, and the pledges they circulated counted as patriotism, among other things, the denunciation of La Follette and working "against all supporters of La Follette." It became dangerous to mention La Follette or any of his words or acts except by way of denunciation. Accusations were levelled at the State University for pro-Germanism because the faculty failed as a body to denounce La Follette, and La Follette became a welcome objective for the katharsis of the repressed war emotions of faculty members. An article in an Eastern weekly led finally to a resolution prepared by a section of the faculty's "war committee," but not formally passed by the faculty. The resolution was signed by all but three per cent. of those to whom it was submitted, signed by many because they dared not refuse. The whole comedy was distinguished by neither courage nor sincerity, and formed simply another episode in the pitiful demoralization of the academic world. For a time the State underwent something like an inquisition and a terror. The most recent episode was the summoning to a "conference" *in camera* of the proprietors of the Watertown *Times* by the Governor and State Council of Defence for having criticised the conduct of the former.

Meanwhile that gentleman was preparing to call a special session of the Legislature. And preparatory to it there took place the other day a bye-election in Marathon County, wherein is the city of Wausau. This city is a point of concentration for the water-power and lumber interests. It belongs to a district which has an immemorial record for stalwartness. Yet it has, for the first time in the history of the State, returned a Socialist to the Assembly, with an unheard-of majority over the "loyal" candidate. When the "German" vote and all the other "local" factors have been counted, his majority is still so great that the cause even for the sportive political fancy must be sought elsewhere than in either of those two influences. In another region, a similar election returned a Democrat. The special session at which these men will sit will have to consider, among other things, a proposed law which will in effect give the Governor power to control what individuals or newspapers may say about him and his Administration. But the most important thing it will be called upon to do is to provide for a bond issue of one million dollars to meet the extraordinary expenses of the war. It is significant that the call allows the Legislature no discretion as to *how* the money is to be raised, and it is significant also that there are reports of alternative proposals, among them the persistent rumor of a State surtax on incomes exceeding $25,000.

Take it all in all, the political situation in Wisconsin is not atypical of that in the rest of the country. There is the complication of the difficult personality of La Follette, with the personal hates and enmities centring around it; but if it be remembered that this same difficult personality has for almost a generation been identified, in the State even more than in the country, with a very definite political and fiscal policy, the complication is dissolved. In Wisconsin, as elsewhere, the tories took the saddle to ride the State to the wars. In Wisconsin, as elsewhere, they seek to ride at the same time into political power and pecuniary profit. In Wisconsin, as elsewhere, any resistance of labor, any dissenting utterance of the individual or press, became branded as "pro-German" and "disloyal." In Wisconsin, as elsewhere, the President's original inhibition of free discussion delivered the progressives into the hands of the tories. And in Wisconsin, as elsewhere, the hysterics of feeling and fancy which wars always breed reinforced the tory control and justified the terror. It did so the more easily because political liberalism had there been identified largely with the name of one man, and that man had by his uncontrolled utterances put himself under a not unnatural suspicion which further played into the hands of the tories. The results were also not unnatural. The tories overplayed their hand. As the evidence in the La Follette libel suits slowly trickles out to the public, his strength with the voters of the State appears to grow. At most twenty per cent. of these are "German," and many of the "German leaders" are among his bitterest enemies. There is no "pro-Germanism" in the sources of his strength. If a Senatorial contest were held to-day on a clean-cut issue of "pro-Germanism," anybody truly guilty of favoring the Germans would be overwhelmingly defeated. In politics, however, the actual meaning of "pro-German" may be "pro-excess-profits-tax" or "anti-universal military service" or "pacifist," and so on. At the base of La Follette's strength is the essentially "progressive" outlook of the great majority of the State's voters. Then there is the general impatience with the high-handedness of the State's "war Administration." Finally there is the general discontent of all consumers on wage or salary and of a large proportion of the labor world with the fiscal situation. Not so long ago liberals were afraid that we might come out of the war the most tory nation among the democratic allies. The political situation in Wisconsin may, for the present, at any rate, serve a little to mitigate this fear.

Postscript: Since this article was written the Wisconsin State Legislature has convened. It promptly passed the Wilcox Bond bill, to raise a million dollars by a surtax on annual incomes of over $15,000. The Governor as promptly vetoed the bill. Whether it can be passed over the Governor's veto has become doubtful, and for this reason: Mr. Phillip had asked of the Legislature action empowering him to appoint a United States Senator in the place of the late Senator Husting. Early in the session it became clear he would not get this power. Rather than face defeat on the issue, he withdrew his opposition to an election. This election, primaries and all, will be over within a month. Its imminence immediately complicated the situation.

For one thing, it made the personality and action of La Follette an issue. Prior to the convening of the Legislature, the factions of the Republican majority had held a caucus in which it was agreed to say nothing either for or against La Follette. But with the imminence of a political campaign and its implications the agreement, apparently, was only a scrap of paper. On February 21 the Assembly had rejected, by a vote of 76 to 15, a resolution denouncing La Follette. Betwen the 21st and the 27th, the certainty of a Senatorial campaign intervened. The Senate passed an anti-La Follette declaration. A local paper announces "sensational disclosures involving the use of money by profiteers to attack La Follette in Madison."

So the merry jig is on. There will be a bitter partisan fight over the Senatorship. Patriotism and loyalty will be dragged through the mud of politics to confuse the fundamental issue, which is—equitable taxation.

WISCONSIN AND LA FOLLETTE[3]

To the Editor of the Nation

Sir: The statement of our colleague, Mr. H. M. Kallen, in your current number, that the fundamental issue in Wisconsin to-day is "equitable taxation" is so wide of the truth that it would not be entitled to a denial had not you given it the publicity of a leading article. The philosophical tangle of statements through which the author proceeds from the assertion that reactionaries still dislike Senator La Follette to the conclusion that all who now oppose him are reactionaries resembles the confusion of mind existing with those who believe it possible to fight all measures proposed by the Government of the United States and yet not retard the progress of the war. Wisconsin is to-day trying to define the term loyalty, and trying to connect theory with performance. As your contributor asserts, the great bulk of our people are entirely loyal. They are now beginning to think.

The opponents of James Thompson, of La Crosse, the "La Follette Republican" candidate for the Republican nomination as Senator, do not include any person whose ideas of taxation are fundamentally different from those of Senator La Follette. Most of Wisconsin, including the present Governor, believe in a policy of rigorous taxation differing only in detail from the desires of the present Senator. Many of them have a bitter grievance against Senator La Follette because he has placed himself in such a position as to nullify his right to fiscal leadership in the United States Senate. Congressman Lenroot is likely to support, as Senator, a searching and rigorous basis for our finance. He has not allowed his distrust of wealth to run him off his feet, but he is in full acceptance of the "Wisconsin Idea" of corporate control and modern taxation. Victor L. Berger, in the primary as a Socialist, is equally radical. In the Democratic primary no one could accuse

[3] Letter to the Editor of *The Nation*: Frederic L. Paxson and Carl Russell Fish, "Wisconsin and La Follette," *The Nation*, 106 (March 21, 1918), 319.

Charles McCarthy of favoritism to wealth; he has written progressive taxation planks by wholesale and believes in them. His opponent, Joseph E. Davies, late of the Federal Trade Commission and once Commissioner of Corporations, is a progressive Democrat of the school that La Follette trained to follow his financial leadership when he was Governor a dozen years ago. The only entry in the primary who has not a long and well-built record in favor of "equitable taxation" is the "La Follette Republican" candidate, James Thompson. He alone has a reputation entirely intrastate and even local. If any of the candidates in the primary of March 19 favors big business or swollen fortunes, he is well concealed.

The fact seems to be that Mr. Kallen has simply missed the point. Wisconsin came slowly into the current of conviction that has taken us to war. Our people, heavily of foreign stock and largely rural, responded slowly. Old ties with Germany held many for a while. Berger, in his Congressional canvass of 1914, used two whole pages in several languages in his Socialist daily, the Milwaukee *Leader,* on the eve of election to fight the canard that he, a German, was disloyal to the Fatherland. And Senator La Follette saw in the war—and still seems to see—only a conspiracy of wealth to save England. "Germany has been patient with us," he declared to the Senate as recently as April 4, 1917; and the context of the sentiment shows that he meant it.

In the crisis of opinion that Wisconsin is now going through, large numbers of men who have been loyal supporters of La Follette have been jarred loose from their dependence upon his judgment. They are beginning to think for themselves, and his friends are trying desperately to deceive them with the cry that all he wants is equitable taxation. Many of his bitterest critics to-day have been his followers in the past and are still hostile to the conservative Republican group that has always fought him. But they have come to believe that a new issue has appeared in which he will not, or cannot, lead. The issue cannot be reduced to the simple formula of "equitable taxation."

The real issue in Wisconsin is this: Since the death of Paul Husting, Wisconsin has not had a Senator who gives affirmation to the loyalty of the State. Group after group, professors, school superintendents, county boards, and even the Legislature itself, have demanded that the new Senator must be a man who believes this war to be just, and who is in favor of prosecuting the war until it is won, and who will not tie up the hands of the nation in order that he may profiteer for himself by urging some pet reform.

FREDERIC L. PAXSON

CARL RUSSELL FISH

MAX OTTO, "I MEET SENATOR LA FOLLETTE."[4]

According to the author's note, the following entry taken from his diary for January 1920 was written shortly after his first meeting with Robert M. La Follette in whose Washington home he had been a guest. At this time Max Otto was a young member of the Department of Philosophy at the University of Wisconsin. He had refused to sign the anti-La Follette round robin letter and had aroused further hostility in some quarters by his alleged anti-religious teachings. Because of his friendship with young Philip La Follette, he had been invited to stop with the family for a visit after a research trip to the east. It was with considerable trepidation that he accepted the invitation.

So I came to Washington—with much uneasiness. Phil met me. That helped. However I was not completely reassured. It was the others—father and mother—I shrank from meeting. I met Mrs. La Follette at the breakfast table, and to my surprise, that was a boost. "But," I said to myself, "there is still the Senator." I have known about Senator La Follette, of course, for many years and have seen him in action. I have long had a kind of apologetic admiration for his fighting qualities and great admiration for his mind. Like many other people, I was repelled by what I regarded as a ruthless streak in him. I had heard him mercilessly brand men in public life, some of whom I admired.

Presently, Bob, Jr., and Ralph S.[5] came down. They were very pleasant fellows, radiating good nature and warmth. We got on easily enough. Still, there was the Senator to come. I did not relish the thought of sitting next to "Fighting Bob."

Then he came.

We shook hands and he looked at me with friendly, affectionate eyes, not at all the platform eyes with which I was familiar. All stiffness vanished. He won me over immediately. If "immediately" is not quite the correct word, that is because his first gaze was searching, disconcerting.

At any rate, my impulse after breakfast was to run upstairs and

[4] From Max Otto, "Washington, the 20's," *Wisconsin Magazine of History,* Winter, 1958–59, pp. 109–11. Reprinted by permission of the State Historical Society of Wisconsin, holders of the copyright, and The Macmillan Company, publishers of *Robert M. La Follette, 1855–1925* (New York, 1953), by Belle Case La Follette and Fola La Follette, copyright 1953 by Fola La Follette, in which quotations from the Otto diary first appeared.

[5] [Ralph G. Sucher, friend of Philip and husband of Mary La Follette.]

write a card to everybody I knew, and another one to the world at large, saying to them all: "I have met Senator La Follette and I am his without reservation!" It was almost as if I had returned to my boyhood and had met my first hero.

This first impression will wear down; such impressions do; yet one thing will doubtless remain, for that has passed into an intellectual judgment. The Senator is a man of generous feeling and sympathy. I have always recognized his extraordinary intellectual ability, but now I know that he feels, that there is a tender, affectionate side to him, and that this drives him into action. And I understand now better than I did then what I witnessed some years ago in Madison. It was between one and two in the morning. A few of us, graduate students at the University, had gone to a restaurant after watching a political fight in the State Capitol where, on this occasion, the La Follette Progressives were badly defeated. Two young men, completely done up emotionally, came into the restaurant sobbing as if the last hope had gone from the world. "God!" said one of them between his sobs, "What a set of pirates, that Connor gang!" And the other, overcome anew as he tried to say the words: "Bill, I'd go through hell like that a dozen times for Bob."

As I sit here, I have been meditating on the hospitality of this home. Hospitality is unique: there is no weighing one kind against another. Still I have been in other homes where there was much show of the etiquette of hospitality and where the reality, so conspicuous in 3320 16th St., Washington, was lacking. All who live here are individual persons; the father, the mother, the children. There is spontaneous, obvious appreciation of the Senator as a great man, but they all speak up, they disagree, they give advice. They seem to be doing the job as a group. Even the maid is a person. A guest is naturally himself in such a home.

Senator La Follette is the biggest human being among men of affairs I have met on anything like a personal basis. He is simple, hearty, and cordial, where so many are pompous, posey, and no more hospitable than is proper. While they appear uneasy as if about something hidden, he seems to be not in the slightest degree afraid that you might find him out.

Dinner enhanced my good impression of him. For one thing—and it happens that I think it to be a great thing—he listens when others speak. How he listens! Most men, big and little, but especially the men who "do things," never listen. They occasionally keep still, if they are the polite kind, but they do not really listen to what is said. They are preoccupied with their own profound thoughts or with the important schemes they are to put over. Some of them seem asleep and so accustomed to posing that they pose even in their sleep. This man listens with such intensity that, when he listens to you, you have a hard time remembering what you intended to say. And when he replies, you have the evidence that he heard what was said; heard, it almost seems, beyond what was said some of the things which were only thought. His own speaking is of an almost explosive directness and force, going at once to the nub of the matter, with an economy of words, with wit, and not without humor.

What made the deepest impression upon me is his complete faith in his fellow men. That faith seems so profound, strong, and dynamic that it caused me to think of the passage in Hebrews which says, "Of whom the world was not worthy." Several times, as he sat there listening to the talk about the table, he would allow statements to pass which he did not agree with, half-smiling to himself. But if there was any expression or any suggestion of a lack of faith in the common man, in "the plain people," a fighting look came into his eyes and a vibrant ring into his voice, and a stream of arguments, which he seemed almost unable to restrain, overwhelmed the unhappy critic.

I have wondered about the genuineness of the Senator's interest in "the people," as others have, perhaps for no better reason than that he was in politics. Did he really believe what he seemed to believe when making a political speech? I no longer have a doubt. It is his religion—basic, compelling, all-illuminating, all-directing, forever trying to express itself in words and act and forever falling short. If anything goes wrong, if the people vote for "the system," seem to "sell out," or when they turn against him in hate, it is because they are misinformed, misled. His faith stirred me to greater faith, but as it did so I could not but wonder, remembering his own bitter trials, whether such faith is justified by the fact or is a noble illusion.

After dinner he read, Mrs. La Follette and I being the audience, from *Darby O'Gill and the Good People*. His Irish brogue is delightful, he has an excellent sense of the dramatic, and his strong sympathetic nature easily gets into the situation. I shall long remember him seated there by the mahogany table, the mellow light of the lamp falling on his strong, mobile face, introducing me to some of the most charming characters I have come upon in literature.

And then, aided and abetted by the children who had returned, he took me in hand and cross-questioned me. What did I teach? What reasons could I give for the position I held? What social justification was that for doing the job I did? His attitude was kindly, fatherly, but the bite of his intelligence was extraordinarily keen, and he was informed, strangely so, since the questions were philosophical. The sheer impact of his questioning and the relentlessness of his criticism made me feel as if I had been operated upon by an expert surgeon, and that when I healed I'd be a better teacher and a better man.

FREDERIC A. OGG, "ROBERT M. LA FOLLETTE IN RETROSPECT" [6]

Frederic A. Ogg first came to Wisconsin in 1913 where he carved out a distinguished career in the field of Political Science. His studies in the special area of comparative government and especially his textbooks on American Government made him famous both nationally and internationally. As a student of government and as a voting citizen of La Follette's state, Ogg had followed "Fighting Bob's" career with more than ordinary interest. Although critical in places, Ogg's article is balanced and shows considerable insight regarding La Follette's contributions to the American political system.

In a single generation our kaleidoscopic American democracy has thrust the torch of political leadership into the hands of a colorful and daring Roosevelt, an urbane and cautious Taft, a determined and dominating Wilson, a suave and meaningless Harding, a placid and enigmatic Coolidge, a voluble and superficial Bryan, an expansive and captivating Smith, a serious-minded and business-like Hoover. It has done more; it has cheered and cursed across the stage the dynamic, indefatigable and implacable La Follette. Without him the gamut would not have been full run.

Three or four of these national figures have already pretty well settled into the places which history holds for them. Certainly this is true of Harding, of Coolidge and of Bryan. Probably it is true of Taft. The verdict is not made upon Wilson. Hoover and Smith have yet to bring the record of their achievements to a close. La Follette reached the end of his labors some five and one-half years ago. What of him?

The question is not an easy one. To begin with, few political careers in our time have covered so long a period, touched so many major problems or exhibited so great stress and intensity. "It is hard," remarked Senator Borah upon hearing of his colleague's death in 1925, "to say the right thing about Bob La Follette. You know, he lived 150 years." In the second place, only Wilson has been so played upon by cross-currents of opinion. No twentieth century leader among us has been lauded more extravagantly by his friends and denounced more vehemently by his foes. Ardent devotees, scornful enemies—these are all. Nobody ever took La Follette casually and disinterestedly. In the third place, the things that La Follette stood for are by no means wholly of the past. The political and economic order for which

[6] From Frederic A. Ogg, "Robert M. La Follette in Retrospect," *Current History*, 33 (February, 1931), 685–91.

he fought may or may not eventually come to realization. We shall not altogether know how to place him until we see the America of 1950 or 1975.

Necessary even to the tentative estimate here proposed is an understanding of the world in which La Follette found himself when he entered public life. Born in a log cabin near Madison in 1855, dividing his early years between attending a district school and working on a farm, going forth with his degree from the University of Wisconsin in 1879, he became District Attorney of his home county (characteristically defying the local organization in doing so) and in 1885 entered the National House of Representatives. Losing his seat after three terms in a Democratic landslide he held no public office from 1891 to 1901. But, elected Governor of his State in the last-mentioned year and advanced to the United States Senate in 1906, he was continuously in public life until his death in 1925—an unbroken stretch of practically a quarter of a century.

Hardly any period of similar length in our national history has witnessed an equal amount of social and economic change. Certainly none ever brought greater developments in the business life of the nation and in the relations between business and government. The World War, was, of course, responsible for a good deal that happened in the period. But, after all, the major underlying trends and tendencies were well established before the war and were affected only rather incidentally by our share in that tragic adventure. Even at the turn of the century the United States had grown rich and strong. The devastating Civil War and its aftermath had been left behind. Though hardly realizing it, we had become a world power. Relieved of apprehension aroused by the campaign for the free coinage of silver, business had taken on a fresh lease of life and was growing by leaps and bounds. The age of "big business" was indeed upon us. Railroads had been pushed into every section of the country and were being consolidated into widely ramifying systems. Captains of industry were building large corporations, which in turn were being combined in still larger "trusts." The Standard Oil Company, the United States Steel Corporation and dozens of other vast industrial combinations were in the hey-day of their earlier prosperity.

"Big Business" is not inherently or necessarily bad; an increasing amount of our business in the future will probably be of that character. But a generation ago the ambitious and expanding industrial, commercial and financial interests of this country had not altogether learned what it means to treat competitors with common fairness or to have decent regard for the public well-being. Competition was often ruthless and deadly; new and more ingenious methods of warfare were almost daily brought into play; in many lines monopoly was the confessed goal, and lacked no great distance of being attained;

public regulation was scant and commonly ineffective. Moreover, government was largely at the beck and call of "the interests." In State after State the corporations and the political bosses were hand in glove. Members of Legislatures were nominated and elected as corporate interests dictated; United States Senators were named by the legal departments of railroads; Legislatures were induced—or bribed—to pass laws that the corporations wanted, to defeat measures that they did not want, to manipulate taxation so as to favor the interests, to grant away privileges and rights of inestimable value. Men in control of the great industries who would have been perfectly honest in their individual dealings saw nothing wrong in robbing the government or the public or, if they had compunctions, felt and openly said, when challenged, that the things that their organizations were doing were necessary and inevitable. Most people accepted the situation or at all events were not excited about it.

The stage could not have been set more perfectly for a rising and ambitious young politician of La Follette's particular aptitudes; and it was a matter of no difficulty for him to formulate and declare a set of principles calculated to stir the fight that he loved and to win the favor that he coveted. Whatever, he proclaimed, was unfair and dishonest in dealings between individuals was unfair and dishonest in dealings between corporations and between corporations and individuals. If it was wrong for a man to steal a dollar from his neighbor, it was just as wrong for a corporation to steal a million dollars from the people of a State by refusing to pay its fair share of the taxes levied to support the government. If it was reprehensible in an individual to employ fraud or intimidation to prevent his neighbor from exercising the suffrage, it was equally reprehensible when the same result was accomplished on a grander scale by control of the machinery of government by the great business interests of the land. If it was wrong for an individual wantonly or recklessly to maim or kill one of his fellows, it was just as wrong when the same result was accomplished wholesale and more impersonally by large employers of labor who refused or neglected to use available devices and means to protect their employes against accidental injury and death.

On grounds of simple logic it is not easy to take exception to these fairly axiomatic propositions. At all events, La Follette never doubted their complete validity; and one cannot correctly appraise his life and work without remembering that they formed not only the talking points of his political program but the warp and woof of a social and economic creed to which he was honestly and passionately devoted.

The first field, or area, in which La Follette found opportunity to put his hand to the task of reducing these theorems to practice was his own State of Wisconsin, which, if the truth be told, stood quite as much in need of reform as did most other parts of the country.

Having fought his way up to the Governorship in 1901 in defiance of corporations and bosses alike, no one knew better than he how largely the political life of the State had become an agency of the moneyed interests—especially the railroad and lumber companies—and how difficult it was for any man, however qualified, to win public office without the endorsement of the political machine which those corporations controlled. No one, too, knew better how difficult it was to stir the people to a realization that anything could be done about the matter. But with fervor and pertinacity which he never failed to bring to a cause in which he believed and with the Governorship as a lever, he launched and in a few short years carried through what amounted to a revolution in the political, economic and social life of the State. Though in both program and method there was plenty for many people to disagree with, the undertaking stirred the interest and the outcome commanded the respect of the country and the world.

Of things tangibly achieved, only a few can be mentioned. In 1902 an antipass amendment to the State Constitution forever did away with the previously notorious corruption of public officials by the lavish distribution of free railroad passes. In 1903 the first State-wide direct primary law in the country was enacted. In the same year a railroad tax law replaced a percentage tax on alleged gross earnings by a tax computed on a physical valuation basis, as in the case of other property. The same measure created a State railroad commission, which in 1907 was given jurisdiction over public utilities generally. With the new taxation of railways was bracketed also, in 1905, a progressive tax upon inheritances. Simultaneously a vigorous railway rate-making law was passed and likewise an act introducing the merit system in the State civil service. The first legislative and bill-drafting service in the country was established; corrupt practices in elections and primaries were defined and penalized; the notorious "third house," or lobby, was for the first time brought under control; the extension service of the State university was created; laws in the interest of workmen's compensation, pure food, public health and a score of other matters of popular concern found their way to the statute book in swift succession and the country's earliest industrial commission was created to administer them. That time and thought went into the preparation of these measures is evidenced by the fact that, although with hardly an exception they were challenged in the courts, not one was ever pronounced unconstitutional. Amplified and strengthened, all are still in operation, and not one but has been influential upon the legislation of other States.

From Wisconsin La Follette, elected United States Senator in 1905, passed to the broader domain of national affairs. As a newcomer and especially as one with an established reputation as a trouble-maker, he was relentlessly "hazed" in the Senate; and though elected as a

Republican and regarding himself as one, he found himself obliged to play a lone hand until, in the course of a few years, he drew round himself a group of eight or ten colleagues willing to be known as "progressives." During some nineteen years of service at Washington he was less familiar to the public as a proponent of new measures than as a foe of pending measures of which he disapproved. The explanation lies, not in any lack of aptitude for constructive policy, but rather in the way the stage was set. Appearing on the scene when the "trust busting" period inaugurated by Roosevelt in 1901 was passing into history, he sat in the upper house through eight years (1909–13, 1921–25), when the Republican conservatives, under Taft, Harding and Coolidge, were enacting laws which in most instances he could not endorse, and through eight other years of Democratic rule, for which he bore no responsibility. Moreover, during six of those Democratic years, wartime conditions and measures diverted Congressional and public attention from the great tasks of political and economic reform in which he was principally interested. In addition, there was the heavy handicap of ill-health during much of this later period.

Far from barren, however, were these Senatorial years. Following up his Wisconsin experience, the Senator bore a conspicuous part in the framing of railroad, banking and labor laws, including the creation of the Department of Labor, the Federal Trade Commission and the Federal farm loan system. In particular, he bore main responsibility for (1) the hours of service act of 1907, limiting the number of consecutive hours during which railroad employes may be kept continuously at work; (2) the employers' liability act of 1908, abrogating or modifying, in favor of railway employes involved in personal injury actions, the harsh common-law rules evolved under primitive industrial conditions when the employe or servant had few if any rights which the master was bound to respect; (3) the hotly contested section of the postal appropriation act of 1912, requiring the management of every newspaper and other periodical (except scientific, religious, etc.) to file with the Postmaster General semi-annual sworn statements showing the personnel and ownership of the enterprise and, in the case of daily newspapers, the average number of copies distributed among paid subscribers; (4) the railroad valuation act of 1913, directing the Interstate Commerce Commission to ascertain and report the physical value of all property owned and used by common carriers throughout the country; and (5) the seamen's act of 1915, bringing to a peculiarly neglected and helpless class of workers relief from conditions so onerous as to constitute virtual peonage. He likewise sponsored measures under which a legislative reference division was established in the Library of Congress, the right of organizations of Federal employees to petition Congress and to affiliate with unions outside the public service was recognized, and telegraph and telephone companies were brought under more effective regulation. It was he who, near the end of his career, introduced the resolution under which the investigation of the naval oil leases proceeded. Although not one of the acts of Congress chiefly associated with his name was ever declared unconstitutional, he persistently advocated curbing the Supreme Court's powers of judicial review. The proposal, however, got no further than did another of his bold ideas, namely, the outlawry of war. A list of measures or projects which he fought on the floor of the Senate—to mention only a few, the Payne-Aldrich and Fordney-McCumber tariff bills, the Taft project for reciprocity with Canada, President Wilson's declaration of war against Germany, America's entrance into the League of Nations—would almost be tantamount to a catalogue of twenty years of national legislative activity.

"A lifetime on the front pages"—such was La Follette's epitomized biography as phrased by a contemporary eulogist. What of the record which the front pages—and likewise the statute books, the Parliamentary debates, and the unwritten annals of politics—disclose? What sort of place does this record justify assigning the man in the history of our times?

To a figure such as La Follette there are two main tests to be applied. One is that of political leadership; the other, that of statesmanship. Political leaders, unhappily, are not infallible statesmen.

All in all, there can be little hesitation about ranking La Follette among the cleverest political leaders of his day. Any man who by his unaided efforts can capture a State from an entrenched and determined enemy, hold it against all comers for a quarter of a century, make himself the idol of uncounted millions throughout a country the size of the United States and win 5,000,000 votes as a candidate for the highest office in the land may be set down as possessing unusual powers of attraction and command. It is true that in pressing his program of political and economic reform La Follette did not have to break ground entirely new; to a degree, the way had been prepared by other men both in Wisconsin and in the nation. More than any other person he, however, put the breath of life into the "progressive" movement, organized and energized it, and piloted it to such victories—of no mean proportions—as it achieved. It is of the essence of political leadership to perceive, as he did, the character of the times, to understand the public temper, to capitalize the change and to take advantage of the mistakes and weaknesses of the opposition.

As a leader La Follette had no lack of weighty assets. Sprung from the soil, he knew the common people, sympathized with them and believed in them. "The people," he was wont to say, "have never failed in any great crisis in our history." In the second place, the things he happened to be interested in were things which great numbers of people consciously desired, or at all events could be stimulated to want.

Few men's lives have touched through politics so many hopes—and, shall we add, so many fears—in the lives of others. High in the list, too, stands the man's indomitable energy. Though handicapped—more than most people knew—by nervous and digestive disorders which produced recurring breakdowns and at times threatened complete collapse, La Follette was for thirty years the most spirited, resourceful and relentless fighter in the American political arena. Having learned the political game from his enemies in Wisconsin, he from first to last fought the devil with fire.

Even more important, La Follette had the faculty of impressing friends and foes alike with his honesty, sincerity and devotion to the public well-being, combined with an extraordinary capacity for inspiring affection among his followers. There were shortcomings; and in his later years they stood out so prominently as to cost him the support and even the friendship of many of his earlier associates in his home town, his State and the nation. He was egotistical. He was over-ambitious to reach the Presidency. He had an excessive flair for publicity, and was not always above practicing the arts of the demagogue. He fought and slew bosses, only himself to become a boss of the first water in his own State. He allowed disappointment to make him petulant, morose and bitter. The credit cannot be denied him, however, of having principles from which he could not be shaken, of repeatedly choosing the harder course when the easier would have led to preferment, and of being motivated fundamentally by a desire to serve the larger, better interests of the country as he understood them. Superlative oratorical powers, an exceptional memory for names and faces, and an unfailing sense of the dramatic were still other assets as a leader. The winsome personality known to his friends and associates never, however, came as close home to the general run of voters throughout the country as did that of Al Smith, or perhaps even that of William H. Taft. For a tribune of the people La Follette was sometimes singularly reserved and aloof.

Finally comes the question of the man's statesmanship. That there were large elements of statesmanship in him admits of no doubt. To start with, he was an indefatigable student of the political, economic and social problems with which he sought to deal. He believed in proceeding only on the basis of carefully authenticated information, and was never so much at home as when surrounded with colossal collections of reports, diagrams, graphs, statistics and similar materials from which to fashion the devastating arrays of facts that so often made his speeches long and dry, but also unanswerable. Furthermore, he believed most thoroughly in the use of the expert in government. Putting experts to work in the interest of economy and efficiency was, indeed, the central feature of the "Wisconsin idea" as developed during his six years in the Gubernatorial chair. He had no lack, too, of far-reaching and coherent plans for promoting the public well-being in his State and in the nation. Sometimes his temper and policies seemed mainly destructive. Day in, day out, he criticized, deplored, condemned and attacked. From his student years until his death he was agitator, reformer, crusader; and not infrequently his zeal drove him to unreasonable lengths. But, in the main, he would destroy only to rebuild; and whatever one may think of the structure he would erect—in the interest of more popular control over government or of more equitable relations between corporate interests and the people or of improved conditions of life for the masses generally—the fact cannot be blinked that he at least had definite, and as a rule studiously matured, constructive plans and procedures.

Not all his policies and contributions have worked out as he hoped. The direct primary has proved a disappointing piece of political machinery. The physical valuation of the nation's railroads has turned out a costly and not particularly useful undertaking. The seaman's law, though justifiable on grounds of humanity, has hampered the development of American shipping. The oft-expressed notion that "the real cure for the ills of democracy is more democracy" has been pretty thoroughly exploded. Even the serviceableness of so-called experts in government has been found subject to some rather serious limitations. It would be futile, however, to expect from statesmanship 100 per cent wisdom and infallibility; and enough of La Follette's reforming and constructive work has stood the test to give him an impressive record of achievement.

Two main limitations remain to be mentioned. The first was a certain lack of capacity for adjustment to the realities of a changing situation. La Follette was most truly in his element as an insurgent Republican of the Rooseveltian era. It was that era that first gave him scope, and he never really outgrew it. Apparently he hardly perceived—or, if he did, he was indifferent to the changes that came over the country in the next twenty years. By 1924 a large part of what he had fought for had been won by his own efforts or otherwise. Yet in the campaign of that year he is found instinctively reiterating the battle cries and formulas of an earlier day. There were still, of course, plenty of things worth fighting for; but the tone and methods and ideas of the campaign did not reveal the fresh orientation that might have been expected.

A second defect was the lack of what may be termed world-mindedness. This was perhaps but a phase of the tendency to live in the past which has been mentioned. Until 1906 La Follette's horizon hardly reached beyond the bounds of his own State. After that date it was broadened to take in the United States. But it was never stretched beyond the seas. The same thing is true, of course, of most of his colleagues in the Senate and of a very large proportion of his fellow-countrymen everywhere. Becoming world-minded has been a very painful process for Americans generally and most of them have not yet accomplished the transformation. A man of La Follette's vision might, however, have been expected to see more clearly than he gave evidence of seeing the larger consequences of the war and its aftermath for America and the world. The point is not that he opposed our entrance into the war and condemned the Versailles treaty. The treaty, at all events, is something of which few intelligent people nowadays are proud. The criticism is merely that in his general outlook upon world affairs La Follette did not display an insight or appreciation marking him off as wiser than the general run of Americans or than the short-sighted and provincial politicians by whom he was surrounded at Washington. For example, he slipped as readily as others into the error of supposing that the short cut of outlawing war, without putting anything in war's place, would take care of the most persistent and difficult of all world problems.

To conclude: La Follette was a political leader of the highest or nearly highest rank. His leadership was preeminently that of the crusader and reformer. It was directed toward those elements of society that commonly incline toward the left in politics, yet without ever going the full lengths of radicalism. In the fields of public action, which he made peculiarly his own, namely, the democratization of government and the regulation of economic life, he reached a high level of constructive statesmanship. His statesmanship was, however, less rounded than that of, let us say, Woodrow Wilson or Ramsay MacDonald. He was never tried in the Presidency. The Presidency, it is hardly necessary to add, is not for such as he. His role was that of an awakener of thought, a stimulator of action, a purifier of the public life. There was sacrifice in it, and suffering. There was also satisfaction. It is the only role that a Robert M. La Follette could have played.

PART THREE

LA FOLLETTE IN HISTORY

Recent historians have usually treated La Follette with respect, according him a place in the pantheon of Progressive leaders. They have differed, however, in their interpretation of his contributions and his role in twentieth-century America. Some have seen "Fighting Bob" as essentially an old-fashioned Jeffersonian, grim and tight-lipped, engaged in the crusade to save the country from itself. Others have seen him as the culmination of the granger–greenback–Populist tradition, uncomfortable in urban America, backward-looking rather than forward-looking, with perhaps an unconscious residue of nativism associated with the nineteenth-century Midwest. Still others have seen in his programs the beginnings of social planning, his use of experts from the university as the model for brain trusts elsewhere, and his stance on war and intervention as a new democratic foreign policy a generation ahead of his time. To this group his campaign for the Presidency in 1924 was not the afterglow of the Progressive Era but the harbinger of the New Deal. To many, La Follette's philosophy has a timeless quality which makes his decisions and views as applicable to the solution of problems in a later period as to his own. His attitude on the First World War, the draft, and the sending of conscripted men overseas, for example, might be instructive to students of the sixties. His demand for the reform of election machinery is as timely today as in the twenties. Whatever the historians' view of La Follette, he was not a man to be ignored. The shadow which he cast over the twentieth century was much too long.

10

Russel B. Nye: Midwestern Progressive Politics[1]

In writing Midwestern Progressive Politics, *Russel Nye developed the thesis that the Midwest Progressive was distinct*

[1] From Russel B. Nye, *Midwestern Progressive Politics: A Historical Study of Its Origins and Development, 1870–1950* (East Lansing, Michigan, 1951), pp. 220–24. Reprinted by permission of the publisher, The Michigan State University Press.

and differed from the Eastern liberal or the West Coast reformer. And in the task of reconciling the divergent sections the Midwest was best equipped to take the lead. Before completing this study, Nye published a biography of George Bancroft *and a volume entitled* Fettered Freedom: Civil Liberties and Slavery. *In this selection, Nye views La Follette as a Jeffersonian liberal, a typical representative of the Midwestern, agrarian, frontier tradition.*

La Follette's own political philosophy was grounded on an old fashioned American individualism of agrarian-Jeffersonian origins. He was a defender of capitalism against itself, he said, believing that capitalism, unless checked, was almost certain to commit suicide, dragging democracy down with it. To him, the preservation of democracy depended upon the people themselves. "Get and keep a dozen or more of the leading men in a community interested in and well-informed upon any public question," he wrote, "and you have laid firmly the foundations of democratic government." In the press, on the Chautauqua platform, at hundreds of county fairs and Grange meetings, from the back of a wagon or later a Ford, La Follette always went directly to the people. "I don't know how the people will feel toward me," he said on his death bed, "but I shall take to the grave my love for them, which has sustained me through life."

The direct primary, the initiative and referendum, the abolition of the caucus and convention, these and other reforms to him were simply devices by which the people might speak. "To insure a more direct expression of the people's will," La Follette said, "in all things pertaining to government, is the dominating thought in American politics today." But having once spoken, the people needed assurances that their voice would be heeded. Special privilege, the *bête noire* of Midwest politics since 1870, must not intervene—the machine, the corporate interest, the self-seeking class. Thus the responsibility of the elected official to the voter, and of the party to the voter, became a La Follette shibboleth. An officeholder, to his mind, represented the individual citizen in person and the party in the aggregate; he could not therefore play fast and loose with either personal or party obligations. Political parties made a contract with the voters, expressed in party pledges. The party which adopted a program and the candidate who endorsed it were honor bound to observe the contract. Violation of it or failure to execute it was not only "an assault upon party honor," but "a betrayal of the public." This, in La Follette's view, was the chief danger to democracy—not the people's inability to govern themselves, but the betrayal of the people by their representatives.

To beat the machine and the boss, La Follette depended upon the people's wisdom. Therefore a free press, a free and extended educational system, and pitiless publicity of campaign and corporate financing were fundamental to the democratic process. Recalling his own career, he wrote: "Machine control is based upon misrepresentation and ignorance. Democracy is based upon knowledge. It was clear to me that the only way to beat the boss and ring the rule was to keep the people thoroughly informed." So he fell into the habit of placing but one major issue at a time before the people, keeping the air clear, allowing opportunity for popular judgments to form without confusion. It was the machine and the boss, of course, who interposed between the people and their representatives—the machine and the boss, controlled by the "special interests," tariffs, banking, trusts, monopolies, plunderers of national resources. "If we would preserve the spirit as well as the form of our free institutions, the patriotic citizenship of the country must take its stand," he wrote in 1905, "and demand of wealth . . . that it shall not corrupt, but obey, the government that guards and protects its rights." Government provided the necessary—in effect the only—weapons in battle of the people against "special privilege . . . , the allied forces of wealth and corruption."

La Follette's forty-four years of public service coincided with the anti-monopoly era, and his progressivism was an extension of the Anti-Monopoly–Greenback–Granger struggle with the giant corporation. Modern business, he said in his message of 1904, needed large concentrations of capital to operate, but it should never be allowed to use that capital to destroy competition, control prices, milk the public, or corrupt government. Self-interested, organized, economic power was a threat to public welfare and to democracy, too strong to be curbed by any agency other than the state. Government therefore must regulate business in the public interest, and if necessary, break it. "It's plain as a pikestaff," he said, "that you cannot yoke private monopoly with honest, impartial public service." Nor can you live under an economic and industrial oligarchy and retain political freedom. "We may have the privilege of the ballot, we may have the form and semblance of democracy," he remarked, "but in the end industrial servitude means political servitude."

His method of dealing with monopoly was concrete, factual, and objective. Let us take as an example, he said, United States Steel. Let a government commission ascertain the valuation of its holdings and its actual investment in business. With this sum in mind, figure a reasonable rate of return, ascertain a fair price for its products, and publish it. U.S. Steel would then know what price it could justifiably charge; if it did not charge that price, the government could use more drastic methods of inducing it to do so. Railroads, whose rates should be calculated on the basis of a fair return for investment and service, could be handled the same way. In the case of natural public resources such as oil, coal, iron, timber, and so on, the government should own them and either operate or lease them, controlling both production and price. Private enterprise, La Follette thought, ought always to be allowed to do its job fairly, but if it did not, government ownership or operation was the only other alternative.

As a practicing politician, La Follette ranked among the best. An organizer of great ability, he built up from scratch a party (or a "machine") that controlled Wisconsin for a quarter-century, one whose influence was apparent in state politics for more than twenty years after his death. If he did not always inspire affection in his followers, he certainly inspired loyalty and respect. His party was always held together by the force of his own personality and the trust its constituents placed in him. Supreme as a leader, he yet lacked certain qualities to enable him to develop a national following, as Bryan and Theodore Roosevelt did. The austerity and rigidity of his nature and his inability to adjust to changing political and human situations narrowed his appeal. His thinking was "Midwestern"—typically so, reflecting the prejudices and the traditions of his state and region; the nation and the world were to him merely bigger Wisconsin. He lacked what historians call the "world view"; it was characteristic of him to remark, after his trip to Russia in the twenties, that he wished the Soviets could "come to Wisconsin to see what a real people's commonwealth was like."

La Follette was closer to the people and closer to the Midwest than any politician after Bryan. Unlike Bryan's, his appeal to the public was rational, rather than emotional. He had none of Bryan's crowd-swaying hypnosis, speaking instead in a rapid, intense fashion, flooding his audience with statistics, figures, and examples. The fact that he could keep a crowd of farmers on the edge of their seats for three hours by reciting tariff schedules and tax rates (as he once did on Chautauqua) is a tribute to a skill less flamboyant than Bryan's but one certainly equally effective. He once spoke for fifty-three consecutive nights, without the slightest flagging of his own energy or the audience's interest, a political feat only Bryan himself could equal.

La Follette was a small, wiry man, with a shock of black (later iron-gray) hair and a tendency toward swift and sharp gesture. He was honest, serious, almost inhumanly intense, and thoroughly uncompromising. He was perfectly willing to jeopardize his career, as he did a dozen times, to keep his principles, and the hate and vituperation that often came his way affected him not one iota. "I can no more compromise, or seem to compromise . . ." he said, "than I could by wishing it add twenty years to my life." His principles were always clear, his course equally so. Cold, severe, almost austere in manner,

La Follette did not invite easy friendship. He never had fun in politics (as Theodore Roosevelt did), nor did he inspire the dog-like devotion that Bryan did. It would be difficult to choose, from the group of men who knew him best and followed him, one who was a really close friend, for his complete and selfless dedication to his cause wrapped him about like armor. In truth, with his solid, lined, granite face, his tremendous idealism, his rigid indifference to any blandishments of friendship, party, place, profit, or power, La Follette was a trifle frightening. No one ever took Bob La Follette lightly or disinterestedly. "The politician cannot exist without absolute, unyielding, uncompromising honesty," he said, and he lived it out to the letter.

La Follette's Wisconsin cut the pattern, and the whole Midwest copied it. Progressivism after 1900 at one time or another had complete control of every state but Illinois, Michigan, Ohio, and Indiana. For that matter, it spread elsewhere under the leadership of men like Hiram Johnson in California, Charles Evans Hughes in New York, Woodrow Wilson in New Jersey, Bass in New Hampshire, and so on. But in the middle West, where it started, progressivism was considerably more than simply a swing toward honest government. It was a definite and coherent political philosophy, a concept of democracy that grew naturally out of Grangerism and Populism. Behind it were Weaver and Bryan, Donnelly and Lloyd, Altgeld, Pingree, and Simpson, and a distinctively Midwestern, agrarian, Jeffersonian, frontier tradition.

11

Claude G. Bowers: Beveridge and the Progressive Era[1]

Claude G. Bowers was a widely-known journalist who combined newspaper work with historical writing and a diplomatic career. In addition to his biography of Albert Beveridge, he was the author of studies of the Jackson period, Jefferson and Hamilton, and the post-Civil War era in American history. Between 1933 and 1938 he served as American Ambassador to the Spanish Republic. In this sketch Bowers depicted La Follette as he appeared as a colleague in the United States Senate with Albert Beveridge during the Taft years.

The senators who, with Beveridge, confronted Aldrich in the epochal struggle over the tariff of 1909 were all men of character and ability, and some among them had more than a spark of genius. They had arrived at insurgency by different routes and some by winding ways. The five who bore the brunt of the battle were more than merely emotional enemies of injustice. They were dominated by their intellectual processes, and they knew their facts because of herculean labors. Differing widely in personal traits, they fought as one man through that dreadful summer of 1909 for a principle.

The senior in insurgency was Robert M. La Follette, at this period a striking figure, short, stockily built, with a large head covered with a great mop of hair, brushed upward. His eyes were keen, penetrating, remarkably expressive; and anyone watching him in battle would note their capacity to express scorn, amazement, contempt, anger, and humor. His smoothly shaven face was strong in all its features, and in combat it was the face of a bulldog. He would walk into the Senate Chamber with a virile stride, and, seated at his desk listening to a debate, he was frequently found in the pose in which Joseph Davidson, the sculptor, has shown him in the vivid, animated statue now in the Capitol—his face alight with intense interest, his hands clasping the

[1] From Claude G. Bowers, *Beveridge and the Progressive Era* (New York, 1932), pp. 324–27. Reprinted by the permission of the publisher, the Houghton Mifflin Company.

arms of his chair as in the act of springing to his feet. No one on the floor, noting that pose, was ever quite comfortable.

La Follette had entered public life years before as a regular, if not content with the *status quo,* not quite realizing what it was. Elected to Congress in his thirties, he had played his part usually after the fashion prescribed by political tradition. He had, in the course of time, learned of things and methods that shocked and irritated him, but he had not crossed the Rubicon entirely.

It was in the gubernatorial office in Wisconsin, which he attained only after bitter contests with one of the most reactionary of machines that long had dominated the politics of the State, that he first attracted national notice. The reforms wrought in the regulation of the railroads in the days of the Granger Movement no longer protected the people against extortion; and the railroad interest completely controlled the State through its domination of the political machine. No longer were the roads subjected to a regulation that interfered in the slightest degree with their plans of greed; and they were immune from full taxation. They dictated to the machine; controlled the major portion of the press; influenced the banks; and through intimidation actually forced an acquiescent mood upon the shippers and merchants, who, no less than the consumers, were robbed in rates and methods. To challenge the power of this combination of political and financial interests, supported by the greater part of the press and superabundantly financed, called for temerity almost beyond the human; and young La Follette challenged it.

Arousing the great unorganized mass of the people, he organized them, and plunged with his fiery zeal into a crusade for the democratization of the government—a crusade as fundamental as those led long before by Jefferson and Jackson. He took the enemy by storm.

Then had followed a series of reforms calculated to make democracy a reality in Wisconsin. He ended the literal stealing by the roads of millions in taxes belonging to society; and when he foresaw the inevitable purpose to transfer the taxes to the consumers through increased rates, he met them there with a scientific method of regulation.

These, however, were but symbolical of the things he did. He found children of tender age in factories and he made that unlawful and sent them back to the playgrounds and the schools. He found workingwomen laboring under intolerable conditions, and he stopped that too. The factories, without a sanitary code, operated to the serious detriment of the workers, and he forced sanitation into the shops. He learned that food adulterators were poisoning the people for profit, and he made that a crime.

No single man, perhaps, ever did more within the limitations of a State to reform abuses, political and social, or to make democracy something other than an academic dream. Thus did he incur the deadly enmity of the forces of privilege and pillage, and these were to hound him with unthinkable fury throughout his life. When the people transferred him to Washington, the embryo plutocracy, with knives in their hands, was waiting for him at the Senate door.

For more than a century, America had referred to her democracy, and yet La Follette was almost unique in his day in that he was a democrat. His political creed largely was that of Jefferson and Jackson —hostility to privilege. To him the only government fit to live was that which acted as an agency of the average man in working out his inalienable right to life, liberty, and the pursuit of happiness. He saw that privilege in government had made a mockery and a mess of democracy, and with a gay gallantry he fared forth to battle against privilege all along the line.

He differed from many others, sincerely devoted to democratic ideals, in that he was superbly equipped and munitioned for his crusade. His sympathies for the average man motivated his action, but there was more than emotion behind his blows. There was an intellect and a genius for research. There was industry of the most appalling sort behind the intellect. He never declared war on any evil until he had studied and mastered its meaning and methods in all their ramifications. This meant for him the most intensive labor with the aid of experts. Mobilizing all the facts, he studied them closely for their effects. Only when his preparation was complete did he declare war; and it was war to the death.

Where the average senator of commanding influence is satisfied to master some one subject—banking, railroads, the tariff, foreign relations, trusts—La Follette made a specialty of them all, because he sought the common thread of privilege running through them all. He spoke with equal thoroughness on each; and most of his major speeches literally were treatises. Each speech reflected enormous work and was so buttressed with authoritative facts that none were seriously challenged on the floor of the Senate. When his enemies were unable to meet the argument, they had recourse to the old device of sneaking out into the cloakrooms. "I see a great many vacant seats in the Senate today," he said one day with a smile to the crowded galleries. "Many of the seats now temporarily vacant will be permanently so after a while." He did not mind the absentee insult; he was using the Senate chamber as a sounding-board to reach the millions in the corn rows and shops.

To pursue this course required ineffable courage and a rare capacity to bear up under misunderstandings, misrepresentations, and loneliness. A woman who had never seen him before, but had admired his public conduct from afar, once met him in the capitol grounds walking alone with his head bowed. As she greeted him she burst into tears. He stopped startled. "You seemed so lonely," she explained. "Yes," he replied reassuringly, "it is a little lonely sometimes, but we can stand it." He always did.

Few men in American history have had greater moral courage. He could stand absolutely alone with an approving conscience. He never counted the cost. He was willing to save his life by losing it. He was never tempted to compromise with his convictions for the sake of a meaningless victory. Had he been of a more compromising nature, he might have won more battles, but the victories would have been dead-sea fruit. He sought the substance or nothing.

As an orator he was overwhelming before a popular audience. Summer after summer found him on the circuit speaking to great audiences for three hours in tents, under the boiling sun or the stars, and holding them spellbound, not with glittering rhetoric, but by a marvelous dramatic marshaling of facts. He had the art of an actor; and in his youth he hoped for a histrionic career. He had won the Interstate Oratorical Contest when in college with a brilliant analytic study of Iago. This instinct for the play stood him in good stead on the platform. He spoke with great vehemence—action, action, action. His modulation itself often was eloquence. In the Senate he did not vary his method greatly, and with the senators sourly seeking the cloakrooms as a storm cellar, the galleries hung upon his words. "Fighting Bob" his friends called him, and he never winced under a blow, and never failed to strike with all his might.

12

Arthur M. Schlesinger: The Crisis of the Old Order[1]

Arthur M. Schlesinger, Jr., is a brilliant and penetrating historian of the New Deal. In addition to his studies of the Age of Roosevelt, *he has written, among other works,* The Age of Jackson, *and a biography of John F. Kennedy under whom he served as Special Assistant to the President. In this volume,* The Crisis of the Old Order, *he interprets La Follette and the Progressive effort of 1924.*

Where T.R. and Wilson had walked down the path of nationalism and war, where Bryan had succumbed to Chautauqua evangelism and Florida real estate, La Follette, austere and mistrustful, had kept the faith. Under his leadership Wisconsin had established the first modern income tax law, the first effective workmen's compensation law, the first modern labor legislation, the first legislative drafting service. In the complacent twenties, he was now demanding increased inheritance taxes, an excess profits tax, public ownership of railroads and water power, and abolition of the labor injunction. He was particularly exercised about the Supreme Court—"the actual ruler of the American people," he called it in 1922—and he suggested that Congress be given power to re-enact statutes nullified by the Court.[2]

Insurgency had been bubbling up elsewhere in the farm belt since the war. In North Dakota the Nonpartisan League, with its Socialist organizers and editors, had begun moving through the grain states demanding state-owned elevators, flour mills, and packinghouses; by 1920 Nonpartisan Leaguers helped found the Farmer-Labor party in Minnesota. And organized labor too was discontented: in 1922 the fifteen railroad brotherhoods called a Conference for Progressive Po-

[1] From Arthur M. Schlesinger, Jr., *The Age of Roosevelt,* Vol. 1, *The Crisis of the Old Order* (Boston, 1957), pp. 100–102. Reprinted by permission of the publisher, the Houghton Mifflin Company.

[2] E. N. Doan, *The La Follettes and the Wisconsin Idea* (New York, 1947), 103–4, 111–12.

litical Action in Cleveland. Out of the spreading unrest there were emerging the materials for a third party.

But the war had bred new perils for American liberalism. The American Workers' party, operating under orders from the Comintern in Moscow, saw its opportunity in the La Follette enthusiasm. The Communist-dominated Farmer-Labor Federation accordingly called a convention to nominate La Follette in the spring of 1924. But the grizzled old fighter had no illusions about the Communists. Their only purpose in joining the Progressive movement, he said, was to further the chaos they required for their ultimate aims. "I believe, therefore, that all Progressives should refuse to participate in any movement which makes common cause with any Communist organization." [3]

The Progressive convention in July was a reunion of a generation of reform. From General Jacob Coxey on, they came to Cleveland, New Nationalists and New Freedomites, social workers and social gospelers, trade unionists, Nonpartisan Leaguers and Socialists. La Follette received the nomination by acclamation; and Burton K. Wheeler, the radical Democratic senator from Montana, joined him on the ticket. "Between Davis and Coolidge," said Wheeler, "there is only a choice for conservatives"; during the campaign he called them the "Gold Dust Twins." The convention platform stood pretty much in its proposals for western radicalism of the old antimonopoly type. In its affirmations (contributed by the Bull Mooser Donald Richberg), it spoke in the accents of the New Nationalism, condemning "the principle of ruthless individualism and competition" and backing "the progressive principle of cooperation." [4]

The Progressive ticket won the support of the Scripps-Howard press, the American Federation of Labor, and most of the reformers. La Follette concentrated largely on the monopoly issue, though he added enough attacks on Wilson's war policy to alienate many Wilsonians and attract many German-Americans. But, despite the Progressives, it was a listless campaign. The combination of Coolidge and prosperity was invincible. Together the Progressives and the Democrats polled about two million fewer votes than the Republicans. La Follette while carrying Wisconsin and beating Davis in a few other states ran about three and a half million votes behind him in the nation.

The Progressive party of 1924 had even less future than the Progressive party of 1912. The railroad brotherhoods pulled out early in 1925, leaving the organization to a tug-of-war between the western

[3] *New York Times,* May 29, 1924; for La Follette on the Soviet Union see Lincoln Steffens, *Autobiography,* 2 vols. (New York, 1931), II, 806.

[4] *Labor,* July 26, 1924; Donald Richberg, *Tents of the Mighty* (Chicago, 1930), 137–38; R. B. Nye, *Midwestern Progressive Politics* (East Lansing, Mich., 1951), 325–47.

agrarians and the Socialists. Someone saw La Follette early in 1925, lying on the couch in his office, his face lined and anxious, puffing at his pipe. "I believe in democracy," the old man said, "but will it ever work?" With his death a few months later, his party crumbled away. It had no center of faith or doctrine to hold its parts together—nothing but the scraps of thirty years of agitation. "Throughout this period," said Donald Richberg, looking back a few years later, "the progressive forces in American political life had only the vaguest ideas of where they were going." [5]

[5] B. C. Marsh, *Lobbyist for the People* (Washington, 1953), 6; Richberg, *Tents of the Mighty*, 138.

13

Kenneth C. MacKay: The Progressive Movement of 1924[1]

Kenneth C. MacKay's study of The Progressive Movement of 1924 *is the standard work on this twentieth century third party crusade. In this chapter entitled "After La Follette" MacKay finds that much of La Follette's platform of 1924 eventually found its way into the statute books under Franklin D. Roosevelt. To this author, La Follette's campaign of 1924 kept the reform spirit alive during the prosperous and materialistic twenties. It was the forerunner of the New Deal.*

AFTER LAFOLLETTE

Senator LaFollette, who had been for the greater part of his career the embodiment of progressive ideals: dynamic, indefatigable and implacable, was coming to the end of the road. His days beyond the last CPPA conference were numbered. The strain of the campaign, added to his seventy years and coupled with a recent period of frail health, proved too much.

LaFollette lived long enough to give the Republicans the satisfaction of punishing him for his political heresy. As reprisal, the party regulars ousted him from Republican caucus, consequently depriving him—and the score of other Republican congressmen who had supported him in the election—of committee rank. LaFollete's 1924 bolt had provided the party leaders with a splendid opportunity to replace him with a dependable, conservative regular, James Watson of Indiana on the important Interstate Commerce committee in the Senate.

The final personal blow to the CPPA came on June 18, 1925, when, exhausted and weary, unable any longer to resist the maladies afflicting him, Senator LaFollette passed away at his home in Washington. The hopes for a third party in 1928 died with Senator LaFollette. He

[1] From Kenneth C. MacKay, *The Progressive Movement of 1924* (New York, 1947), pp. 243–64. Reprinted by permission of the publishers, The Columbia University Press.

would have been too aged to lead another political revolt himself, but the devotion of his admirers might have endowed the progressive movement with the cohesive quality without which, after 1925, the whole conglomeration of agrarians, Socialists, liberals and labor men fell apart and disappeared.

It was fitting that Senator LaFollette should pass away at the moment when America had chosen to accept the materialistic creed of the 'Twenties. LaFollette's faith in the common man seemed out-of-date in a nation spellbound by the exploits of wealth and bigness. His capacity for vigilance and criticism seemed unwanted by a people which had condoned corruption in high places. His Jeffersonian distrust of the powerful few, the oligarchy of rank and riches, struck a discordant note in the market-place, the market-place where all Americans, of course, could become millionaires by buying the right stock, the same market-place which assured a chicken in every pot and two cars in every garage.

LaFollette had left his mark upon the American political scene. His contribution might be better assayed, not in 1925, but in 1940 or 1950. It was going to take the American people a long time to evaluate the man properly. LaFollette's life had been long filled to overflowing, with both the fury of combat and the remorse and sorrow of defeat. "His role was that of an awakener of thought, a stimulator of action, a purifier of the public life. There was sacrifice in it, and suffering. There was also satisfaction. It is the only role a Robert LaFollette could have played." [2]

The collapse and disappearance of the progressive movement after the 1924 election cannot be fully explained in terms of the particular conditions and circumstances which blighted the LaFollette campaign. To establish—let alone win elections—a third party is a Herculean assignment; a task multiplied many times when the new organisation (sic) is liberal or radical, as was the case in 1924. The two-party system is so strongly ingrained in the structure of American politics that efforts to coalesce the opposition elements are likely to accomplish little beyond reaffirming the strength of the old parties. If the principles and policies espoused by the third party are unpopular, the leaders of the major parties can safely denounce or ignore them. If the new party has a live issue, capable of attracting votes, the old party leaders will probably steal it. In either case, a new party's lot is not a happy one. Unless it chooses, like the Socialist and Prohibition parties, to continue tasting the bitter dregs of defeat in election after election, a new party is almost certainly doomed to an early death. In dying it may often be

[2] Ogg, F. A., "LaFollette in Retrospect," *Current History Magazine,* 33:5, Feb. 1931, p. 691. [See also Syre, W., *Robert M. LaFollette, A Study in Political Methods,* Unpublished Doctor's Thesis, N.Y.U., 1930, for a brilliant appraisal of Senator LaFollette.]

comforted by the thought that its policies, having been kidnapped, are in safe and strong hands.

To be permanent, a party must be organized from its roots upward. The hasty collapse of the Bull Moose movement, a decline quite as meteoric as its rise, is eloquent testimony to the temporary nature of parties which appear fullgrown from the brow of some great political hero. The pathetic lack of organisation of the Progressives in 1924 is further evidence that, in a nation with the geographical scope and magnitude of the United States, the groundwork for the construction of a new political party is a gigantic undertaking. Considerations of local office-seeking are of such vital importance in determining the success of an entire party ticket that it becomes futile for a national candidate to expect success without diligent preparation in county and precinct spadework.

To the dismay of the Progressives, the 1924 experience demonstrated the effectiveness with which the various state election laws hamper—intentionally or not—the efforts of a third party movement. Running for office is not merely a matter of placing one's name in space provided on the ballot. Long, wearisome days of legal study and consultation, precious—and expensive—weeks collecting signatures and perhaps even funds for election fees are prerequisites for getting one's party on the ballot. The election machinery, in the hands of members of the old parties, is manipulated so as to discourage, if not to prevent, the appearance of a new party column on the election ballot.

And the plans, ambitious as they must be, of a third party take money and willing hands. In a country where campaigns last for several months and millions of dollars are spent on traveling expenses, rentals, campaign literature, radio time and all the incidental expenses, success at the polls must be predicated upon ample and sufficient financial support. Those affluent enough to finance a new party, even if not frightened off by the purposes of the rebel group, will hesitate to contribute to a party which can hold out little promise of success. The *quid pro quo* arrangement, which so often is a determining factor in campaign donations, is hardly applicable when the chance of rewarding the party angels is so remote. Thus a kind of vicious circle restricts the new party from achieving results. Because it has no money, it is unable to organize. Because it is unorganized—and likely to lose, it attracts little financial support. The "cohesive power of public plunder" cannot be generated for any prospect so lean as the political dividends of a protest vote.

What has been said of money applies equally to political workers. With his characteristically pragmatic approach, the politician is unwilling to associate himself with a losing cause. After all, he is primarily interested in winning his own—or his own candidate's—election. If supporting a new party jeopardizes his prospect of winning, then, naturally, it will have to wait to secure his endorsement; wait until it has demonstrated its ability to win elections. The bandwagon did not go out of date with the horse and buggy. In 1924, neither Senator Borah nor Senator Norris, notwithstanding their personal admiration and friendship for LaFollette, campaigned for him. In fact, while Norris remained silent, Borah endorsed Coolidge and the Republican ticket. There is evidence that both these great Western leaders, while probably unmoved by selfish considerations, were convinced of the futility of a third party. Among politicians less powerful and less independent than men like Borah and Norris there was the fear of reprisals after Election Day when the old parties would still be around, working at the same old stand.

It seems a practical impossibility for a new party to erect a national organization, penetrating into the smallest towns and counties and supported by experienced local politicians or leaders capable of getting out the vote. To do so takes time, patience, volunteers and money far in excess of the amount produced by the progressive crusade of 1924. The Bull Moosers of 1912, with Munsey and Perkins funds behind them, were at least in possession of one of these much needed ingredients for success. The LaFollette Progressives, of course, were in dire financial stress all the time. In fact, if we may judge from 1924, the only effect, from a financial viewpoint, of the emergence of a liberal third party like LaFollette's is to facilitate the task of the revenue collectors of the old parties. Just when the major parties were in need of some extra cash, LaFollette or Wheeler would considerately blast again at the Supreme Court or "big business" and the flow of checks and money orders into Republican and Democratic headquarters would resume.

Moreover, for many persons, voting the old ticket has become an environmental or cultural characteristic. Such persons would no more think of deserting their party than their families. Their political behavior is as predictable as the salivary response of a conditioned dog in Prof. Pavlov's laboratory. "To many good Americans, there is something peculiarly sacred about the two party system. It is like the decalogue, or the practice of monogamy, or the right of the Supreme Court to declare a law of Congress unconstitutional." [3] In striking contrast to social politics abroad, the United States has never witnessed any permanent, effective alliance of farmers and laborers. Perhaps the singularly dynamic development of the nation, with its abundance of cheap land and pioneer opportunities, has been chiefly responsible for this. Occasionally—when their immediate interests coincide, as in 1932—farmers and workers vote together, but more frequently they are opposed.

[3] Hicks, J. D., "The Third Party Tradition in American Politics," *Mississippi Valley Historical Review,* 20:I, June 1933, p. 3.

> The farmers want lower freight rates, while railroad employees demand higher wages. Daylight saving meets the need of city workers, but is objectionable to the farmers. Higher prices for farm products do not seem reasonable to workingmen in cities. The farmer is individualistic and capitalistic in his views. He is group-conscious, but not class-conscious. Only when some emergency arises does he turn to the state for help.[4]

Whether the cause is to be found in some such tangible conflict of interest or as a result of the farmer's preoccupation with his property interests, the net effect is an almost complete lack of the class feeling noticeable in Europe. Farm-labor political alliances have been temporary expediencies here, with the two groups finding common cause in opposing conservative forces but falling apart as soon as more definite and positive policies take shape. "What it takes to arouse resentment and revolt they have; what it takes to go forward on a line of action they have not." [5]

American farmers, clinging to a political habit which contradicts Marxist concepts of group solidarity, have persistently declined to identify their own welfare with that of the industrial proletariat. American farmers "disbelieve in industrial evolution." [6] They prefer to adhere to their faith in a Jeffersonian Utopia, where each man has his plot of land and the right to buy more land. Their panacea for the social and economic ills of the nation lies not so much in extensions of government controls as in limitations and safeguards upon the freedom of the industrialists to convert the nation into a bustling urban community of factories, technological skills and hired workers. Their reluctance to co-operate politically with the proletarian victims of the industrial process has been a consequence of their refusal to accept, in their thinking and political attitudes, this condition of change. Mid-West farmers may have voted for LaFollette because his principles reminded them of Populism, or because his swing around the circuit was Bryanesque, or because, like Mary Lease, they just felt like raising less corn and more hell. To them, LaFollette was in the tradition of those great champions of the soil of that West whose economic conditions and grievances had cradled so many rebel party movements. To them, LaFollette's party was another party of agrarian dissent, a latter-day collection of Free-Soilers, Greenbackers and Populists. They voted for LaFollette because he seemed to express so abundantly their wrath

[4] Haynes, F. E., "The Significance of the Latest Third Party Movement," *Mississippi Valley Historical Review,* 12:2, Sept., 1924, p. 182.

[5] Tugwell, R. G., "Is a Farmer-Labor Alliance Possible," *Harper's Magazine,* 174:1044, p. 651.

[6] Macmahon, A., "Political Parties—The United States," *Encyclopedia of the Social Sciences,* Vol. II, p. 599.

and their loathing for the malefactors of great wealth who had tinkered with the order of things.

The Progressives did not receive a full measure of support from organized labor. Labor's original reluctance to endorse LaFollette and Wheeler before alternative courses were exhaustively explored, its wavering, inadequate support during the campaign, its early retreat in the face of defeat, its indecent haste to abandon the progressive movement and humbly solicit the old parties for a share of the political swag once more, all of this demonstrated that organized labor—at least, large and controlling sections of it, particularly in the American Federation of Labor and the Railroad Brotherhoods, were not prepared to face the logical consequences of a real break with the entrenched political machines.

Looking back on 1924 now, we can discern certain difficulties of this particular third party—features which, in all probability, would also hamper other progressive movements. First of all, there was not time enough. From July 4 to November 4 was inadequate for the construction of a new political organization. Painstaking time and energy must precede the actual launching of a national party.

Then, too, prosperity—the Coolidge variety—beckoned with too many material comforts. Attuned to the low emotional vibrations of Coolidge's negative policies, the nation was in no mood to hear the Progressive plea. Indeed, theirs were voices crying in a wilderness, a wilderness crowded with popular-priced automobiles, golf courses and service club outings. LaFollette and the Progressives raised their voices when the business interests were apparently more thoroughly entrenched, in both political power and public esteem, than at any time since the days of Harrison and McKinley. Despite the wishful dreams of intellectuals, the nation was not ready for a counterpart of the British Labour Party in 1924. Neither the intellectuals, who had failed to prepare the way as the Fabians had done in England, nor the labor unions, which were still frankly opportunistic, were adequately equipped to launch the new party. Major political movements are the products of their times, with economic and social factors strong enough to compel changes in voting behavior and to remold party lines. There was no such compulsion about 1924.

There were too many dissensions within the CPPA. LaFollette's mixed army went in too many directions, all at once. The heterogeneous nature of the movement undermined confidence. Not only was there the obvious difficulty of conciliating trade-union ideas with Western agrarian principles and non-Partisan League practical politics with the idealism of Eastern intellectuals, but there was always the fear on the part of each group that it might be swallowed up by the others. This feeling implanted in all of them a sense of inferiority, a need for being on guard. The Socialists distrusted the labor unions;

the unions feared Socialism. The farmers were hostile to the Socialists and in economic disagreement with the labor unions. Jockeying for position in the new organization, the different parts of the CPPA found difficulty in watching the common enemy. One effect of the internecine dissensions was to make the movement more and more dependent upon LaFollette. The temporary basis for agreement among agrarians, labor unions, intellectuals, Single Taxers, the Committee of Forty Eight and all the rest had been the endorsement of LaFollette and Wheeler. It was both a strength and weakness of the movement. The extent to which the CPPA was dependent upon LaFollette and submissive to his desires was shown when it permitted him, as its candidate, to dictate the platform. As the campaign progressed, it became increasingly the "LaFollette movement" and the terms "Progressive" and "CPPA" were much less in evidence. While a tribute to his personal magnetism and the force of his character and personality, such a development heightened the impression that the progressive effort was a one-man show, which, instead of laying the foundation for a new party, would culminate in victory or defeat for LaFollette on Election Day. The 1924 progressive movement, under these circumstances, became as vulnerable and as mortal as LaFollette.

In spite of LaFollette's attempts to make monopoly the major issue, there was no paramount issue in the campaign.[7] This coincided with Republican strategy to divert attention from the Harding scandals. LaFollette often lashed out against "the interests"; Wheeler generally denounced "the Ohio Gang." Frequently, the Progressive leaders would condemn imperialism or high tariff policies. Often they called for agricultural relief. But none of these appeals had political glamour in 1924. The apathetic electorate seemed bored by the charges of Republican scandal and corruption. Monopoly was not the torch word LaFollette expected it to be. At best, it was an issue which lacked constructive character, largely negative by nature. LaFollette seemed to be thinking still in terms of 1905 or 1910, little aware that the problems of the 'Twenties called for remedies more complex than the dissolution of trusts and the elimination of the private monopoly system. In the campaign, as he denounced monopoly, LaFollette was constantly reiterating the battle cries and suggesting the panaceas of an earlier day. Trustbusting days were over, but the Senator did not realize it. "In final judgment the veteran warrior turned again to the veteran issues —and decided to march his legions out to familiar shell-torn battlefields." [8]

Issues which LaFollette did not intend to emphasize were cleverly accentuated by the old-line politicians. In particular, three issues stand

[7] See Sullivan, M., "Looking Back on LaFollette," *World's Work,* 49:3, Jan. 1925, p. 326.

[8] Richberg, D., *Tents of the Mighty,* p. 135.

out as distinct liabilities to LaFollette. They were the Court issue, LaFollette's alleged pro-German sympathies, and the threat of an election deadlock. The first of these, as we have already seen, alienated countless sincere voters concerned about the dignity of the Court or the preservation of civil liberties. In the minds of many substantial God-fearing citizens, the members of the Supreme Court were close to demigods. Any attack, even indirect, upon them approximated blasphemy. Mark Sullivan has described how some voters made up their minds. After describing the venerable, dignified justices in their solemn robes he says:

> The voter looked on the photograph of the Supreme Court and saw all that. Then the same voter turned to the campaign photographs of LaFollette, some of which were not of LaFollette at his best, he saw in LaFollette something of that unusualness, that aberration from the conventional, which is frequently a deterrent from confidence in the average man's mind, the pompadour hair that suggests emotional excitability—the voter turned from one photograph to the other and decided to stand by what seemed to be the picture of greater stability.[9]

It may be amusing to think of anyone to whom campaign issues and choices can all be simplified into a comparison of two photographs. Nevertheless this psychology must have been effective in swelling the Coolidge total on Election Day.

Allusions to LaFollette's war record, as already indicated, were frequent and effective. LaFollette's poor showing in Missouri may be evidence that his lack of ardor for the Allies lost him more votes among patriots whose enthusiasm had not yet abated than it gained for his ticket in German sections.

The apprehensions over the possibility of a deadlocked election served the Republicans well. The fearful picture drawn by the nimble imagination of many a Republican editor of the disastrous confusion sure to follow in the event of an indecisive electoral count seemed to provide tangible evidence of the dangers foreseen by George Harvey when he cried out that the paramount issue was "Coolidge or Chaos." [10] By "Chaos," as he was careful to point out, Harvey meant the paralyzing consequences of a deadlocked electoral college. That George Harvey's exuberant desire for Republican success in the election temporarily exceeded his faith in the American constitutional system was obscure to many alarmed voters.

Although its leader had passed away and its official organization was stillborn, the ideas and the men of the progressive movement marched on. From 1925 until the coming of the New Deal, it was the

[9] Sullivan, M., *op. cit.*, p. 331.

[10] Harvey, G., "The Paramount Issue—Coolidge or Chaos," *North American Review*, 220:824, Sept. 1924, pp. 1–9.

undercurrent of reform and rebellion, an undercurrent dramatically re-emerging in the places of the mighty in 1933. Intermittent efforts to organize a third party of Progressives on a national scale continued. Progressive leaders concentrated, in the late 'Twenties, on maintaining and enlarging the liberal bloc in Congress, a group sufficiently large and influential enough to embarrass the Coolidge and Hoover Administrations. As a Congressional group it reflected in large part the agrarian policies of Northwesterners like Shipstead and Frazier. Perhaps its greatest victory was the passage of the McNary-Haugen farm relief bill, although President Coolidge killed the bill by veto.

The 1928 national election provided no opportunity for progressives to offer their program to the country. Confused by irrelevant issues and misled by whispered canards, the American voter found himself on a holiday from thinking, his choice at the polls often determined by Al Smith's pronunciation of *radio* or the latest rumor about the Free Masons or the Knights of Columbus.[11] Repeating again and again the pragmatic idiom, Mr. Hoover sought and secured election as the guardian of material comforts, of prosperity, and the American way of life. These major issues of 1928—prosperity, religion and Prohibition—cut directly across ordinary political affiliations. Kansas farmers suspected Al Smith's Tammany connections; Herbert Hoover lost the votes of thirsty Republicans in the great cities of the East.

On Mar. 11, 1931, a conference of progressives was called in Washington by five liberal Senators—G. W. Norris of Nebraska, Edward Costigan of Colorado, Bronson M. Cutting of New Mexico, Robert M. LaFollette, Jr. of Wisconsin, and Burton K. Wheeler of Montana. By 1931, the depression, which had begun early in the Hoover Administration, had deepened. Liberal and reform groups, despairing of any assistance from the White House, were calling upon Congress to assert itself in taking positive steps for the alleviation of the nation's economic ills. In such a political climate, so different from that of 1924, these liberals met. The purpose of the meeting was "to outline a program of constructive legislation dealing with economic and political conditions for presentation to the first session of the 72nd Congress." [12] Unlike the CPPA, this group explicitly announced that the meeting would not consider a basis for a new party. Rather it was to be devoted to an exchange of ideas looking solely to the formulation of a sound legislative program for liberals. Many names familiar to the 1924 Progressive campaign reappear at this conference. From Congress came men like Brookhart, Cutting, Norris and LaGuardia. From the ranks of labor came William Green, Sidney Hillman and D. B. Robertson.

[11] See Peel, R. V., and Donnelly, T. C., *The 1928 Campaign,* pp. 112–28, for an analysis of the factors in this election.

[12] *Proceedings,* Conference of Progressives, Washington, D.C., Mar. 11–12, 1931, title page.

LaFollette men of 1924 like Donald Richberg and Joseph Bristow joined with farm representatives like Milo Reno and George Huddleston. Present were such intellectuals as Charles Beard, Bruce Bliven and E. A. Ross. While accomplishing little more than afforded by the opportunity to meet each other and exchange ideas, the progressives of 1931 found common ground in their uncompromising and unreserved disapproval of the Hoover Administration. The 1931 conference was a suggestion of the shape of things to come, when farm and labor voters would join to oust the Republicans from control of the national government.

Spasmodically between 1928 and 1932, liberal groups had sought to prepare the way for another progressive electoral campaign. Even before the great depression had underlined the need for social and economic reform, Paul Douglas and others, in 1928, had organized the League for Independent Political Action, devoted to the principles of increased social control and fundamental realignment of the American party system.[13] John Dewey became its Chairman and Howard Y. Williams its national organizer. The League was intended to act as a co-ordinating agency, rather than to become a new party itself. The response to the formation of the League was disappointing. Prominent liberals, like Norris and Cutting, preferred to remain within the old parties and to work as regulars for a more liberal program. As the 1932 presidential election approached, the League for Independent Political Action presented a program of progressive policies—called a "Four Year Presidential Plan"—which was largely an anticipation of the program which Franklin D. Roosevelt was later to unfold.[14] During the 1932 campaign, the League endorsed the Socialist candidacies of Norman Thomas and James Maurer.[15]

How much did the 1924 Progressives contribute to Franklin D. Roosevelt's victory in 1932? To what extent did the LaFollette Progressives move into the Democratic party as the Populists had entered the Democratic ranks in 1896?

As the Democratic national convention of 1932 approached, it became increasingly apparent that the delegates would divide into two opposing factions: those supporting Governor Roosevelt's presidential candidacy, and those opposed to it, the latter drawn together by their common desire to "stop Roosevelt." In this group were the loyal followers of Al Smith, Governor Ritchie of Maryland, Newton D. Baker of Ohio, James Reed of Missouri and a host of others. Although the issues were blurred, as they usually are at a national political convention, by maneuvering and hotel-room deals, it is probably cor-

[13] See Douglas, P. H., *The Coming of a New Party.*

[14] "The Four Year Presidential Plan," complete text of the L.I.P.A. platform, *The Nation,* 134:3476, Feb. 17, 1932, special section.

[15] *The New York Times,* July 11, 1932.

rect to say that the opposition to Roosevelt came chiefly from conservatives already alarmed by some of Roosevelt's measures of social reform in the State of New York, and city bosses anxious to deadlock the convention in order to nominate a candidate more directly obligated to them than the ambitious Franklin D. Roosevelt. Thus, Democrats like John W. Davis and Boss Hague joined to stop Roosevelt. Jim Farley, Roosevelt's energetic campaign manager, had been busy collecting votes before the delegates assembled. Roosevelt's success in the state conventions and preference primaries brought him into the convention with a majority, but not the requisite two-thirds.[16]

The convention itself provides no clear-cut lines to the behavior of progressives in 1932. Occasionally there was an indication that progressive sympathies lay mostly with Roosevelt. The Roosevelt forces supported Tom Walsh of Montana for permanent chairman, action which precipitated one of the early tests of strength of the respective Roosevelt and anti-Roosevelt forces. The balloting for the presidential nomination disclosed the liberal-conservative division in the 1932 convention. The opposition to Roosevelt—expressed as votes for Smith, Reed, Ritchie, Baker or some other of the Stop-Roosevelt group—came largely from boss-dominated states like New York, New Jersey and Illinois. The states like Wisconsin, the Dakotas and Minnesota, where LaFollette had been strong in 1924, voted for Roosevelt.[17] A rather dramatic portent of the position many progressives would take in the forthcoming election was provided when the assembled delegates, awaiting Roosevelt's arrival to accept the nomination, were informed that the party's candidate had received the unqualified support of George Norris of Nebraska, grand old man of the Progressive bloc in the Senate.[18]

Partly, perhaps, as the result of a natural desire to get on the bandwagon, and partly because of general—though unexcited—approval of Roosevelt's program as it was slowly revealed through campaign speeches, the progressive element lent support to the Democratic ticket during the campaign. In Wisconsin, the LaFollettes came out in complete endorsement of the Democratic candidates.[19] As the campaign progressed, such outstanding liberals as Norris of Nebraska, Cutting of New Mexico, Richberg and Manly of Illinois, and Frank Walsh of New York were actively campaigning for Roosevelt. Paul Anderson, one of the most acute political observers of the 'Thirties, had been extremely skeptical about the Democratic candidate. But, by early October, he was writing that one of the "most heartening aspects of

[16] Farley, J., *Behind the Ballots,* pp. 112–22.

[17] *The New York Times,* July 2, 1932.

[18] *Ibid.,* July 3, 1932.

[19] Evjue, W. T., "Wisconsin Turns to Roosevelt," *The Nation,* 135:3513, Nov. 2, 1932, p. 425.

the 1932 campaign is (Franklin D. Roosevelt's) demonstrated eagerness to associate himself openly with progressives of . . . unquestionable sincerity." [20] The Norman Thomas Socialist vote, which had appeared so substantial in numerous straw ballots, was inconsequential on Election Day. There is a strong likelihood, as one magazine supporting Thomas suggested, that many Thomas supporters, alarmed by Republican claims of a "ground swell" for Hoover as the election approached, voted for Roosevelt. Needless to say, the reports of a "ground swell" for Hoover were, like the news of Mark Twain's death, greatly exaggerated!

How much did the 1924 Progressives contribute to the New Deal in power? Most certainly, whatever the contribution has been, the New Deal and its leaders have never acknowledged it. A comparative study of the Progressive platform of 1924 and the policies enacted into law by Franklin Roosevelt and his New Deal would indicate that, perhaps unintentionally, much of the latter was plagiarized. The Progressives get no credit line for the TVA, the "rapidly progressive" income (and inheritance) tax schedules, the Wagner Labor Relations Act, the various New Deal aids to agriculture, the Securities Exchange Commission and the abolition of child labor. Yet all these demands, and others later incorporated as a part of the body of the New Deal legislation, are to be found in the Progressive platform of 1924.[21] What prophets those distressful and dismal days in March 1933 made of the LaFollette insurgents who, in the midst of prosperity and complacency, foresaw the inevitable consequences of reckless financial manipulation and shameless exploitation! Undismayed by threats of coercion and unreceptive to seductive promises of lush materialism, the Progressives of 1924 saw their apprehensions confirmed by the disastrous events of the depression years.

In their hour of economic and social peril, the American people, reacting in accordance with the prescribed practice of American political behavior, had decided to "turn the rascals out" and to elect a Democrat as President. Perhaps H. L. Mencken's hardy Chinaman could have been elected in 1932 provided he had been running as a Democrat. But the choice of the Democrats was Franklin D. Roosevelt, Governor of New York, generally regarded as sympathetic to those people, farmers, laborers, small business men, who had felt the full brunt of the depression. His plan of action, reluctantly and only partially disclosed during the campaign, was "an indistinctly liberal program, patterned generally after the progressivism of his late cousin and of the late Robert LaFollette." [22] But, for the large part, Roose-

[20] Anderson, P. Y., "Roosevelt Woos the Progressives," *The Nation,* 135:3510, Oct. 12, 1932, pp. 331–332.

[21] See Appendix 4.

[22] Allen, F. L. *The Lords of Creation,* pp. 420–21.

velt was elected not because his program incorporated progressive policies. The American people were chiefly motivated, as they voted for him by the millions, by their resentment at Hoover and the Republican Party and a feeling, born of pathetic desperation, that any change would be a change for the better. Preoccupied by their powerful urge to change administrations, they had little time to make a reasoned choice. Hence the kind of providential luck which had assisted Calvin Coolidge on so many occasions thrust Mr. Roosevelt and his advisers into positions of great responsibility. That these advisers were often Progressives, of the 1924 variety, was not the result of an expression of preference on the part of the American electorate so much as it was the deliberate choice of advisers made by the new President, choosing men like David K. Niles to serve as Executive Secretary, Harold L. Ickes as Secretary of the Interior, and Basil Manly as a member of the Federal Power Commission. A veteran of many sessions of Congress noticed the connection.

> If one will take the trouble to examine the platform of 1924 on which Robert M. LaFollette ran for Senator (sic) he will find very many of the identical propositions embodied that are now being put into execution by the administration of Franklin D. Roosevelt and, furthermore, a closer examination will reveal the fact that many of the very men who are now engaged in aiding President Roosevelt were in Wisconsin at that time helping LaFollette.[23]

Support, sometimes even before the party had nominated him, from such respected liberals as George Norris, Burton K. Wheeler and young Bob LaFollette was sufficient evidence to many a progressive voter that Roosevelt had challenged the power of the vested interests.

But progressivism had changed in shape—though perhaps not in substance—by 1932. Progressivism as an independent movement of farmers and workers had disappeared, only to reappear as a powerful and influential wing of the resurgent Democratic party, carrying weight among the leaders close to the ear of the Chief Executive. That the term "Progressive" was drowned out in the torrent of political discussion and debate over the "New Deal" should not obscure the thread of continuity which connects 1924 with 1932 and 1936. The overwhelming support which Roosevelt received from farmers and workers, in 1932 and 1936, proves that these groups will unite when a coherent program appealing to both of them is presented and when the leadership is adequate.[24] "The LaFollette movement has never died."[25]

[23] Watson, J. E., *As I Knew Them,* p. 297. Copyright 1936. Used by special permission of the publishers, Bobbs-Merrill Company.

[24] Tugwell, R. G., *op. cit.,* p. 655.

[25] *Ibid.*

Roosevelt, with some less liberal program, would have won in 1932—the tide against Hoover was so strong—but not with such an overwhelming endorsement from farmer and worker. Perhaps that endorsement strengthened the hand of those progressives around the President who guided and charted a course for the new Administration.[26]

The overwhelming Roosevelt landslide in 1932 and the subsequent preoccupation of the New Deal with matters of social and economic reform retarded the development of Paul Douglas' idea of a new party of progressives in the 'Thirties. Many liberals, as we have noted, were playing an active role within the Administration. Even those who were not identified with the New Deal hesitated to divide the forces of reform by joining a party whose votes would be drawn from supporters of President Roosevelt. In 1933, a futile attempt had been made to coalesce the elements left of Roosevelt at a conference held in Chicago.[27] Despite the able and energetic support of Alfred Bingham's *Common Sense,* which had, to all intents and purposes, become the official organ of Douglas' League for Political Action, the conference did little except hear an excellent speech delivered by Thomas Amlie of Wisconsin. In 1935, another attempt was made, again in Chicago.[28] With some of the old timers of 1924 like Ray McKaig and Nathan Fine in attendance, a much more serious effort to launch a new party came to the same end. Lured by William Lemke's presidential candidacy, some Non-Partisan League supporters sought temporary sanctuary in Father Coughlin's ill-starred potpourri of dissidents called the Social Justice Party in 1936. That same year, liberals within New York State organized the American Labor Party.[29] In 1938, a new effort on the part of progressives led by the LaFollettes, quickly produced both a name—the National Progressive Party and an emblem—a red, white and blue design.[30] But the November elections—so satisfactory to the Republicans throughout the nation—swept Phil LaFollette from the Governor's chair in Madison and put an early end to the national aspirations of the progressives.[31] Undeterred by what they considered

[26] Oswald G. Villard vigorously dissents from this opinion that the New Deal has been influenced by progressive ideals. Correspondence, O. G. Villard to author, 1944.

[27] Bingham, A. M., "The Farmer Labor Political Federation," *Common Sense,* 2:4, Oct. 1933, pp. 18–20. *Common Sense* (1932–1944) is a rich source of material on the progressive movements of the 1930's.

[28] See Amlie, T. R., "The American Commonwealth Federation," *Common Sense,* 4:8, Aug. 1935, pp. 6–7. This issue of *Common Sense* also includes the complete platform of the "American Commonwealth Federation" organized at Chicago by the progressives.

[29] *The New York Times,* July 17, 1936.

[30] *The New York Times,* April. 29, 1938. The Wisconsin Progressive Party had been founded in 1934.

[31] See LaFollette, P., "They Wanted Something New," *The Nation,* 147:43, Dec. 3, 1938, pp. 586–87.

to be temporary setbacks, the Wisconsin progressives—with little encouragement from the rest of the nation—continued to dwell upon ways and means of expanding their organization into a national political structure.

The fate of third parties in American History—to expire after their contributions have been adopted (or stolen) by one of the major parties—has blinded many students to their real significance. "Looked at from the social point of view, the chief function of third parties has been to bring new issues before the people; they force new policies upon the older parties, and after accomplishing their work, they pass away." [32] The major parties, dominated by the prime consideration of effecting a majority on Election Day out of countless sectional and economic blocs, cannot afford to be so definite or articulate in facing the issues of the day. As a rule, only a minor party can afford the luxury of expecting defeat at the polls; it can afford to be recklessly courageous. Our weakest parties are our most unequivocal parties. In contributing new issues, the third parties become the trial horses of the American party system. When a good race is run, the horse may find himself suddenly transferred to one of the elegant stables of the old parties. Hence the value of a third party must be accepted in terms of its effects upon the other parties rather than by an exclusive history of its own efforts and achievements. There is no way of evaluating the influence of the 1924 Progressives upon the New Deal beyond recognizing the familiar faces and comparing the LaFollette program with the Roosevelt record. But, basically, the same social and economic forces which were responsible for nearly five million votes of protest in 1924, manifested themselves in the formulation of that program of recovery and reform which we have come to refer to familiarly as the New Deal. Without that base, how firm a foundation would the New Deal have had at the beginning of Franklin Roosevelt's administration?

The real political alignments in America are local, consisting of innumerable parochial factions whose interests are often in sharp conflict. The American party system has evolved as an ingenious device for creating national majorities out of conglomerate local interests and particularist groups. The American political party is a kind of huge circus tent beneath whose broad canopy a startling variety of characters perform, some of them acrobats, others skilled actors and a great many well-paid clowns. The only practical substitute—and would it be so practical?—is a multiple-party system under which the United States would be exposed to the irresolute and vacillating fruits of bloc government. The two-party system in America represents not a consolidation of the various local factions, but rather a working union

[32] Haynes, F. E., *Social Politics in the United States* (New York, Houghton Mifflin, 1924), p. 154.

in which the common objective of victory is more of a cohesive factor than the various group interests.

> That the two-party system does not under these conditions produce a direct conflict of principle is understandable. The victorious faction has not only to conciliate the defeated faction in its own party but it must bid for the movable vote in the other party. Therefore, the progress of an election campaign tends to show a steady closing up of issues that would divide men, a steady approach to the same apparently popular cries, a constantly increasing neutralization of the conflict. I have often thought during a national election that if it ran another six months the candidates would be using each other's speeches.[33]

Viscount Bryce was noticing the same feature of the American party system when he commented that the parties in the United States are pure home growths, developed by the circumstances of the nation.[34] Woodrow Wilson recognized the role of our parties in holding together disconnected and dispersed elements and in lending coherence to the action of political forces which might otherwise have a disruptive effect.[35] The anxiety of the average politician to conciliate the groups which might turn against him reminds one of the remark in *The Bigelow Papers*—

> Every fool knows that a man represents
> Not the fellers that sent him but them on the fence.

What, then, becomes the role of a third party like LaFollette's in 1924? If the major party organizations in America are sufficiently flexible and embracing to absorb movements of protest and revolt, how can a group like the Progressives hope to make any contribution, beyond swelling the vote for one of the old parties? The answer lies in the concessions and alignments which go to make up the substance of a political party. In 1932 Governor Roosevelt aligned himself, first, to secure the Democratic nomination, and later, to win the election, with progressive elements from industrial centers and the agrarian West. In doing so, the nominee of the Democratic party added progressive spice to the Democratic pie. It is no curious coincidence that it was those states of the Middle Border, where long the banners of progressivism had been displayed, which supported Mr. Roosevelt most loyally at the 1932 Convention. In one of those marriages of convenience so characteristic of American political behavior, progressives were joining city boss-dominated machines, like Kelley's and Hague's,

[33] Lippman, W., "Birds of a Feather," *Harper's Magazine,* 150:898, Mar. 1925, p. 409.
[34] Bryce, J., *The American Commonwealth,* Vol. II (1927 edition), p. 5.
[35] Wilson, W., *Constitutional Government in the United States,* p. 206.

the overlords of the South, Democratic state organizations and a horde of discontented resentful voters in a determined, united effort to get rid of Hoover. Thus, in 1933, on a memorable day when a new President was inaugurated, the remnants of the progressive movement of 1924 provided one of the mosaics in the baffling, sometimes inharmonious, but unvariably vivid pattern of that New Deal which was to contribute such a lengthy chapter to American history.

14

Earl Warren: "Robert M. La Follette, Sr."[1]

This address commemorating the one hundredth anniversary of Robert M. La Follette's birth was given at the State Historical Society at Madison, on June 19, 1955. At this time the Hon. Earl Warren was Chief Justice of the United States Supreme Court and the centennial celebration was attended by dignitaries from many parts of the United States, members of the La Follette family, and a number of scholars and students of the American past. Prior to his elevation to the high court, Warren had served as a district attorney in California, Attorney General of the State, and Governor of California. In 1948 he had been the Republican Party's nominee for the Vice Presidency of the United States.

You do me great honor in permitting me to speak at this official centennial of the birth of your most distinguished citizen. I appreciate your hospitality the more because of the intimacy of the meeting here in the presence of members of the La Follette family, in the presence of old companions and lifelong believers in his principles of public morality; and because the meeting is sponsored by this learned and patriotic Wisconsin Historical Society. Lastly I appreciate it because it is being held in your capital city where, as Governor, many of his great accomplishments were made and because here at your great University he received not only his intellectual inspiration but he met and married his mate, companion, and lifelong source of inspiration.

In such surroundings and under such auspices, one who did not have even the privilege of a personal acquaintance with the honoree, must be doubly conscious of the hospitality that is being shown him in permitting him to participate.

I am not here to recount the life and works of Bob La Follette. I take it that none of us are here for that purpose. The people of Wisconsin and particularly those who are here know his life, chapter and verse.

[1] From Earl Warren, "Robert M. La Follette, Sr.," in *The Wisconsin Magazine of History* (Summer, 1955), pp. 195–98. Reprinted by permission of the publisher, The State Historical Society of Wisconsin.

It was so inseparable from the growth and the development of your State that his good works are everywhere around us today: your great University; the majesty of the law as represented by your state capitol; the institutions under which you live as contained in the journals of the Legislature; and above all the abiding affection that people still have for his memory.

What I do believe we are here for is to rekindle the flame of his memory, in gratitude for his long and distinguished public services and because his dynamic principles and his fighting spirit are as needed today as they were in his hey-day.

It was not my pleasure to have known him. I saw him on the platform on occasions and, while still a college student, I once heard him from the gallery of the Senate Chambers pour out his heart from the floor of the Senate.

But I feel I knew Bob La Follette. I acquired something from him as did other Americans who perhaps never saw him, but who believe that the substance of our government is not to be found in its form but in the eternal principles upon which it is based, and which if preserved must be fought for by courageous men and women in every generation. "Let fools for forms of government contest; that which is administered best is best."

It has been my great privilege to serve the public most of my adult life. I too had the responsibility as Governor of my state to make our institutions serve the best interest of all the people. I know the pressures that Bob La Follette found it necessary to resist and overcome in order to give our democratic process the broad base it must have to serve its purpose. Every governor knows those pressures because they are in every state capitol. And they will probably always be there because as long as we have free government, of necessity, we will have pressures of selfishness, greed, and intolerance as well as those for the common weal.

There are times in the life of every public servant when the feeling of frustration becomes almost overwhelming. It is at such times that we come to know and appreciate the indomitable spirit of souls like that of Bob La Follette. It was in that way I came to know him, although I assumed my first public office almost at the precise time of his death thirty years ago.

Some historian has referred to our state governments as forty-eight laboratories for the development of our institutions. I believe that to be true. The old states, of course, built the foundation for our system, but it remained for Bob La Follette, one of the last of our log cabin statesmen, to turn the searchlight upon our social problems and to grind out with mortar and pestle the answers to them. And he suffered the same treatment that courageous men of vision in all ages have suffered. He was called a radical, a disrupter, a Socialist, a subverter, and perhaps the only reason he was not called a Communist was because that term had not then been popularized as a term of opprobrium. But Bob La Follette was a lifelong Republican, steeped in the tradition of that party which was born in this State the year after his birth. He believed in the party system.

He believed in parties and his party in particular as a party of the people—farmers, workmen, small businessmen; and not as an oligarchy of dominant interests.

He believed in private property and he said this about it:

"Property, whether the modest home of the artisan or farmer, or the great fortune of the masters of finance, if it be honorably acquired and lawfully used, is a contribution to the stability of government, as well as to material progress."

He believed in the private ownership of utilities, but he believed in regulating them for the public good:

"The owners of railroads and the holders of railroad securities must be protected in all of their rights. They must not be wronged in any way. They are entitled to such remuneration as will enable them to maintain their roads in perfect condition, pay the best of wages to employees, meet all other expenses incident to operation, and in addition thereto enough more to make a reasonable profit upon every dollar invested in the business. To preserve all these rights, they are entitled to the strongest protection which the law can afford."

He believed implicitly in our system, in our system of government and in our system of free enterprise, but he believed it belonged to the people, that it should not be shackled and that every hindrance should be removed from it in order to enable it to progress so that it might produce a better life for every man and woman and their children. This is the way he stated the issue:

> The supreme issue, involving all others, is the encroachment of the powerful few upon the rights of the many.

These were the undergirding principles of the Wisconsin Idea of which he was the father. These were the motive power in his laboratory of human problems.

How detestable those experiments of his were to some people of his day. How commonplace they are now. How much a part of American life they are. These are some of them:

> The Direct Primary giving control over government to the people instead of to the bossism.
>
> The Corrupt Practices Act preventing the pollution of the election process.
>
> The establishment of a comprehensive civil service to destroy the spoils system.

The registration of lobbyists act—not to prevent them from functioning but to bring them out in the open because as he said: "Evil and corruption thrive best in the dark."

The equalization of taxation between the individual citizen and the powerful corporate interest. "Equal and just taxation," he said, "is a fundamental principle of republican government."

An inheritance tax and a graduated income tax based on the ability to pay.

The regulation of utilities to prevent indirect and unjust taxation from burdening the people.

The right of working men to join unions and bargain for their rights. He was determined that there should be no submerged class of industrial workers.

The health and safety of the people through pure food and other laws and the compensation for industrial accidents through an industrial accident commission.

The development of the University and a sound system of general education.

These were the ingredients of the Wisconsin Idea. It is for these things Bob La Follette was called a "dangerous radical." Was it a radical program? Is it radical today?

While it has found acceptance in the hearts and minds of most Americans, I am sure there are those who still believe it is radical, and are nostalgic for the so-called "good old days." There are still among us those who could call it socialism; those who refuse to make any distinction between socialism and social progress; that kind of individual whom Lincoln described as being unable to distinguish between a horse chestnut and a chestnut horse. There will be such in every generation. That is why under our system every generation must fight for the kind of society and economy it desires to have, and the standards of the government it is to live under.

If the Wisconsin Idea was radical, it was so only in the sense that freedom itself is radical. And freedom was so considered when the founding fathers brought our nation into existence. It was radical only if the idea of government "of the people, by the people, for the people . . ." is radical.

But also it must be remembered that the party of Bob La Follette—the Republican Party—was considered radical when it was founded. Think of it. It proposed to prevent the spread of slavery; to open up the great public lands of this Western country to settlement by families; and to give the average man a greater stake in society and in his government. That was radicalism at the time Bob La Follette was born.

Bob's difficulty came from the fact that he took the principles and platforms of his party at face value. He believed it was a party of the people and he determined to make it serve that purpose. But he realized that these things could not be done overnight. He wanted it all to come by peaceful means. He wanted it done through reform. He was not in a hurry to push the nation into reforms for which it was not prepared. On the contrary, he said: "Everything worthwhile takes time, and the years teach us all patience."

Again he was squarely in the American tradition, with its reliance on the idealism and innate reasonableness of men. He had an old-fashioned faith in the sovereign power of reason in human affairs.

But preeminently, Bob La Follette was a dissenter—a dissenter in the finest sense of the word.

He did not dissent through mere obstinacy. He dissented in righteous indignation when he thought the objectives of our government were being subverted. He satisfied what is said to be the acid test of dissent, namely the ability to get itself accepted finally as the truth. In this respect no statesman in our history has succeeded better. I have often wondered if he as a boy heard the advice given by Disraeli to a young politician. When asked what he could best do to serve the public well, Disraeli replied: "Associate yourself with a just, but unpopular, cause." How many times Bob La Follette did that. Often his voice sounded as one in the wilderness because the most successful and most respectable in the nation were carried away at that time with the doctrine of *laissez faire*. They believed that our new industrial society, if not interfered with by government, would lead to Utopia for them. Bob reminded them, however, that merely an abundance of materials did not represent true progress; that progress implied the progressive enlightenment of the people, the humanization of our institutions, and the free application of intelligence in the evolution of society. He reminded them that in their enthusiasm for material gains they were breaking with the ideals of an earlier day. It was often a thankless task. But it needed to be said, and he said it. He was called wrong, short-sighted, and unfair. But no one ever called Bob La Follette dishonest. And when he died in 1925 he enjoyed the respect of everyone.

How important it is that we keep alive this type of dissent in America! It is as important now as it was then. We must test all of our public actions by dissent. The majority may always be right but it does not always discover the right answer until it has been tested by dissent.

The term "Fighting Bob" to the uninformed might connote a man in uniform, a general or perhaps a admiral. Particularly would that have been true in days gone by when the history of nations was written in terms of their wars, their most glorious achievements in terms of battles won, and their heroes in terms of conquerors of other people. Not so with Bob La Follette. He was a man of peace; not a pacifist but a fighter for peace. He fought for peace with the same steadfastness of purpose that he fought for other things. And he was not cowed by the majority view. He was satisfied to live with his own conscience.

Yes, he was scathed for it, but he died with the respect of everyone.

The day before yesterday I participated in the unveiling of a statue of a former Chief Justice in the rotunda of our National Capitol. There were the images—two from each state—of the most beloved men and women of American History. I noticed that the vast majority of them were civilians rather than military men; there were statesmen, there were social workers, there were men of the Cloth; there were philanthropists, there were scientists, and humanitarians of various descriptions. They were all citizens of peace. And even those men who were there cast in their uniforms were placed in that gallery not so much because of their military exploits, but because of the way in which they satisfied their obligations of citizens of this land. In the forefront of these was the statue of fighting Bob La Follette, most beloved son of Wisconsin. Instantly my thoughts flew back to the turbulent days of his career and what people then said of him, and then it occurred to me how understanding Americans are on sober second thought, how willing they are to make amends for harsh appraisals made by them in times of crisis; and how the objects of their lasting affection are those who have tried to make life more rewarding for everyone. I could not help noticing how stalwart Bob La Follette appeared in that company. And today to see the affectionate regard in which he is held in his own State, thirty years after his death, produces a thrill of pride and feeling of well-being.

I trust that 100 years from this day the people of Wisconsin will gather in this same spot to rekindle the flame of his memory. His accomplishments should then stand out even in bolder relief. The need for his understanding of people, his devotion to their interests, his fighting faith in our free institutions, will be equally as great as it is now.

It will give the people of Wisconsin then, the same feeling of well-being that we have today.

15

Robert S. Maxwell: "The Legacy of La Follette"[1]

In addition to his work on La Follette and the Rise of the Progressives in Wisconsin, *the writer of this essay has contributed articles on La Follette and Progressivism to a number of scholarly periodicals, and the sketches on the La Follette family in the* Wisconsin Dictionary of Biography. *In April 1964 he was invited to give a series of lectures on Progressivism at Lakeland College, Sheboygan, Wisconsin, in honor of the late Dr. H. A. Muehlmeier, the first president of the College. "The Legacy of La Follette" is a shortened version of the second of these lectures.*

Few men have been able to exert an influence upon their time which lasted much longer than their own lifetime. Robert M. La Follette, Sr. was one of the few. To Wisconsin and the nation he left a legacy that was many-faceted, a legacy that, after more than a generation, remains a pole-star for the man in public life, the person seeking a career in public service. In his home state, La Follette and Wisconsin have become so entwined that they are almost interchangeable. The La Follette family developed into a potent political dynasty which still plays an important part in the life of the state after three generations.

The founder of this political dynasty was "Fighting Bob" La Follette. Blocked by the stalwarts in his early efforts for reform, La Follette developed his own loyal progressive organization which was capable of defeating the conservatives at the polls and enacting his reform program in the legislature. Combining elements from "soil, shop, and seminar," La Follette welded together old Populists, trade union groups, idealistic crusaders, ambitious youngsters, university intellectuals, Scandinavian, German and other ethnic groups, social planners, progressive farmers, and even a disgruntled millionaire or two, to form the Progressive Machine. This machine he kept intact, despite periodic defections, through his entire life and it was responsible for

[1] This paper was first given in a somewhat expanded version as one of the H. A. Muehlmeier Lectures at Lakeland College, Sheboygan, Wisconsin, in April, 1964.

the enactment of the array of reform legislation which has come to be associated with the "Wisconsin Idea."

The central figure in the Wisconsin Progressive Machine was, of course, La Follette. He was a dynamic public speaker who possessed that magnetic quality that inspired devotion and drew men to him, old and young alike. He developed effective political techniques, such as concentration on a few important issues, presenting issues in moral terms and identifying himself with specific reforms, and reading the "roll call" on his opponents' records. Though his speeches were long, they were seldom, if ever, dull. People would drive for miles and stay all day to hear Bob La Follette speak.

La Follette was also a vigorous party organizer. In all aspects of politics he was a strict disciplinarian, demanding loyalty and support from his followers. In turn, he would drive himself to the verge of collapse in behalf of friends or causes that he had embraced. In every essential, he was a "reform boss." Far from the "grim, unsmiling, La Follette" that some associates have pictured him, "Fighting Bob" possessed a charm and grace which on occasion could completely captivate an erstwhile opponent or an entire audience. Though he grew old in the public service, La Follette remained essentially a young man's candidate. In his early campaigns he organized university students and recent graduates in his support. Even in his final race for the Senate in 1922 and in his campaign for the Presidency in 1924 on the Independent Progressive ticket he drew numbers of young men to his cause. Far from a mere echo of the past, La Follette was consistently the prophet of the future. As a Wisconsin political leader he was without peer, and his comprehensive program of reforms placed the Badger state in the forefront of the Progressive Movement.

In the United States Senate, a seat La Follette held for almost twenty years, he compiled an impressive record of constructive legislation. In the field of labor legislation three major groups of employees: railroad workers, civil service employees, and merchant seamen, were indebted to him for laws which significantly improved their condition. He was responsible for the law limiting continuous duty on the railroads to sixteen hours (1907) and later (1916) he was instrumental in the passage of the Adamson eight hour law. La Follette was also the author of the "anti-gag" law which restored the right of appeal, guaranteed the right to organize, and provided protection from summary dismissal for federal civil service employees despite executive orders which tended to shut off appeals for relief. The La Follette Seamen's Act extended to sailors on American merchant ships the same fundamental rights and protection which American industrial workers enjoyed. All of these were landmark advances in the history of labor legislation in America.

La Follette's legislative contributions ranged along the entire gamut of public questions. He sponsored the act to provide for the physical valuation of railroad properties as a basis for ratemaking. He pushed the adoption of the Nineteenth Amendment to extend the suffrage to women. He proposed legislation calling for publicity of campaign contributions and expenditures. Few men in public life have made so many constructive contributions to the public good. Most of his proposals eventually found their way into the laws of the land.

But La Follette's legacy included more than a brilliant record of reforms as a state executive or an impressive array of constructive legislation during a long tenure as United States senator. He was the example of the independent man in politics. He would not bend to expediency. If he thought it wrong, he would not follow a popular cause though he found himself a minority of one; nor would he condone wrongdoing or waywardness on the part of friends and old acquaintances. In a very real sense he was the "Conscience of the Republican Party."

Perhaps La Follette's greatest legacy was his abiding faith in American ideals. He really believed that democracy could be made to work. The great system of primary election laws which he fashioned to extend from local offices to the Presidency were predicated on his belief that the people should be allowed to choose. He was certain that only when all artificial barriers were removed would "the will of the people [truly] become the law of the land."

La Follette was far from a sacrosanct political saint. He was a rugged, and at times ruthless, partisan politician, a skilled parliamentarian, and a brilliant debater. His opponents feared and respected his barbed wit as much as his encyclopedic knowledge of the issue at hand. La Follette was not one to accept a "half loaf" or to give quarter in a political struggle. His opponents often became personal foes and his trail was strewn with his adversaries, including some of his onetime colleagues who had supported him in earlier battles. But through all of the sound and fury, La Follette stood steadfastly for popular control of the political machinery, an informed electorate, and the well-being of the individual against the claims of the corporation and the state. It is a legacy of which Wisconsin can well be proud.

16

John F. Kennedy on Robert M. La Follette[1]

John F. Kennedy, then U.S. Senator from Massachusetts, was selected as chairman of a Senate committee to choose five senators who by their outstanding records in the upper house would entitle their portraits to hang in the new Senate lounge. The Committee chose Henry Clay, John C. Calhoun, Daniel Webster, Robert A. Taft, and Robert M. La Follette. Other senators gave longer orations in praise of La Follette but Senator Kennedy's brief word picture at the time of the portrait presentation epitomized the character of "Fighting Bob" and denoted a kinship of spirit between the two.

"Robert M. La Follette, Sr. of Wisconsin, a ceaseless battler for the underprivileged in an age of special privilege, a courageous independent in an era of conformity, who fought memorably against tremendous odds and stifling inertia for the social and economic reforms which ultimately proved essential to American progress in the 20th century."

—John F. Kennedy

[1] From remarks by (then Senator) John F. Kennedy at the presentation of the portraits of five outstanding senators for the newly redecorated Senate Lounge, the *Congressional Record,* Vol. 105:3976 (March 12, 1959).

Bibliographical Note

The starting point for any study of Robert M. La Follette is his own account of his career found in *La Follette's Autobiography: A Personal Narrative of Political Experiences* (Madison, 1913). Long out of print, this valuable personal memoir has been recently republished (1960) by the University of Wisconsin Press. Because it is now again readily available, the present writer has chosen to prepare this biographical study without including material from *La Follette's Autobiography*. Supplementing and completing the saga of "Fighting Bob's" career is the family biography written by Belle Case La Follette and Fola La Follette, *Robert M. La Follette, June 14, 1855–June 18, 1925*, 2 vols. (New York, 1953).

To date there is no good critical biography of the Wisconsin senator, in part because of the restrictions which still prevent the use of the La Follette papers in the Library of Congress dealing with his later career. His role as progressive leader in Wisconsin is described and analyzed in Robert S. Maxwell, *La Follette and the Rise of the Progressives in Wisconsin* (Madison, 1956); and his early career is discussed in David Paul Thelen, *The Early Life of Robert M. La Follette, 1855–1884* (Chicago, 1966). Other works of a biographical nature, largely uncritical, include Edward N. Doan, *The La Follettes and the Wisconsin Idea* (New York, 1947); Albert O. Barton, *La Follette's Winning of Wisconsin* (Madison, 1920); and Ellen Torelle, ed., *The Political Philosophy of Robert M. La Follette* (Madison, 1920).

Books by and about the men around La Follette, friend and foe, are important in gaining a full and rounded picture of the man. In addition to the works quoted in this study, useful accounts include Theodore Roosevelt, *An Autobiography* (New York, 1913); William Allen White, *Autobiography* (New York, 1946); Joseph Lincoln Steffens, *Autobiography of Lincoln Steffens* (New York, 1931); Charles McCarthy, *The Wisconsin Idea* (New York, 1912); Henry F. Pringle, *Life and Times of William Howard Taft*, 2 vols. (New York, 1939); Robert S. Maxwell, *Emanuel L. Philipp: Wisconsin Stalwart* (Madison, 1959); Arthur S. Link, *Woodrow Wilson*, 5 vols. to date (Princeton, 1947–1965); George W. Norris, *Fighting Liberal* (New York, 1945); and George E. Mowry, *The California Progressives* (Berkeley, 1951).

More broadly based studies which treat the social, cultural, and intellectual aspects of Progressivism include such well-known works as Harold U. Faulkner, *The Quest for Social Justice, 1898–1914* (New York, 1931); Eric F. Goldman, *Rendezvous with Destiny* (New York, 1952); Richard Hofstadter, *Age of Reform: From Bryan to F.D.R.* (New York, 1955); George E. Mowry, *The Era of Theodore Roosevelt,*

1900–1912 (New York, 1958); and Arthur S. Link, *Woodrow Wilson and the Progressive Era, 1910–1917* (New York, 1954).

In addition there are numerous editions of personal memoirs, letters, and diaries which shed light on Robert La Follette and the Progressive Movement. Excellent examples are Elting E. Morrison, ed. *The Letters of Theodore Roosevelt,* 8 vols. (Cambridge, Mass., 1951–1954); and the less-well-known Nils P. Haugen, *Pioneer and Political Reminiscences* (Evansville, Wisc., 1930). The standard historical quarterlies such as *The American Historical Review* and *The Journal of American History* contain a variety of articles dealing with the Progressive Era. The files of the *Wisconsin Magazine of History* include a veritable mine of material on the La Follette family and the Progressive Movement.

These notes for further reading are intended to provide merely a suggestive guide limited to generally available materials. More detailed bibliographies on specialized topics may be found in most of the works cited. Eventually there should be a multivolume edition of the papers and letters of Robert M. La Follette.

Index

GREAT LIVES OBSERVED

Gerald Emanuel Stearn, *General Editor*

Other volumes in the series:

Churchill, *edited by Martin Gilbert*

Cromwell, *edited by Maurice Ashley*

Frederick Douglass, *edited by Benjamin Quarles*

Garibaldi, *edited by Denis Mack Smith*

William Lloyd Garrison, *edited by George M. Fredrickson*

Hitler, *edited by George H. Stein*

Jesus, *edited by Hugh Anderson*

Lloyd George, *edited by Martin Gilbert*

Mao, *edited by Jerome Ch'en*

Robespierre, *edited by George Rudé*

Franklin Delano Roosevelt, *edited by Gerald D. Nash*

Stalin, *edited by T. H. Rigby*

Booker T. Washington, *edited by Emma Lou Thornbrough*